Praise for Herman Schw

Packing the Courts: The Conservati
Rewrite the Constitutio..

"Herman Schwartz, one of our most informed and impassioned constitutional scholars, documents and analyzes the shocking story of the Reagan right's attempt to rig the courts and the Constitution. A sad but critical tale."　　　　　—Victor Navasky, *The Nation*

"A highly readable political and legal adventure story."
　　　　　—Carl Stern, law correspondent, NBC

"A scathing but accurate history of the Reagan Administration's single-minded plan to reshape the federal judiciary in its image."
　　　　　—Lee Dembart, *The Los Angeles Times*

The Rehnquist Court: Judicial Activism on the Right
"If the past is prologue, then surely Professor Schwartz's compilation of the Rehnquist Court's record, category by category, is 'must' reading, not just for lawyers, but also for concerned citizens."
　　　　　—Patricia M. Wald, former chief judge, U.S. Court of Appeals for the District of Columbia Circuit

"A timely and incisive set of essays by an impressive group of intellectuals and activists, *The Rehnquist Court* is a rich resource for anyone interested in how the current Supreme Court's jurisprudence is changing the face of justice. It has never been more important for more Americans to become Court-watchers. This book is the essential field guide."
　　　　　—Nadine Strossen, President, American Civil Liberties Union

The Struggle for Constitutional Justice in Post-Communist Europe
"A must read for those who follow international legal issues. Lively in prose style, tightly developed in argument line, there is not a dull moment in this ride across the recent legal history of five countries."
　　　　　—Frederick Quinn, *Legal Times*

"It would be hard to overestimate [Herman Schwartz's] contribution to constitutionalism in Central and Eastern Europe. He is deservedly revered, admired, and appreciated . . . probably more than any other Western scholar."
　　　　　—Wojciech Sadurski, *International Journal of Constitutional Law*

Also by Herman Schwartz

*The Struggle for Constitutional Justice
in Post-Communist Europe*

*Packing the Courts: The Conservative Campaign
to Rewrite the Constitution*

Edited by Herman Schwartz

*The Burger Years: Rights and Wrongs
in the Supreme Court, 1969–1986*

The Rehnquist Court: Judicial Activism on the Right

RIGHT
WING
JUSTICE

The Conservative Campaign
to Take Over the Courts

Herman Schwartz

NATION
BOOKS

ꜱHT WING JUSTICE: *The Conservative Campaign to Take Over the Courts*

Copyright © 2004 by Herman Schwartz

Published by
Nation Books
An Imprint of Avalon Publishing Group
245 West 17th St., 11th Floor
New York, NY 10011

Nation Books is a co-publishing venture of the Nation Institute and
Avalon Publishing Group Incorporated.

Library of Congress Cataloging-in-Publication Data is available.

ISBN 1-56025-566-8

9 8 7 6 5 4 3 2 1

Book design by Paul Paddock
Printed in the United States of America
Distributed by Publishers Group West

CONTENTS

*To Susan, Sean, and little Ben, and to
the memory of Danny*

Introduction

Three social revolutions took place in the middle years of this past century. The New Deal established the principle that the federal government has a direct responsibility to care for the welfare of those in need, and that the government also has a responsibility to regulate and manage the economy. Then, in the aftermath of World War II, a social and cultural revolution took place, highlighting the human rights movement and the change in women's roles.

Many Republicans and others have never accepted these revolutions. Not only did they attack the New Deal while it was being put into effect, they have continued to assail the measures that have embodied it over the years. Many have responded similarly to the social and cultural changes of the past half-century. The first signs of an organized counterrevolution began with the Goldwater and Reagan speeches at the Republican National Convention in 1964. When the Right gained political power with Ronald Reagan's presidency in 1980, it began to undo those advances. With the ascendancy of House Speaker Newt Gingrich in 1994, the victory of George W. Bush in 2000, and the rise of House Majority Leader Tom

DeLay, the Right has now gained full control of the Republican Party. Today, with all three branches of the federal government under tight Republican control, that counterrevolution is fully under way, and full control of the courts is a central goal.

The specific legislative goals of the Bush administration and its allies are to privatize Social Security and Medicare, to largely eliminate or shrink public welfare programs, and to weaken environmental, health and safety, antimonopoly, and other regulatory measures designed to tame a market relentlessly driven by a search for profits. As *New York Times* columnist Paul Krugman put it, this crusade is powered by "an ideology that denigrates almost everything other than the national defense, that the government does." It is intended to turn the clock back as much as possible to the 1920s, and even earlier to a time when the federal government did relatively little and "dual federalism" doctrines governed. In its most extreme version its goal is, in the words of Grover Norquist, the powerful archconservative president of Americans for Tax Reform, "to shrink government to a size where I can drown it in a bathtub."[1]

Civil and political rights are also under attack, particularly those touching on personal autonomy like abortion and the rights of gay people to live normal lives without being ostracized. Also targeted are the protections created for the many racial and ethnic minorities, women, those who are disabled or elderly, illegal aliens, and others shortchanged by life.

What the Right hopes to achieve was set out by Judge Douglas H. Ginsburg in a speech in September 2002 to the Cato Institute, a conservative libertarian group. Ginsburg is a Reagan appointee to the federal court of appeals in Washington, D.C. whom Reagan had also nominated for the Supreme Court after the Senate rejected Robert Bork but was forced to withdraw because Ginsburg had smoked marijuana with students at Harvard.[2]

In the speech Ginsburg bemoans what he calls an absence of fidelity to the text of the Constitution. As he sees it, this "infidelity" started with the New Deal Court in 1937 when it wrongly sustained congressional power under the Commerce Clause to regulate activities like union-management relations and other activities that substantially affect the national economy. Ginsburg praises the nineteenth and early twentieth century decisions that narrowly restricted the federal government's power to transportation and related facilities, and blocked federal regulation of manufacturing, no matter how great the impact on the national economy or how difficult, if not impossible, it would be for the states to deal with the problems. Under Great Depression and New Deal pressures, the "wheels came off," according to Ginsburg. For him, the current conservative Court is not conservative enough. He condemns its recent unanimous decision allowing Congress to delegate broad powers to administrative agencies, urging instead a doctrine that the Court has consistently rejected except for two 1935 decisions by the pre-New Deal Court; in this regard, he is apparently echoing the views of Northwestern University law professor Gary Lawson who has argued that the post-New Deal administrative state is unconstitutional and its validation by the legal system is nothing less than a bloodless "constitutional revolution." He also criticizes the current Court's refusal to force federal, state, and local governments to use an ambiguous constitutional provision, the "Takings" Clause, to compensate property owners when environmental and other regulations reduce the value of the property. If that clause were applied as Ginsburg would like, the costs would be staggering and few state or local governments would dare to adopt such regulations.[3]

In his lament for this golden age, Ginsburg omits to mention that these constitutional interpretations were developed at a time when American capitalism was at its most rapacious and irresponsible, coinciding with the crude excesses that Mark Twain named the Gilded Age and Vernon Parrington called "The Great Barbecue." Parallels between these times and today are not hard to find.

Although Ginsburg is primarily an economic and regulatory specialist, he also castigates the Court for recognizing new rights like the 1965 decision allowing married couples to use contraceptives, as well as its recent ban on executing the mentally retarded. And he called on judges and scholars to renew "fidelity to the text"—a return to the constitutional doctrines that prevailed from the 1880s to 1937 that disabled the federal government from dealing with the most fundamental problems facing this country, problems that state and local governments could not possibly cope with.[4]

How successful the Right's counterrevolution will be is not clear at this time. Much depends on the 2004 presidential election. No matter who is president, however, it is certain that the right will not discontinue its campaign and that the effects of what it achieves will continue for a long time to come.

Even to approach the realization of these goals and to ensure that those effects do continue, it is necessary not only to pass legislation and issue executive orders but to control the courts, for many of these issues wind up in the courts, especially human rights. Many of the rights in question were first established by the courts and all need to be implemented and enforced by the courts. What judges have done can be undone or cut back by other judges.

Who sits on the bench is also important to Republican electoral success. Since enactment of the 1965 Voting Rights Act, which made it possible for African-Americans to vote in large numbers, the South has become the Republican base. That region has become almost as solidly Republican as it used to be Democratic and, in both cases, very conservative. Many of these Southern constituents are still hostile to black progress as well as to the cultural changes of the past fifty years. These voters are now indispensable to Republican success in gaining the White House and in controlling Congress. Ronald Reagan also managed to get the votes of socially conservative blue-collar Democrats, but Vice President Al Gore regained a majority of these in 2000, and the Republicans want to win them back.

Control of the courts is equally necessary in order to undo the regulatory and welfare revolution. This is necessary to take care of the pocketbook interests that make up the more traditional wing of the Republican Party and provide the necessary campaign funds. These groups are concerned about the interpretation and enforcement of regulatory and tax statutes, as well as the challenges to these programs, and many of these issues are decided by judges. The so-called states' rights movement to undermine the constitutional basis for many social and environmental programs is a judge-made product, crafted by the five conservative justices on the Supreme Court, conservative lawyers, and others, most of whom are prominent and active members of the Heritage Foundation and the Federalist Society.

The campaign to control the courts did not begin with the George W. Bush presidency. It began twenty-four years ago with the Republican platform of 1980, which called for the overturning of *Roe v. Wade* (the 1973 abortion decision) and much of the work of the Supreme Court during the preceding decades. This involved reducing access to the federal courts for the redress of grievances, allowing greater state involvement in religious matters, weakening the rules requiring fairness in election district reapportionment, striking down voluntary and other kinds of affirmative action, diluting the laws against race and sex discrimination, virtually eliminating most legal protections for the accused, and dismissing challenges to public or private authority for violation of statutory or constitutional rights by Medicare patients whose funding is terminated without a hearing, public assistance claimants, handicapped people, antitrust plaintiffs, and anyone suing under a Civil Rights Act provision.[5]

To fulfill this agenda, soon after his election in 1980 Reagan, guided by his chief counselor, Edwin Meese, nominated young right-wing ideologues like Robert Bork, Antonin Scalia, and Richard Posner to the federal appellate bench where much of our law is made. George H.W. Bush continued what Reagan and Meese had started, appointing such hard-right ideologues as Clarence Thomas and Michael Luttig. There was a brief eight-year hiatus during the Clinton administration, but George W. Bush has nominated conservatives even farther to the right than Reagan and Bush Sr., like Janice Rogers Brown and William Pryor.

If this right-wing campaign succeeds, it will have momentous consequences for the way Americans live now and for what they take for granted. Consider the following situations:

In 1962, Sherri Finkbine, a Phoenix, Arizona, television personality and mother of four, became pregnant for the fifth time. While she was pregnant, frightening reports began to circulate that taking the drug thalidomide produced deformed babies, without arms or legs. Finkbine had taken tranquilizers containing thalidomide. She immediately tried to get an abortion, but Phoenix hospitals refused, because Arizona, like almost all other states, had made it a crime to perform an abortion unless it were to save the life of the mother. Finkbine then flew to Sweden to get the abortion. Other women seeking an abortion could not afford to do so, and it is estimated that the death toll from badly performed self-abortions and from illegal abortionists was about a million women annually then.

Fast forward twenty years later to 1982: Sherri Finkbine would not have to fly to Sweden anymore. American women could now obtain a safe and legal abortion at hospitals, clinics, and other authorized providers.

Fast forward twenty years again to 2002: Women like Sherri Finkbine who live in Phoenix, Arizona, can still get a legal abortion, but women who don'tlive in big cities probably cannot. Eighty percent of Arizona counties have no abortion provider. Nationwide, it is becoming more and more difficult and burdensome to obtain an abortion. Although abortion is still legal, many clinics, doctors, and other abortion providers have stopped operating because state and local governments have imposed waiting, informal consent, reporting, and other burdensome requirements that make it prohibitive, expensive, and difficult to operate. As a result, women who are poor or young can no longer obtain a safe and legal abortion.

Each of these immense changes in the lives of women resulted from a decision by a few politically connected lawyers appointed to be judges who are empowered to make such decisions for the rest of their lives, and who are accountable for these decisions to no one but their own consciences. The first major shift, of course, was the 1973 decision in the *Roe* case, in which seven Supreme Court Justices established a woman's right to an abortion and virtually prohibited states from raising obstacles to abortion in the early months of pregnancy, which is when the overwhelming number of abortions are done. The change between 1982 and 2002 also resulted from court decisions: the 1992 Supreme Court decision in *Planned Parenthood of Pennsylvania v. Casey*, preserved the right to have an abortion but allowed states and localities virtually unlimited discretion in erecting barriers like waiting periods and notification and consent procedures. Most of these barriers were then upheld by the lower courts with no further review by the Supreme Court.[6]

Abortion is but one example among countless others of the immense power we have always given our courts. Recent examples include:

- The school desegregation decision in *Brown v. Board of Education* of Topeka, Kansas, which launched the civil rights movement. This showed that major social change could be achieved through the courts, and it stimulated legal action by women, the gay rights movement, prisoners, and many others who had long suffered from prejudice and discrimination.
- *The electoral district reapportionment decisions* that reshaped American politics when the Supreme Court ruled that the courts could insist on the "one person one vote" principle, so that the votes of some would not count for more than the votes of others.
- *The school prayer decisions* that barred officially mandated religious observances in schools.
- *The gay rights decisions* that first barred states from denying gay people the right to fight for statutes protecting them against discrimination and then prohibited making criminals of them.[7]

But judicial power has not always been benign. For example:

Child labor. In 1919 the Supreme Court prevented the federal government from moving against the scourge of child labor in *Hammer v. Dagenhart.*

The Depression. In the 1930s, the Court struck down numerous efforts by the president and Congress to cope with the ravages of the Great Depression in the *Butler* and *Carter* cases.

School desegregation. In 1974, in *Bradley v. Milliken*, the Court refused to require Detroit suburbs to participate in desegregating the Detroit schools, with the result that our cities have become increasingly populated by impoverished minorities with pressing needs for social services but with a decreasing tax base.

Worker health and safety. In 1905, *Lochner v. New York* struck down an effort to improve the health and safety of bakers in New York by limiting their working hours. In 1923, the Court nullified minimum wage statutes in *Adkins v. Children's Hospital.* Until the 1930s, courts consistently ruled against labor union efforts to organize and to strike.

Overtime pay. In 1999, in *Alden v. Maine*, the Court prevented probation officers employed by the state of Maine from suing the state for violating their rights to overtime pay under the federal Fair Labor Standards Act.

Violence against women. In fall 1994, Christy Brzonkala, a freshman at Virginia Polytechnic Institute, was brutally raped by two members of the school's football team. The school did little about it, so Christy sued one student under the federal Violence Against Women Act. The act had been passed with the support of some thirty-eight states who told Congress they could not deal with the problem because of local sexism. In 2000, a 5-4 majority of the Supreme Court threw out Christy's suit, finding the statute unconstitutional. The majority did not think violence against women substantially affected interstate commerce despite what dissenting Justice David Souter, appointed by President George H.W. Bush, called a "mountain of data assembled by Congress" detailing the billions of dollars violence against women cost the national economy each year.

The heritage of slavery. And then there were two of the most infamous decisions in American history, *Dred Scott v. Sandford* in 1857, which ruled that Blacks could never be citizens, and *Plessy v. Ferguson* (1896), which stamped America with racial segregation for the next sixty years.[8]

Most of these decisions are constitutional rulings, but the courts' power to interpret statutes is equally important, for in many cases a court's interpretation of a statute or regulation is decisive. The legislature can reverse the Court's decision, and sometimes does. That is what happened in 1991 when Congress overturned eight Supreme Court decisions that had seriously weakened enforcement of the laws against racial and gender discrimination in employment. In most cases, however, politics, inertia, and a lack of time or attention make the judicial interpretation final.[9]

This judicial conservatism is not unusual. Although the federal courts' performance since 1954, the date of the school desegregation decision, may have led many people to believe that the courts usually lead the struggle against injustice and inequality, for most of our history they have not. Indeed for most of American history, the federal courts have been a bastion of conservatism rather than a leader in protecting human rights and promoting social justice. They were probably intended that way, at least by some of the Framers. Except for relatively brief periods, the courts have been primarily concerned with protecting the haves against the have-nots—the poor, workers, farmers, blacks, and women—and upholding official action.

There have always been significant exceptions to that conservatism throughout our history. But a sustained commitment to liberty, justice, and equality did not take place until the last three quarters of the twentieth century. It started in the 1930s, hit a peak with *Brown* and the decisions of the 1960s, and concluded with the important rulings in the 1970s and 1980s establishing a woman's right to an abortion and protection against discrimination in general, approving affirmative action for minorities and women, and promoting school desegregation and church-state separation. By 1988, that period was largely over. The next chapter will explore the history of the federal courts more closely.

All the decisions described above were decided by the Supreme Court. In our hierarchical judicial structure, the Supreme Court sets the basic rules within which the lower courts and the state courts must operate. But the Supreme Court decides very few cases, and a good proportion of those are from state courts. From 2001 to 2003, the Court decided an average of only sixty-five federal cases per year. By contrast, the thirteen federal appellate courts have been deciding approximately 28,000–30,000 per year. Although the overwhelming proportion of these cases—perhaps as many as 90–95 percent— are nonideological and noncontroversial, all require time, money, effort, and the expenditure of scarce judicial resources, and all are important to the people involved. In the criminal cases, liberty and public safety are at stake; in the civil cases, substantial amounts of money, because federal appeals are expensive, and in many cases today, must involve at least $75,000. For litigants in these cases, the thirteen Courts of Appeals are the courts of last resort for all but a tiny handful.

In deciding these appeals, the lower courts have a good deal of discretion at both the trial and appellate levels. All court decisions, including and perhaps especially Supreme Court decisions, leave a great deal of room for interpretation and application, and many statutory and other issues never even get to the High Court. For example:

- In 1998, a divided panel of the Court of Appeals for the First Circuit in Boston struck down the affirmative action plan adopted by the school system's renowned flagship school, the Boston Latin School, to increase the number of minority students who would otherwise not be able to gain admission to the elite high school.

An affirmative action plan to integrate a magnet elementary school in Montgomery County, Maryland, was struck down by the Fourth Circuit in Richmond in *Eisenberg v. Montgomery Cty. Pub. Schls.*[10] On the other hand, in *Brewer v. West Irondequoit Central School District* (2000), a split panel of the Second Circuit in New York upheld a similar plan involving transfers from Rochester to suburban schools. None of these cases was reviewed by the Supreme Court, which has not dealt with affirmative action in education below the college level.

- In 2000, the Supreme Court struck down a Colorado constitutional amendment that barred any state or local action to protect gay people against discrimination. Cincinnati had earlier adopted a local charter amendment barring any municipal antidiscrimination action against gays. Despite the Supreme Court decision in the Colorado case, the Court of Appeals for the Sixth Circuit in Cincinnati upheld the charter amendment and the Supreme Court declined to review the decision.

- In 1933, the federal court in New York declared that James Joyce's great novel *Ulysses* was not "obscene." Americans could now read one of the greatest novels of the twentieth century without having to smuggle it in past customs inspectors, and publishers could print it without facing criminal penalties.[10]

Even when the Supreme Court does get around to deciding an issue, it may be years after the lower courts have grappled with the problem, for it often waits to see how the appellate courts have viewed the issues. Until the Supreme Court decides the case, many litigants and others who lose in an appellate court decision may have lost opportunities and benefits to which they would otherwise be entitled. For example, in 2003 the Supreme Court ruled that a university could use racial preferences in their admissions process in order to achieve racial diversity in *Grutter v. Bollinger*. In 1996, however, the Court of Appeals for the Fifth Circuit had ruled otherwise in *Hopwood v. State of Texas*, and for seven years, many minority students have had difficulty attending universities in Texas, Mississippi, and Louisiana during their normal educational years, particularly the graduate schools. For example, the percentage of Mexican-American and black law students at the University of Texas Law School dropped from 19.9% in 1995 before the *Hopwood* decision, to 6.5% in 1997, and reached only 9.25% in 2002, after years of intense recruiting.[11]

One reason for the power of the American judiciary was suggested by Tocqueville's much-quoted observation that "scarcely any political question arises in the United States that is not resolved, sooner or later, into a judicial question." This is now truer than ever, for America is probably the most litigious society in history. It has always been that way, even in colonial times.[12]

Another reason for the power of the judiciary is that legislatures, and particularly Congress, have usually been dominated by powerful racist, sexist, and business interests, and have failed to meet such pressing needs as ending racial and gender discrimination, gun control, monitoring corporate dishonesty, reducing cigarette smoking, and enacting meaningful campaign-finance reform and affordable health care, to mention but a few examples. Our system of separated powers has contributed to these failures, since for most of the past half-century the White House and Congress have been in different hands, and inter-branch and even House-Senate competition have often resulted in deadlock. Some state legislatures have managed to move forward on some of these issues like campaign-finance reform, smoking, corporate malfeasance, and prescription drugs, but these are still scattered. Courts have therefore been called upon to fill the vacuum.[13]

These federal judges whose authority is invoked so often are appointed by the president, usually from members of his own political party and often upon the recommendation of senators or other powerful politicians; in most state court systems, the judges are elected. Because judges influence so much about how people live, judicial appointments are political matters, and American judges almost always obtain their offices because of political connections. Judges are often former prosecutors, who in the United States are steeped in politics, since the prosecutor's office can provide high public visibility and is often a stepping stone to either higher office or a judgeship. This is particularly true at the state and local levels where the chief prosecutor is usually elected. Chief Justice Earl Warren is probably the best-known example of such a rise. When serving as District Attorney of Alameda County, California, he was considered one of the ablest prosecutors in the nation. That reputation won him the governorship of California and ultimately the highest judicial office in the United States.

Appointments to the Supreme Court have always drawn a great deal of public and expert attention. Until recently, however, only a few political scientists have studied the way in which lower federal court judges are chosen. This book focuses on that latter process.

At this point, certain disclosures and disclaimers are appropriate. This book is not a value-free exercise. I have been involved as a scholar, lawyer, and writer in many of the constitutional and legal issues discussed in these pages, and have been an active participant in many of the nomination disputes; in 1988, I published a study of the Reagan nominations, much of which is incorporated in this book in Chapter 2. Although I have tried to document and verify the factual assertions that are made, errors have certainly crept in and for these I apologize in advance.

As for my point of view, I am what might be considered an old-fashioned liberal, with no apologies, even though the word "liberal" has fallen into disrepute in some circles on both the Left and the Right. As a rough approximation of my views, I can say that I believe in the necessity of federal, state, and local action to deal with those shortchanged by birth or fortune and those in need; that our Constitution is a "living Constitution" that must respond to the changing needs and obligations of society; and that judges have an obligation to promote "liberty and justice for all." The Constitution gives federal judges the unique privilege of tenure for life without even an obligation to retire. This is a privilege found nowhere else in the developed world, and the only justification for so great a power, if there is any, is to enable our federal judges to defend and promote the great rights enshrined in our constitutional and moral heritage when they are under threat.

These views will not be defended here, for this book is not about whether those views are correct or misguided, but only to state the premises on which this book is written and the judgments expressed. I will simply note that national and international tribunals are being assigned a similar role all over the world.[14]

A final note on my use of the word "ideology." By that I mean what the dictionary says it is: "the body of beliefs that guides a particular individual, class, or culture."

My focus is on the past twenty-five years for reasons that will become clear. Before turning to that, it is important to explore the development of the federal courts in our history. For lack of space, knowledge, and because of the dominance of the

Supreme Court in our judicial system, there will be relatively little discussion of the lower courts in this chapter, but rather it will focus on how the Supreme Court has shaped our law, and particularly on its ideological premises.

• • •

1. For these early constitutional doctrines, see John E. Nowak and Ronald R. Rotunda, *Constitutional Law* (Sixth Ed), p. 162 (2002).
2. The speech, entitled "On Constitutionalism" is reprinted in the first issue of the *Cato Institute's Supreme Court Review*, October 2003, p 7.
3. *Hammer v. Dagenhart*, 247 U.S. 495 (1918) and *Bailey v. Drexel Furniture Co.*, 259 U.S. 20 (1922) (child labor); *NLRB v. Jones & Laughlin Steel Corp.*, 301 U.S. 1 (1937) (labor-management); Assn's, Inc., 531 U.S. 457 (2001). *Schecter Poultry Corp. v. United States*, 295 U.S. 495 (1935) and *Panama Refining Co. v. Ryan*, 293 U.S. 388 (1935) (delegation); *Lucas v. S. Carolina Coastal Council*, 505 U.S. 1003 (2001) ("Takings").The Lawson article is "The Rise and Rise of the Administrative State," 107 *Harvard Law Review*. 1231, 1231, 1237-41 (1994).
4. *Griswold v. Connecticut*, 381 U.S. 479 (1965) (contraception case); *Atkins v. Virginia*, 536 U.S. 304 (2002) (mental retardation).
5. See 1980 Republican Party Platform, available at http://www.presidency.ucsb.edu/ site/docs/doc _platform.php? platindex=R1980.
6. Roe v. Wade, 410 U.S. 113 (1973); *Planned Parenthood n.s.e. Pennsylvania v. Casey*, 505 U. S. 833 (1992).
7. *See Brown v. Board of Education*, 347 U.S. 483 (1954) (school desegregation); *Reynolds v. Sims*, 377 U.S. 533 (1964) (electoral district – reapportionment); *Santa Fe Indep. Sch. Dist. v. Doe*, 530 U.S. 290 (2000); *Lee v. Weissman*, 505 U.S. 577 (1992); *Wallace v. Jaffree*, 472 U.S. 38 (1985); *Sch. Dist. v. Schempp*, 374 U.S. 203 (1963); *Engel v. Vitale*, 370 U.S. 421 (1962) (school prayer); *Romer v. Evans*, 517 U.S. 620 (1996); *Lawrence v. Texas*, 123 S.Ct. 2472 (2003) (gay rights).
8. *Hammer v. Dagenhart*, 247 U.S. 251 (1918) (child labor); *U.S. v. Butler*, 297 U.S. 1 (1936); *Carter v. Carter Coal Co.*, 298 U.S. 238 (1936) (depression); *Milliken v. Bradley*, 418 U.S. 717 (1974) (Detroit schools); Lochner v. New York, 198 U.S. 45 (1905) (working hours); *Adkins v. Children's Hospital of D.C.*, 261 U.S. 525 (1923) (minimum wage); *Alden v. Maine*, 527 U.S. 706 (1999) (overtime pay); *U.S. v. Morrisson*, 529 U.S. 598 (2000) (violence against women); *Dred Scott v. Sandford*, 60 U.S. 393 (1857) (slavery); *Plessy v. Ferguson*, 163 U.S. 537 (1896) (segregation).
9. The Civil Restoration Rights Act of 1991, 42 U.S.C. 2000e (1991). This legislation overruled *Lorance v. AT&T Technologies*, 490 U.S. 900 (1989); *Price Waterhouse v. Hopkins*, 490 U.S. 228 (1989); *McDonnell Douglas Corp. v. Green*, 411 U.S. 792 (1973); *Wards Cove Packing Co. v. Atonio*, 490 U.S. 642 (1989); *International Brotherhood of Teamsters v. United States*, 431 U.S. 324 (1977); *Will v. Michigan Department of State Police*, 491 U.S. 58 (1989); *Jett v. Dallas Independent School District*, 491 U.S. 701 (1989); *Patterson v. McLean Credit Union*, 491 U.S. 164 (1989).
10. See *Wessman v. Gittens*, 160 F.3d 790 (1st Cir., 1998); *Eisenberg v. Montgomery* Cty. Pub. Schls., 197 F.3d 123 (4th Cir., 1999); *Brewer v. West Irondequoit Cent. Sch. Dist.*, 212 F.3d 738 (2d Cir., 2000) (affirmative action); *Equality Foundation of Greater Cincinnati, Inc. v. City of Cincinnati*, 123 F.3d 289 (6th Cir., 1997); (gay rights);

United States v. One Book Named "Ulysses" 5 F. Supp. 182 (S.D.N.Y. 1933), aff'd, 72 F.2d 705 (2d Cir. 1934).

11. *Grutter v. Bollinger*, 123 S.Ct. 2325 (2003); Hopwood v. State of Texas, 78 F.3d 932 (5th Cir. 1996). For the numbers, see www.law.utexas.edu/hopwood.

12. Alexis de Tocqueville, *Democracy in America* (Everyman ed.), p. 280.

13. For the author's views on the current "states rights" decisions, see Herman Schwartz, ed. "The States Rights Assault on Federal Authority" in *The Rehnquist Court,* pp. 155-168 (2002) and "The Supreme Court's Federalism: Fig Leaf for Conservatives," *Annals,* March 2001, p. 119; See generally, Herman Schwartz, *The Struggle For Constitutional Justice in Post-Communist Europe* (2000).

Packing the Courts (1988).

14. See Herman Schwartz, note 13.

Chapter 1

1787–1980

Even a cursory glance at American history shows that a powerful politically shaped and oriented judiciary is nothing new. It has roots deep in our history. Even in colonial times, courts were called upon to resolve serious disputes, for "the colonists were conditioned to a great number of courts and an elaborate system of appeals." During these years, Americans also became accustomed to a form of judicial review of their laws, for the Privy Council in England had the power to veto statutes and ordinances enacted by colonial legislatures.[1]

One theme in the Revolution was an attack on the executive in favor of legislative power, and with it a downgrading of judges, who by 1776 had come to be seen and distrusted as instruments of royal power. During the 1770s, legislative controls over the selection, salaries, and even removal of judges were established. In Vermont, Connecticut, and Rhode Island, judges were elected annually, and in Georgia, the legislature could remove every judge but the chief justice whenever it wished to.[2]

In the postrevolutionary years, economic hardship was widespread, and with it went a substantial growth in the debtor population. State legislatures responded with legislation favoring debtors, including legislative approval of paper money, moratoriums allowing delayed debt repayment, and by occasionally interfering with judicial functions. Many influential people like James Madison, and particularly the more affluent, became hostile to state legislatures. Throughout the Federalist papers, Madison warns against legislative overweening. In Pennsylvania, he wrote:

> The constitutional trial by jury had been violated; and powers assumed, which had not been delegated by the Constitution.
>
> Executive powers had been usurped. The salaries of the judges, which the Constitution expressly requires to be fixed, had been occasional varied; and cases belonging to the judiciary department, frequently drawn within legislative cognizance and determination.

Madison also quotes Jefferson, who in his *Notes on the State of Virginia* complained that the Virginia legislature "have decided rights which should have been left to judiciary controversy."[3]

This hostility to legislative excesses raised the status of the judiciary among the propertied classes. Judges came to be seen among the propertied as somehow representative of the popular will, and not as the antidemocratic institution that they had been considered as earlier, and would be considered to be again. Arguments for judicial review of legislation began to be put forward, with some success. Within a relatively short period judges were raised to a position of eminence they had never before enjoyed.[4]

The provisions in the Constitution providing for life tenure and other protections for judges reflect this elevated status. Other provisions setting out the jurisdiction of the federal courts incorporated the conservative bias that was deliberately intended to be applied by those federal judges. According to John Frank, "It was clearly contemplated that the judges were to be conservative and sound men of property." As Hamilton put it in the *Federalist 78*, the courts would be "essential" to deal with "unjust and partial laws" that would injure "the private rights of particular classes of citizens." Frank also suggests that the jurisdictional provisions, including the diversity clause allowing access to the federal courts for suits by citizens of one state or a foreign country against citizens of another state, was designed to help land speculators. In 1787, "there were fortunes to be made" in buying land cheaply from a state or the federal government and reselling it at an inflated price, and many of the Founding Fathers, including Robert Morris, the "financier of the American Revolution," John Marshall and his brother James, George Mason, Patrick Henry, and many others were avid land speculators. Frank notes that "the Supreme Court aided virtually every land speculator who came before it from 1790 to 1815," and concludes that "one heavy factor in establishing diversity jurisdiction was the consideration of the comparative class bias" of the federal and state systems, for most of the federal judges were expected to be—and were—from among the well-to-do classes. Although most state court systems also became favorable to business interests, the Founders would not be disappointed in their expectations for the federal courts.[5]

The best example of this judicial favoritism for land speculators was *Fletcher v. Peck*, which involved one of the greatest and most colorful land swindles in American history. In 1794 Georgia was in deep financial trouble. It had heavy obligations and its treasury was empty. Its one great asset was the Yazoo territory comprising almost all of Alabama and Georgia, some 35 million acres. In December 1794 the Georgia legislature sold the entire Yazoo territory to four land companies for $500,000 or $7 million 2003 dollars: this amounted to 1.5 cents per acre or about 12 cents in today's money. Every member of the Georgia legislature who voted for the sale, with one exception, as well as other public officials and notables, had been bribed by the land companies.

The land companies promptly resold the land at huge profits; many of the purchasers knew nothing about the bribery. The Georgia voters were outraged and threw out the "Yazooist" legislature. The new Georgia Assembly tried to undo the sale by repealing the law authorizing the sale. Political controversies continued for many years, and the matter finally reached the Supreme Court. In 1810 the Supreme Court struck down the Georgia repeal statute on the ground that it violated the constitutional ban on states "impairing the obligation of contracts." The case was almost certainly made up by the parties who were not really adversaries, for both sides were involved in the Yazoo land companies and brought the case in order to get a ruling from the Court to settle matters.*

The *Fletcher* case has been described as a vital "link between capitalism and constitutionalism," and it made the contract clause into "the major constitutional limitation on state legislatures in a period when the states were the source of most laws regulating business interests. Between 1810 and 1889 the contract clause was invoked in almost 40 per cent of all cases challenging the validity of state legislation." It was the basis for some seventy-five decisions striking down state efforts to regulate business.[7]

During the first decades of the Republic, federal judges were usually politically prominent figures, who viewed judicial office as one more arena for their political activity. Intensely partisan enforcement of the Alien and Sedition Laws by Supreme Court Justice Samuel Chase, which led to his impeachment and near-conviction, is but one example; there were many others.

The great early battles, as bitter as any since then, were

---

* The decision was also legally questionable because the "contract" was a public grant. It also involved further "obligations" since the grant had already been made.

between the Federalists, the party of the financial and commercial classes, and the agrarian and artisan elements led by Thomas Jefferson, then called the Republicans, who became today's Democrats. Washington and Adams, the Federalist Party presidents, appointed only Federalists to the federal bench. As a lame duck president in 1801, Adams tried to use newly adopted legislation reforming the federal courts to appoint Federalists to sixteen newly created Circuit Court judgeships. These were the well-known "midnight judges," so called because their commissions were signed by Secretary of State and Chief Justice–designate John Marshall just before Adams left office. In one of the few fights over lower court judges in the early years, the Jeffersonians repealed the legislation and removed the judges.

During these years, the Federal government was beginning its acquisitive binge, getting and holding property free from state government control, which was a major concern of the emerging business interests. Courts became a central battleground. As Gordon Wood writes:

> Judges now became the arbiters between the emerging separate spheres of public power and private rights. Law became more and more of a science removed from politics and comprehended by only an enlightened few who needed to be educated in special professional law schools. The desire for an independent expert judiciary was bred by the continuing and ever renewed fears of democratic politics.... Efforts to carve out an exclusive sphere of activity for the judiciary, a sphere where the adjudicating of private rights was removed from politics and legislative power, contributed to the remarkable process by which the judiciary in America suddenly emerged out of its colonial insignificance to become by 1800 the principal means by which popular legislatures were controlled and limited. The most dramatic institutional transformation in the

early Republic was the rise of what was called an "independent judiciary."[8]

So powerful a role for an unelected and unaccountable institution is anomalous in a democracy, especially since the incumbents of that institution have life tenure. In the federal judiciary this really means "life," for federal judges are not forced to retire at a set age as in every other modern judiciary. This imperviousness to democratic control can be justified only if it is used to protect democratic values that the community considers vital and that majority rule may jeopardize. The courts need their immunity to democratic control when they challenge the majority and overturn the judgments of the electorate on behalf of some unpopular individual, group, or cause.*

For most of our history, however, the rights most protected by the courts have been the rights of the haves, or in more legal language, the rights of property. Here another factor comes into play: the ubiquitous and powerful role of lawyers in American life. Again, Tocqueville said it best:

> If I were asked where I place the American aristocracy, I should reply without hesitation that it is not among the rich, who are united by no common tie, but that it occupies the judicial bench and the bar.
>
> As the lawyers form the only enlightened class whom the people do not mistrust, they are naturally called upon to occupy most of the public stations. They fill the legislative assemblies and are at the head of the administration; they consequently exercise a powerful influence upon the formation of the law and upon its execution.[9]

---

* The other great functions of the federal judiciary are (1) umpiring clashes between the other two branches and occasional clashes between the judiciary and either or both of the other two (2) federal statutory construction. In principle, the latter raises few issues of nonaccountability, since a legislature unhappy with a court construction can revise the statute by ordinary legislative process. In practice this is often difficult.

Tocqueville considered this a great piece of good luck for the United States because he believed that lawyers—including those on the bench—would be a conservative force. As Gordon Wood wrote, "The desire for an independent expert judiciary was bred by the continuing and ever renewed fears of democratic politics."[10]

And for much of American history, federal judges have been such a conservative force, drawn largely from the social and economic middle and upper classes throughout the century. Even when the Jeffersonians were in power, the men appointed to the bench were largely conservative in their outlook and committed to protecting the interests of property-holders. For example, Supreme Court Justice Joseph Story was known as a conservative even before his appointment to the Court by the Jeffersonian Madison. It was Story who wrote *Swift v. Tyson* (1842), the decision that made the federal courts readily accessible to large business interests looking for federal judges who would apply business-friendly federal law in order to escape the often more populist state courts.[11]

Swift dealt with the federal courts' diversity jurisdiction: suits between citizens of different states. Like *Fletcher v. Peck*, *Swift* involved a fraudulent land deal. Two men sold some Maine property that they did not own to Tyson for $1,450 (about $20,000 today). Tyson gave them a draft drawn on himself in payment, and they transferred the draft to Swift to satisfy a debt they owed him. Swift, who knew nothing of the fraud, tried to collect on the draft from Tyson, who refused to pay. Under the 1789 Judiciary Act, in diversity cases the federal courts were supposed to apply the relevant state law, for in these cases the litigants are in federal court only because they come from different states. Under New York law, Tyson would have won, but Story ruled that federal law applied except where state statutes were involved, and Tyson had to pay Swift.[12]

Swift v. Tyson shaped the course of American commercial law for almost 100 years until it was overturned in an opinion by Justice Louis D. Brandeis in 1938 in *Erie Railroad v. Tompkins.* It enabled businesses that operated in many states to escape state laws and judges who were often more sympathetic to worker and agricultural interests. *Swift* was especially useful to insurance companies because the federal courts developed legal doctrines in the diversity cases that were far more favorable toward insurance companies than state laws. The federal courts also developed their own tort law, the law that decides who is liable for the damages when there is an accidental or intentional injury. This was particularly important in connection with on-the-job injuries. The federal courts decided that if a worker was hurt because the mistakes or some other action of another worker contributed to his injury, even if only marginally, the employer was not liable. This doctrine, known as the "fellow servant" doctrine, was developed in the steel industry where injuries were commonplace. It left most workers hurt on the job without any recourse, for most of these cases wound up in the federal courts. Even if the injured worker wanted to sue the other worker, the latter rarely had any money to pay for the medical bills, lost wages, or other damages resulting from the injury.[13]

Perhaps inadvertently, Congress also got into the act by enacting a general "removal" statute in 1875 to protect blacks and Southern Unionists, though some senators almost certainly had other goals in mind. Under the 1875 law, any litigant in a state court case in which the plaintiffs are in states different from the defendants or in which federal law or the Constitution are involved could "remove" the case from the state court to a federal court. Although blacks and Southern Unionists wound up getting little benefit from this statute for a long time, railroads, insurance companies, and other interstate corporations quickly and enthusiastically resorted to removal in order to get into the business-friendly federal courts and to evade state judges and legislatures increasingly resentful of eastern capitalists. Not until the 1960s civil rights movement was removal used primarily to protect blacks and civil rights workers.

The federal courts were not only biased toward business with an often blind faith in the market, but they were also expensive and inconvenient, giving the big multistate corporate litigant, who could remove the case from the local court to a distant federal court, a great advantage.

Diversity jurisdiction was only one of many pro-business tools. The tight ties between business and the Republican Party, together with Republican control of the White House during all but sixteen of the sixty-seven years between 1865 and 1932, resulted in a militantly pro-business judiciary led by the Supreme Court, which used not only diversity but other federal court doctrines and powers to the fullest. For example, in 1875 Congress also authorized suits raising federal questions to be brought in the federal courts. As a result, the federal courts became the principal forum for litigating issues that arose under either Congressional statutes or the federal Constitution. As Judge Patricia Wald has observed, "After the turn of the twentieth century, as the business of federal courts began to deal less with patents and admiralty and more with politically volatile issues such as antitrust, labor disputes, child labor, corruption, and due process challenges to governmental regulation, issue-oriented politics increasingly intruded on judicial selection." And since the federal judges were largely chosen by presidents who were sympathetic to business, so were the courts.[14]

The *Swift v. Tyson* doctrine in diversity cases gave the federal courts the power to shape *private* commercial law. During the period between the end of Reconstruction and before the arrival of the New Deal Court, the *Swift* case was supplemented by the due process and commerce clause cases which gave the federal judges a weapon against *public* action. Using the due process clause of the Fourteenth Amendment adopted in 1868 primarily to protect the freed slaves, the Court struck down much state social legislation. The 1905 *Lochner v. New York* decision, which nullified a New York law limiting the working hours of bakery workers is the best-known example; the Court did not believe the statute was a "reasonable" health measure. The Court's decisions narrowly construing the federal commerce clause and the federal taxing powers also undermined the few federal efforts to deal with such problems as child labor and huge industrial combinations.[15]

Not surprisingly, unions were a particular target of the federal judiciary. Two favorite anti-union weapons used by business lawyers were the injunction prohibiting certain activities, and "yellow-dog contracts," in which employers required prospective employees to agree not to join a union, or to quit their jobs if they did. Both the federal government and some states had tried to ban the use of these "yellow-dog contracts," but the Supreme Court struck down these efforts as unconstitutional. The federal courts also issued injunctions to stop strikes in transportation, and frequently applied the Sherman Antitrust Act against union activities, many times more often than to the businesses against whom the act was originally directed. In the 1914 Clayton Act, Congress tried to limit the use of injunctions against unions in antitrust and other cases, but the courts nullified that effort as well.[16]

A Supreme Court decision in 1917 in a successful diversity suit by mine owners against the United Mine Workers shows how the injunction and "yellow-dog contracts" could be used in tandem.

The UMW was one of the few strong national unions then in the country. When it tried to unionize workers at the Hitchman Coal and Coke Company in West Virginia, the mine owners sued the unions to enjoin activities, charging it with conspiracy and wrongful interference with contract—the "yellow-dog contract." The company's claims were based on state law and were tried in federal court only because the union defendants and the coal company were from different states. In a sweeping decision, six members of the Court, with Justices Louis D. Brandeis, Oliver Wendell Holmes, and John Clarke dissenting, gave the mine owners everything they wanted.

As Edward Purcell writes, the result was that:

> After *Hitchman* the labor injunction swelled to flood tide ... By leveraging diversity jurisdiction, substantive due process, and the independence of federal equity, *Hitchman* expanded the power of the national courts and provided employers with a lethal anti-union weapon. Prior to 1917 yellow dog contracts had not been used extensively, but by the end of the 1920s they bound approximately 1,250,000 workers. To enforce them the courts issued hundreds of injunctions. In the repressive atmosphere, union membership dropped by 1,500,000, while unionized workers fell from 19.4 percent of the nonagricultural work force in 1920 to half that number a decade later.[17]

Between 1880 and 1920, state and federal courts issued almost a thousand such injunctions, with the federal courts especially active. Not until the Depression were the labor injunction and "yellow dog contracts" successfully curbed with passage of the Norris-LaGuardia Act in 1932 by overwhelming majorities in both the Senate and the House. Efforts to eliminate or reduce diversity jurisdiction failed, however.[18]

Injunctions were used by federal judges not only against labor unions but also against state efforts to control the rates of regulated industries like electricity, gas, transportation, and other utility companies that were started in the latter years of the nineteenth century. In 1908 the Court allowed utility officials to enjoin state officials from enforcing rate orders claimed to be "unreasonable" if a court found the rates "confiscatory"— according to a methodology favoring the utility. Like the removal jurisdiction, the right to enjoin state officials became a valuable weapon in later efforts to enforce individual rights against unconstitutional and illegal state acts.

Prior to the New Deal, the federal government made few efforts to control business or to regulate the market. The first significant attempt at federal regulation was in 1887, with the creation of the Interstate Commerce Commission (ICC) to control railroad pricing and to reduce the rampant discrimination and often ruinous competition caused by the harsh economics of the railroad industry. As Robert Rabin notes, however, the Supreme Court was quick to undermine and weaken the ICC. Its assault on railroad regulation began with a decision in an 1889 state case giving courts the authority to review commission-set rates for "reasonableness," what Rabin explains as a reflection of the Court's suspicion that western state legislatures influenced by the Populist movement would not adequately "protect the financial interests of the railroads and their wealthy backers." The judiciary was to be, as in our earliest days as a nation, "a bulwark between popular tyranny and traditional respect for property rights."[19]

Once the ICC got underway, the Supreme Court proceeded to undermine it. The Justices so restricted the commission's rate-setting and policy-making powers that within little more than a decade, an angry Justice John Harlan called the commission "a useless body for all practical purposes." Congress became more involved in regulation with the 1907 enactment of the Food and Drugs Act and the 1914 passage of the Federal Trade Commission Act, but the Court undermined the commissions established to administer these laws as well.[20]

Judicial conservatism was not limited to economic issues. The judiciary was equally conservative on free speech and racial and gender equality. Jim Crow was aided and abetted by the Supreme Court in cases like *Plessy v. Ferguson* (1886), which made "separate but equal" constitutionally acceptable and doomed black people to decades of brutal segregation, and *Grovey v. Townsend* (1935) which allowed Southern whites to exclude black people from primary elections, the only elections that counted in the South back then. Until 1930, restrictions on free speech were consistently upheld by the Supreme Court, despite powerful dissents from Brandeis and Holmes. Until 1940, the Court also refused to protect religious freedom. Few efforts were made to restrain law enforcement or prosecutorial abuses. The many civil liberties abuses during World War I and its immediate aftermath, the Palmer raids, went almost entirely unchecked by the courts, which in some instances, especially those involving labor disputes, actively and sometimes enthusiastically participated in suppressing dissent.[21]

This is not to say that during these years, the federal judges were uniformly hostile to unions, workers, farmers, minorities, and dissenters. Many decisions upheld state and local regulation of business interests. On the federal level, the Supreme Court construed the 1890 Sherman Act to ban most market sharing arrangements among independent entities. Ultimately, though not initially, the Court also allowed the government to strike at some of the trusts like Standard Oil in 1911, though the antitrust doctrines it established still allowed many large conglomerations to go forward. There were also some decisions advancing civil rights for blacks. And reversing its earlier restrictive attitude toward the ICC, the Court began to allow the commission to exercise broad powers, declaring that it would not interpose its own judgment of what was "wise." Moreover, some federal and state judges were not conservative at all. Nevertheless, the overall composition of the federal judiciary and the dominant feature of their jurisprudence prior to the late 1930s strongly favored the haves against the have-nots.[22]

The post-World War I period is well-known. During the 1920s, the conservatism of the nation and witch-hunts against radicals continued. J. Edgar Hoover began amassing his dossiers, and the federal courts continued to strike at state regulation.

In 1929, the bubble burst. Franklin D. Roosevelt took office in 1933 and launched a host of national programs and agencies to deal with the Depression. The courts, including the Supreme Court, were still dominated by conservative Republicans, and they fought a vigorous rearguard action, striking down one New Deal program after another, rendering the nation powerless to deal with the crisis. By 1936, the Court had invalidated six federal laws, including laws for industrial recovery, agriculture, mining, and railway pensions. The lower courts were also busy. According to one estimate, they issued more than 2,000 injunctions against federal programs, mostly against taxes under the Agricultural Adjustment Act, though many other programs were affected. Sheldon Goldman has found that 1,600 injunctions against New Deal programs were issued by the lower courts just in 1935–36.[23]

In 1936 Roosevelt won by a landslide and hostility to the Supreme Court was a major issue in the election. He decided to add new Justices to the Court to overcome the conservative majority. He failed ignominiously, but it made no difference. In 1937, Supreme Court Justice Owen Roberts abandoned the conservatives, and within a few years, they were all replaced by Justices sympathetic to labor and the regulatory state.

The years from 1937 to 1960 reflected the enduring influence of the New Deal in some areas, but produced new crises that New Deal attitudes and doctrines had either been unable to anticipate, such as those arising out of the Cold War, or had not tried to deal with, like African-American demands for true equality.

This transitional period can be divided into four segments: the New Deal judicial revolution, 1937–41; the war years, 1942–46; the immediate postwar period, 1947–50; and the Cold War era, 1951–60. As always, the strict hierarchy in the federal judicial system made the Supreme Court the primary actor.

1937–41. As a result of Justice Owen Roberts's "switch in time" in April 1937, the Court began to turn away from its attack on social legislation. The breakthrough came in the *Jones & Laughlin* steel case, in which the Court allowed Congress to regulate labor relations in manufacturing that could "have a most serious effect upon interstate commerce." Soon, one New Deal law after another was upheld as the Court turned away from trying to monitor laws passed to deal with the national economy, allowing Congress to regulate the farthest corners of the national economy. For sixty years this doctrine held until the arrival of the Rehnquist Court in the 1990s.[24]

Two other early judicial rulings had transformative effects. In 1938, in *Erie v. Tompkins*, the 82-year-old Brandeis finally succeeded in his long campaign to overthrow *Swift v. Tyson*. Henceforth, federal judges would have to apply the substantive law created by state judges and legislatures in diversity cases, though the procedural rules, the rules that determine how a case is tried, would still be a matter of federal law; drawing the line between "substance" and "procedure" would spawn years of uncertainty and litigation over what was substance and what was procedure.[25]

That same year, in the course of undoing the restraints on Congressional authority over the national economy, the Court issued the most famous footnote in constitutional history, footnote 4 of *U.S. v. Carolene Products*. In that case, the Court asserted that economic regulatory legislation was entitled to a presumption of constitutionality. This meant that legislation was not to be overturned unless it was obviously unconstitutional, and the Court made it clear that this would be rare. Of equal importance for the future, the Court suggested in footnote 4 that it would be much more skeptical of legislation encroaching on the specific provisions of the Bill of Rights and other sections of the Constitution that protected individual rights. It also raised the possibility that it might also be concerned about measures affecting racial or other "discrete and insular minorities."[26]

The following year, another of the Court's transformative decisions was issued in a murder case from Connecticut dealing with a state's right to appeal. In one of his last decisions on the Court, Justice Benjamin Cardozo wrote that state and local officials must, like the federal government, honor those rights that go "to the essence of a scheme of ordered liberty" and that "lie at the base of all our civil and political institutions." This became known as the "incorporation doctrine," and in succeeding decades, the Court proceeded to "incorporate" most of the Bill of Rights such as the First Amendment and protections for the criminally accused.[27]

The Court's efforts to impose fair criminal procedures on the states had actually begun much earlier, but only fitfully. In 1936, the Court began to try to eliminate the use of coercion by state officials to obtain confessions, overturning a conviction in a Mississippi case in which a black man had been hanged from a tree by his thumbs to force him to confess. In ensuing years, the Court continued to overturn state convictions in a largely futile effort to stop the police from coercing confessions, culminating with its decision in the *Miranda* case in 1966.[28]

One other area began to be changed by the new Court in this relatively brief period—civil rights for black Americans. Ever since *Plessy v. Ferguson*, and even earlier, the Supreme Court had allied itself more often with the white supremacists than with civil rights advocates. As late as 1935, the pre–New Deal Court had upheld an all-white primary in Texas, after striking down two earlier versions in 1927 and 1932. The 1935 decision was overruled nine years later, but even prior to that, in 1938 the Court told Missouri it could not exclude a black applicant from its law school by offering to pay his tuition at an out-of-state law school, thereby starting the Court on the road to *Brown v. Board of Education*.[29]

The lower courts were also transformed. When Roosevelt took office, according to Sheldon Goldman, he was not overly concerned about the policy views of the lower court judiciary, which in the early years of the New Deal was about three-fourths Republican. But in 1935, when the New Deal became more reformist in response to the continuing Depression, and the Republican-dominated judiciary struck down program after program, what Goldman calls the "policy-agenda" reason for a judicial appointment became much more significant. Goldman found that overall, twenty-four of FDR's fifty Court of Appeals appointments were to further his policy agenda, with twenty of these between 1935 and 1940; most of the rest of his appointments were for partisan political reasons.[30]

During Roosevelt's twelve years in office, the federal judiciary was expanded by some 25 percent to 193 district judges and fifty-nine appellate judges. Of these, he appointed 183 district judges and fifty circuit judges so that by 1945, the federal judiciary had been transformed.

1942–46. During the war years, the Court continued to enlarge federal power over the economy, vigorously enforcing the antitrust laws and giving a broad reading to the Norris-LaGuardia Act, so that labor was largely freed from court injunctions.

The most prominent feature of this Court was, however, its wartime decisions. It is a constant in American history, going back to our first decade, that when the nation perceives a foreign or serious internal threat, the incumbent administration, no matter which party is in power, adopts harsh measures against suspected enemies and all too often against those who merely dissent. In the name of national security, civil liberties are flagrantly violated. So it was in the late 1790s, when the Federalist Party under John Adams and Alexander Hamilton, believing that the revolutionaries in France and their American supporters like Thomas Jefferson and the Republicans would destroy the Republic, passed the Alien and Sedition Laws. With these laws, they prosecuted and severely punished critics of the administration and party foes. One-hundred twenty years later, World War I and then the American reaction to the Russian Revolution and its aftermath also produced a wholesale abandonment of judicial concern for civil liberty. This was repeated during the Cold War era, during the Vietnam years, and now again post–September 11. Almost invariably, the courts have rubber-stamped and sometimes applauded what the authorities did.

The conventional wisdom is that after such abuses, the nation and the courts advance the cause of civil liberty beyond where the nation was before the crisis, thus making overall progress. In fact, that has happened rarely. One such instance was in 1969, when the Court adopted a stringent clear-and-present-danger test whereby speech may be forbidden only if it is "directed to inciting or producing imminent lawless action and is likely to incite or produce such action." But that was during the 1960s, when the Court was in one of its rare reformist phases, and has few if any parallels. Most of the time, there has been little or no such forward movement, but merely a return to the status quo once the hysteria subsided. At times, the situation became worse, both in the society and especially in the courts. The World War I abuses and the cases allowing them were succeeded by the Red raids of 1919–20 which were generally sustained by the courts, and then by the decisions in the mid-1920s on "criminal syndicalism." The World War II cases were followed by McCarthy-era decisions like the *Dennis* case, which in turn were limited somewhat in the late 1950s.[31]

The low point of this period was the infamous Japanese internment case, *Korematsu v. United States* (1944), in which the internment of about 112,000 Japanese-Americans, 65,000 of whom were citizens, was upheld by the Court. This decision has never been overruled and, indeed, was cited as authority in 2001 by the ultra-conservative Washington Legal Foundation and other conservative lawyers to support George W. Bush's Executive Order of November 13, 2001 authorizing the establishment of military tribunals for "enemy combatants."[32]

The earliest World War II decision came in 1942, in *Ex parte Quirin*, a case involving German saboteurs tried by a military tribunal. This case was the primary authority in support of the Bush military tribunal order. In a hastily written decision the Court upheld the use of these tribunals. A year after the war, the Court upheld the death penalty for Japanese General Yamashita in a proceeding rife with gross violations of the most elementary due process. These "enemy combatant" cases have never been judicially questioned, though members of the *Quirin*

Court later expressed unhappiness with the opinion and decision, and legal experts consider the decision poorly reasoned.[33]

During this period, the Court continued to support the New Deal with decisions upholding federal regulatory actions, antitrust enforcement and protection of labor. It began to expand First Amendment protections, suggesting in a 1946 case that these rights occupied a preferred position over property rights, and issued its landmark decision allowing schoolchildren who were Jehovah's Witnesses to refuse to salute the flag during World War II, in deference to the Witnesses' religious convictions.[34]

1947–1960. The postwar period began a new chapter in judicial history. Not only did the issues begin to change, but the composition of the Court changed significantly. New Deal reformism waned, Cold War pressures began, and the Supreme Court began to move to the right again, though this time on different issues.

President Harry Truman was not too concerned about the ideological views of his nominees since by now there was no longer much of a fight over the direction of national economic and social policy. His primary concerns were patronage and friendship. Nevertheless, despite his own liberal leanings, between 1945 and 1949 Truman tilted the Supreme Court to the right. He appointed Fred M. Vinson of Kentucky as chief justice, replacing Harlan F. Stone. Owen Roberts and Roosevelt appointees Frank Murphy and Wiley Rutledge also left the Court, and three new justices were appointed—Harold H. Burton (1945), Tom C. Clark (1949), and Sherman Minton (1949), all of whom were conservative. These joined the liberal Hugo Black and William O. Douglas, and the increasingly conservative former New Dealers Felix Frankfurter, Robert Jackson, and Stanley Reed.

Three crucial judicial developments mark this period: The Court began its tortuous efforts to separate church and state; it barred judicial enforcement of restrictive covenants in deeds that barred the sale of real property to nonwhites; and it issued the first of its Cold War decisions.

In the late 1940s, Cold War hysteria swept the nation, fomented by the Republican Party and led by Senator Joseph McCarthy. The hysteria did not subside until the mid-1950s, and in the second half of the decade, the Court—with new members—began to curb the most extreme of the excesses. By then, of course, countless individuals in all parts of American life had seen their careers and much of their lives destroyed, in many cases beyond repair.

The central judicial event of the decade of the '50s, however, was of course the school desegregation cases. The replacement of Fred M. Vinson as Chief Justice by Governor Earl Warren of California was crucial, for unlike Vinson, he was totally committed to racial justice for blacks.* Upon his accession to the High Court, Warren immediately set about producing an opinion in simple non-legalistic language that would have all nine Justices behind it. The price of unanimity was the follow-up decision in 1955 to allow Southern school boards to desegregate the schools gradually. This approach ultimately resulted in delays of some thirteen years before the South was forced to undertake school desegregation in earnest in 1968.

President Dwight D. Eisenhower was not too interested in the ideology of his appointees, even though Republicans by this time accounted for only about one-fifth of the judges, and the judiciary had a largely liberal approach. The courts had not yet gotten as deeply into social issues as they were to become, and Eisenhower was not interested in reversing the New Deal anyway. He relied heavily on the Justice Department and was primarily concerned with appointing middle-of-the-road

---

* Though not at the time for Asian Americans, having built his political career in part on hostility to West Coast Chinese and Japanese immigrants and citizens. He had been a moving force behind the Japanese Internment of 1942.

lawyers of ability. For this reason, the American Bar Association was brought into the process and its ratings given a great deal of weight.

For the Supreme Court, Eisenhower indicated early on that he wanted experienced appellate court judges, and three of his four appointments came from either the federal courts of appeal (John M. Harlan and Potter Stewart) or in one case, that of William J. Brennan, from the New Jersey Supreme Court; the only exception was Earl Warren.

As a result, some of the most important judicial figures in the civil rights struggle of the ensuing years were Republican lower court judges, such as Frank Johnson, Elbert Tuttle, and John Minor Wisdom, even though Eisenhower himself was unhappy with the Court's desegregation ruling. For these judges, and particularly for the district judges in the trial courts, desegregation required great courage, for it often brought down upon their heads intense anger from longtime friends and associates, social ostracism, and numerous death threats. By contrast, many Democratic judges had been appointed by segregationist Southern senators and were not eager to enforce black rights.

1960–68. Between 1960 and 1968, the final of the three great transformations of the twentieth century took shape. The New Deal created the first two: a change in the relationship between the federal government and the American people, which established a major role for the government in American economic life, both to protect the economically defenseless—labor unions, older people, workers—and to control the excesses of business. The *Brown* case in 1954 started a third revolution, a "rights revolution," in which racial minorities, women, criminal defendants, aliens, and others victimized by our social and legal system fought for fair and equal treatment. Initially, this was achieved through the courts by black groups who demonstrated that the judicial system could be a powerful agent for social change. Black success in the courts led the way for the other groups, as well as for the expansion of the right to free speech, church-state separation, reproductive rights, and more.

At about the same time, in the mid-1960s, Congress acted to implement and expand on the judicial decisions, as well as to create many new social programs, including Medicare, Head Start, and the Legal Services Corporation. This judicial and legislative reformism hit a peak during 1960–68, though the early 1970s saw further regulatory developments on such matters as consumer protection and the environment. The Supreme Court led the way of course, but the lower courts, increasingly staffed by Kennedy-Johnson appointments, really made the decisions of the Supreme Court the law of the land.

The primary concern of Kennedy and Johnson, but particularly of Lyndon B. Johnson, was to ensure that their Court of Appeals and District Court appointees were sympathetic toward civil rights (though in some cases Kennedy was afraid to cross powerful Southern senators and appointed known segregationists). Sheldon Goldman has concluded that each made three appointments to the Courts of Appeals on a "policy basis" (the policy being civil rights), which accounted for 7 percent of Kennedy's appellate appointments and 3 percent of Johnson's. "Partisan agenda" reasons accounted for most of the rest, and usually this also meant liberal Democrats.

In the late '60s, the tide began to turn. The three revolutions had struck at central features of American conservatism: The New and Fair Deals, with their combination of regulation and social welfare, struck at the freewheeling business practices of corporate America and at the pocketbooks of the wealthy; the rights revolution offended the social conservatives and the South, which the Republican Party began to see as the key to its electoral success. Richard Nixon's 1968 "Southern strategy"

a key element of his presidential campaign, was the first of the
continuing Republican efforts to capitalize on the South's hostility to fair treatment of America's blacks.

1969–1980. The accession of Richard Nixon to the presidency began the process of deliberately restoring the federal
judiciary to its traditional conservatism. Nixon reintroduced
ideology into judicial appointments, to a degree not seen since
FDR, in order to promote his law-and-order and Southern
agenda. The rhetorically neutral cover for this was "strict construction," to set up a contrast with the Warren Court's activist
approach. In practice, "strict construction" meant that the
courts would not move beyond already established principles
in their civil rights and civil liberties decisions, and would not
use the courts for social progress. They would work, instead, to
maintain the status quo. This was contrasted with "judicial
activism," which, in practice and as explained more fully
below, meant using the courts to move forward in these areas.[35]

Despite Nixon's intentions, he does not seem to have gone
about the task of picking "strict constructionists" very system-
atically. Although a Nixon staff member urged the establishment of a review procedure for federal judges at all levels, there
seems to be no evidence that a formal vetting procedure was
ever adopted. And though Nixon obviously appointed conservative judges, since he chose Republicans almost entirely, it
does not appear that he was too concerned about the views of
his nominees on anything but criminal justice. Still, Nixon's
appointees did tilt the Court back to the right. It started, as it
had to, with the Supreme Court.[36]

But not yet and not entirely. In some respects, as Tom
Wicker points out, Nixon was a moderate. His four appointments to the Supreme Court turned out to cover a wide spectrum. His first appointment, the replacement of Chief Justice
Earl Warren with Warren E. Burger, was relatively moderate,

at least during Burger's early years on the Court. Nixon's southern strategy stumbled when he failed to put either Judge Clement Haynsworth of South Carolina or G. Harrold Carswell of Florida on the High Court to replace Abe Fortas, who was forced to resign in 1969. Instead, Nixon had to settle for Harry Blackmun, a cautious moderate from Minnesota who developed after a few years into one of the Court's staunchest liberals on everything but criminal justice. Then, when Justices Hugo Black and John Harlan died, one of the two successors was Lewis Powell. Powell was a conservative Democrat from Virginia, but, despite his conservatism, he often voted with the liberals on the most controversial issues, thereby becoming the swing vote as the Court became polarized along liberal-conservative lines. The Court also continued to enforce the antidiscrimination laws of the mid-1960s and to apply the principles of the *Brown* case to Northern schools. In all these areas, the lower courts were crucial, since decisions on Northern school-segregation frequently turned on complex factual disputes about intention and effect that the lower courts had to resolve. If a violation was found, they also had to devise and enforce complex remedies.

Nixon's fourth appointee—William Rehnquist—was something else. Rehnquist opposes almost everything that the federal judiciary has done to advance human rights and government regulation during the past fifty years. He was raised in an extremely conservative family that despised Roosevelt and the New Deal, and from his boyhood days, he planted himself firmly on the far-right end of the political spectrum. Until joined by Reagan appointees Sandra Day O'Connor and Antonin Scalia, he was often alone in dissent, even from his conservative colleagues on the Burger Court.

Rehnquist was a brilliant law student at Stanford and became a law clerk to Justice Robert Jackson. During his clerkship,

Rehnquist wrote a memo to Jackson in a case challenging the exclusion of black voters from a Texas primary in which Rehnquist said, "It is about time the Court faced the fact that the white people in the South don't like the colored people; the Constitution restrains them from effecting this dislike through state action, but it most assuredly did not appoint the Court as a sociological watchdog to rear up every time private discrimination raises its admittedly ugly head." Jackson ignored him.[38]

When the *Brown* case came before the court, Rehnquist urged that *Plessy v. Ferguson* be affirmed, which Jackson also ignored. Rehnquist displayed the same hostility to Warren and Burger Court rulings. An April 1969 memo by Rehnquist when he was Assistant Attorney General, which was not disclosed to the Senate, castigated the Warren Court's criminal justice rulings and expressed disdain for the Court's decisions applying most of the Bill of Rights to state and local officials, the "incorporation" doctrine discussed earlier. In addition, there was evidence that Rehnquist had harassed black voters in Phoenix, Arizona, in the '60s. Rehnquist denied this of course, but there were affidavits supporting the charges from numerous witnesses. One witness had heard Rehnquist say "I am against all civil rights laws." In 1964 Rehnquist challenged a proposed public accommodations ordinance for the City of Phoenix with the comment that "the ordinance summarily does away with the historic right of the owner of a drug store, lunch counter, or theatre to choose his own customers." Despite all this, Rehnquist was confirmed.[39]

During Gerald Ford's brief tenure upon Nixon's resignation, he had one appointment, the successor to William O. Douglas. Ford was not an ideologue and his Attorney General was Edward Levi, one of the most distinguished legal scholars in the country. Levi opted for quality over ideology, and to succeed Douglas, on Levi's recommendation, Ford chose John Paul Stevens, a centrist

Court of Appeals judge in Chicago, who has moved, often unpredictably, from left to right and then back to left again. In the 1990s, he came to identify more and more with the liberals, as the Court's center of gravity moved sharply to the right.

Because he was so often the lone dissenter, Rehnquist had relatively little influence during his first years on the Court. The result was that during the 1970s and for much of the 1980s, before Powell left the Court in 1987, the then-moderate Burger, the increasingly liberal Blackmun, and the occasionally moderate Powell made the Burger Court a surprisingly liberal institution with respect to what were to become some of the most contentious issues of the times—abortion, school desegregation, women's rights, affirmative action, and church-state separation.

This is not to say that the Burger Court did not represent a significant shift to the right. It did, particularly in criminal justice. While not overruling the landmark criminal justice decisions on searches, arrests, and confessions, the Court began a process of chipping away at them by crafting exceptions in lax interpretations of the decisions, a process that has continued to this day. They did not turn the clock back to the time that police were totally unaccountable, but by the time Rehnquist became chief justice in 1986, there were few controls left, and certainly far fewer than had been intended by the Warren Court.

States rights are another area in which the Burger Court conservatives tried to initiate what became a wide-ranging and continuing crusade during the '90s. The goal of this campaign, which has always been a major focus of Rehnquist's efforts, is not so much the enhancement of state authority, except residually, but to curtail federal power, with the primary target the New Deal and other social and regulatory legislation initiated by Roosevelt, Kennedy, and Johnson, and carried forward by subsequent Congresses.

Rehnquist's first victory in his crusade against the federal government came in 1976, when the conservatives cobbled together five votes, including a "not untroubled" Blackmun, to strike down federal minimum wage and hour standards for state employees. The statute violated state sovereignty, said Rehnquist, writing for the Court. His victory was short-lived. The criteria he laid down for applying the decision were so ambiguous and uncertain that after nine years of judicial confusion, Blackmun switched to the dissenters and they overturned the 1976 decision.[40]

Civil rights was another area in which the Court began to move to the right. The most serious setback for the civil rights movement came in a case in the mid-1970s. In a 1974 case from Michigan, the Court prohibited school desegregation remedies that encompassed both an inner city and a suburban school district unless both districts were found to have deliberately segregated their schools. It was rarely possible to prove deliberate segregation by the newer suburbs, in contrast with old inner cities like Detroit and Chicago. The result was to encourage white flight to the suburbs and to doom minority children to racial isolation.[41]

During Gerald Ford's brief tenure he appointed some Democrats, though not to the Courts of Appeals. The primary result of the Nixon and Ford appointments was that the lower court judiciary shifted from 70 percent Democrat to more than 50 percent Republican by 1976.

During the Jimmy Carter presidency, there were two major developments that reflected and influenced the federal judiciary profoundly. One was a nonevent: For the first time in the century, a president had no opportunity to make a Supreme Court appointment. He was thereby unable to significantly influence the nation's constitutional jurisprudence. On the other hand, Congress increased the size of the federal judiciary by almost a third—from 525 to 677, adding 117 district judges and thirty-five appellate judges. This enabled Carter to exercise a strong influence on the makeup of the federal judiciary despite his short presidential tenure.

Carter also tried to reduce the partisan-political aspects by requiring that judicial commissions be established to recommend qualified candidates and to open up the process. Although senators objected to this, Carter was able to establish such commissions for the appellate courts, thus concentrating these appointments in the White House, and leaving the district judges largely to the local Democratic senators, if there were any.

Although Carter had no particular ideological agenda—most of his appointees were middle of the road, and he appointed a number of known conservatives—he was bent on increasing the number of minorities and women. As a result, at the end of his presidency, out of a total of 258 appointments, he had succeeded in appointing forty women, twenty-nine to the trial bench and eleven to the appeals courts, and fifty-five racial minorities, forty-three district judges and twelve appellate judges. Democrats accounted for 60 percent of the lower court judiciary. Because minorities and women tend to be more liberal than others in the general population, which was especially true in the '70s, this gave a distinctly liberal cast to the lower court judiciary. At the close of the Carter presidency, some 60 percent of the federal judges were Democrats, of which 6.9 percent were women. He appointed fourteen Hispanic district judges, two Hispanic appellate judges, and for the first time, there were black judges in eleven Southern and border states.[42]

• • •

1. This section draws heavily on Gordon Wood's two magisterial works, *The Creation of the American Republic* 1776-1787 (1969) ("Creation") and *The Radicalism of the*

American Revolution (1991), ("Radicalism'), on Morton Horwitz, *The Transforma-tion of American Law* (1977) and on Richard Ellis, *The Jeffersonian Crisis* (1971). The reference to the colonists' use of the courts is in John P. Frank, Historical Bases of the Federal Judicial System, 13 L. & *Contemp. Probs.* 3, 12, 18, 23, 27 (1948) ("Frank").

2. Wood, *Creation* 161.
3. *The Federalist* 48, 49 (Cooke ed.) 336-37; see also *The Federalist* 71.
4. Creation 454. This did not happen in France or in Europe which continued to insist that judges be relatively minor civil servants, with as limited a function in law-making as possible. The limits proved to be weak if not actually nonexistent. Because every legal norm requires interpretation when it is applied, particularly to new and unforeseen circumstances, creative interpretation, a disguised form of law-making, is unavoidable. Nevertheless, for the most part, the civil law judge's role in law-making remained modest.
5. The quotations are from Frank at 12, 18, 23 and 27.
6. 10 U.S. 87, 126 (1810). The full story is told in George L. Haskins and Herbert A. Johnson, *History of the Supreme Court of the United States-Foundations of Power: John Marshall 1801-1815*, (pp. 340-53; see also C. Peter Magrath, *Yazoo* pp. 70-84, 107 (1966).
7. Magrath at p. 101.
8. Radicalism 323
9. *Democracy in America*, pp 279-80 (1837) (Everyman Edition, 1994)
10. Radicalism 323.
11. *Swift v. Tyson*, 41 U.S. 1 (1842).
12. The best discussion of Swift v. Tyson is in Edward Purcell, *Brandeis and the Pro-gressive Tradition* (2000) ("Purcell").
13. Friedman and Ladinsky, "Social Change and the Law of Industrial Accidents," 67 *Colum. L. Rev.* 50, 51-58 (1967).
14. Patricia M. Wald, "Some Thoughts on Judging As Gleaned From One Hundred Years of the Harvard Law Review and Other Great Books," 100 *Harv. L. Rev.* 887, 888 (1987).
15. *Lochner v New York*, 198 U.S. 45 (1905); *Hammer v. Dagenhart*, 247 U.S. 495 (1918) (child labor); *Kidd v. Pearson*, 128 U.S. 1 (1888) (commerce clause and manufacturing).
16. Duplex Co. Deering, 254 U.S. 443 (1921).
17. *Hitchman Coal and Coke Co v. Mitchell*, 245 U.S. 229 (1917); Purcell, p.77
18. Id. at 70.
19. Rabin, "Federal Regulation in Historical: Perspective," 38 *Stan. L. Rev.* 1189 (May 1986).
20. Id. at 1230-36.
21. *Plessy v. Ferguson*, 163 U.S. 537 (1896); *Grovey v. Townsend*, 295 U.S. 45 (1935); David Rabban, *Free Speech In Its Forgotten Years* (1997); William Preston, *Aliens and Dissenters* (1963); Zechariah Chafee, *Freedom of Expression,* especially 40-119 (1920).
22. *E.C. Knight Co. v. United States*, 156 U.S. 1 (1985) (1895) (price-fixing illegal); Standard Oil Co. v. United States, 221 U.S. 1 (1911); *Buchanan v. Warley*, 245 U.S. 60 (1917) (civil rights).
23. Purcell 34; Sheldon Goldman, *Picking Federal Judges: Lower Court Selection from Roosevelt to Reagan*, p. 31 (1997) Goldman 1997).
24. *NLRB v. Jones & Laughlin Steel Co.*, 301 U.S. 1 (1937).
25. *Erie RR. Co. v. Tompkins,* 304 U.S. 64 (1938).

26. 340 U.S. 144, 152 n. 4. (1938).

27. *Palko v. Connecticut*, 302 U.S. 319 (1937).

28. *Brown v. Mississippi*, 297 U.S. 278 (1936); *Miranda v. Arizona*, 384 U.S. 436 (1966)

29. *Grovey v. Townsend*, 295 U.S. 45 (1935), overruled, Smith v. Albright, 321U.S. 649 (all-white primary) (1944); Missouri ex rel. *Gaines v. Canada*, 305 U.S.57 (1938) (law school).

30. Goldman 1997, pp. 30-31, 38.

31. *Brandenburg v. Ohio*, 395 U.S. 444 (1969); Zechariah Chafee *Freedom of Expression* 40-119 (1920) (court approval of abuses); *Whitney v. California*, 274 U.S. 357 (1927) (anarchism); *Dennis v. United States*, 341 U.S. 494 (1951) (Communist Party); *Yates v. United States*, 354 U.S. 298 (1957) (limiting Dennis).

32. Korematsu v. United States, 323 U.S. 214, (1944); William A. Glaberson, "A Nation Challenged: The Government's Case," *New York Times*, Dec. 5, 2001, p. B6..

33. Ex parte Quirin, 317, U.S. 1 (1942; In re Yamashita, 327 U.S. 1 (1946); George Lardner, Jr., "Nazi Saboteurs Captured FDR Orders Secret Tribunal," *Washington Post Magazine*, Jan. 13, 2002, p. W2. A critical discussion of the Yamashita case appears in Stephen B. Ives, Jr., "Vengeance Did Not Deliver Justice," *Washington Post*, Dec. 28, 2001.

34. *Marsh v. Alabama*, 326 U.S. 501 (1946) (preferred position); West Virginia State Board of Ed. v. Barnette, 319 U.S. 624 (1943) religious convictions).

35. Goldman 1997, p. 198.

36. Id. at 207.

37. See generally, Tom Wicker, *One of Us* (1991).

38. The memorandum appears in testimony of Julius L. Chambers, Legal Defense Fund, at *Hearings Before the U.S. Sente Committee on the Judiciary on the Confirmation of William Hubbs Rehnquist to be Chief Justice of the United States*, 99th Cong., 2nd sess., p. 896 (1986). The case was *Terry v. Adams*, 345 U.S. 461 (1953) .

39. Rehnquist's memo on *Plessy v. Ferguson* is discussed in Richard Kluger, *Simple Jusice* (1977), pp. 605-06; the April 1969 memo is quoted and discussed in John Dean, *The Rehnquist Choice* (2001), pp. 278-80; Rehnquist's activities in Phoenix are discussed in Herman Schwartz, *Packing the Courts*, (1987), pp. 113-14. The "incorporation" doctrine is discussed on p. 28

40. *National League of Cities v. Usery*, 426 U.S. 833 (1976) (overruled); Garcia v. San Antonio Metropolitan Transit Authority, 469 U.S. 528 (1985).

41. *Milliken v. Bradley*, 488 U.S. 717 (1974).

42. Goldman 1997, pp. 236-84 (the Carter record).

Chapter 2

1981–1988

1981–1984

The double blow of the 1979 oil shock, which produced startlingly high inflation, and the Iranian hostage-taking of Americans were too much for a president who had not aroused much affection or respect. President Jimmy Carter thus had little chance of winning a second term and Ronald Reagan won handily in 1980.

The welfare-regulatory responsibilities undertaken by government, and the revolution in women's rights, sexual practices, and other social attitudes and behavior were both targeted by Ronald Reagan and the conservatives upon their accession to power in 1980. Reagan's prime targets were civil rights—one of his earliest campaign trips was to Philadelphia, Mississippi, where three civil rights workers had been killed in 1964—and the Supreme Court decisions on abortion, school desegregation, affirmative action, school prayer, the rights of prisoners and criminal defendants, as well as antitrust and other economic regulation, including environmental protection. Because the federal courts had been in the forefront on these issues, a takeover of the courts by the right was among the first orders of business. Liberal judges were to be replaced by zealous young right-wingers who believed in "judicial restraint" and would be on the bench for years to come; doctrines expanding the authority of both the federal courts and other parts of the federal government to protect individual and other rights would be cut back; once again, a nearly unfettered market would be king. The architect of this policy was presidential counselor and later Attorney General Edwin Meese III, supported by right-wing think tanks, pressure groups, and the newly established Federalist Society.

The Reagan-Meese strategy depended on two key elements: a systematic ideological screening system for judicial nominations initially recommended to Nixon but not implemented by him, and an emphasis on youth. To promote ideological purity as rigorously as possible, a Committee on Federal Judicial Selection was established and chaired by Counsel to the President Fred Fielding; it included Meese, Attorney General William French Smith, and other top White House and Justice Department officials. A computer data bank containing every available publication by a candidate was set up, and daylong interviews were held with the finalists. The role of the American Bar Association was reduced. More controversially, senatorial influence over the choice of judges was reduced, which often led to sharp clashes between Republican senators and the White House. According to Stephen Markman, who was in charge of judicial selection in Reagan's second term, "the Reagan administration has in place what is probably the most thorough and comprehensive system for recruiting and screening federal judicial candidates of any administration ever. This administration has, moreover, attempted to assert the president's prerogatives over judicial selection more consistently than many of its predecessors."[1]

The goal, according to Meese, was to "institutionalize the

Reagan revolution so that it can't be set aside no matter what happens in future presidential elections. Young conservatives were to be named, wherever possible, so that the revolution would last long after Reagan was gone. Fred Fielding vetoed a sixty-nine-year-old candidate for an appellate slot with the comment, "in view of Judge Neaher's age, appointment runs counter to President's desire to appoint younger judges who will have lasting impact on the judiciary." During Reagan's first term, 11.4 percent of all his appointees were under 40, a higher percentage than under any previous Presidents in recent years; the average age of his appeals court appointees during his first term was 51.5, the youngest average of the past five administrations. Examples of this youth movement included the appointment of the 42-year-old Richard A. Posner, a leading conservative theoretician when nominated, and 35-year-old Frank Easterbrook, both of the University of Chicago Law School, to the Seventh Circuit (Illinois, Indiana, Wisconsin); J. Harvie Wilkinson, 39 when nominated to the Fourth Circuit (Maryland to South Carolina); Kenneth Starr, an assistant to former Attorney General William French Smith, 36 when named to the US Court of Appeals for the District of Columbia; Alex Kozinski, 34 when nominated to the Ninth Circuit, which covers the West Coast; and Edith Jones (one of Reagan's few female nominees) who was 36 when appointed to the Fifth Circuit (Texas, Mississippi, and Louisiana). Despite Reagan's obvious agenda during his first term, there was little opposition to his nominations; it helped that his party controlled the Senate all four years.[2]

Within a few months of his inauguration, Reagan had his first Supreme Court appointment when the ailing Justice Potter Stewart retired. Reagan used the occasion to appoint the first female Justice, an early example of the curious attitude of recent Republican presidents toward affirmative action. While opposing affirmative action in almost all other contexts, both Reagan and George H.W. Bush quite openly chose obscure, undistinguished judges for the Supreme Court, only on the basis of their gender and race—Sandra Day O'Connor and Clarence Thomas. O'Connor's nomination was not based on her legal qualifications or reputation. When nominated, she was an unknown Arizona lower-court judge, with no national prominence and no federal experience, and she was not considered a distinguished judge among Arizona lawyers. She would not have made any gender-blind list of likely Supreme Court nominees.

Clarence Thomas had been chairman of the Equal Employment Opportunities Commission and briefly a judge on the federal appeals court in Washington, D.C.. He had not particularly distinguished himself in either position, and it is highly unlikely that he would have been even considered for the Supreme Court had he not been black. But he was succeeding Thurgood Marshall, and politics required that Marshall be succeeded by another African-American. As events proved, the Thomas appointment was a brilliant stroke. Though it turned out to be very controversial for reasons having nothing to do with his race, many black people rallied to his support, neither knowing nor perhaps caring about his extreme conservatism, which he concealed during his hearing but which he has consistently manifested during his Supreme Court tenure.

Although it was feared by some on the right that Justice O'Connor would not be sufficiently conservative, particularly with respect to abortion, their fears turned out to be unwarranted. Though she has tried to position herself in the center and to exercise the leverage that Lewis Powell had, she has been far more conservative on issues like abortion, civil rights for racial minorities, affirmative action, habeas corpus, and church-state separation. Since joining the Court in 1981, and despite a few swing votes, she has been a leader in shutting the courthouse door to civil rights litigants and others.

On civil rights, numbers tell the story best. In her first sixteen years on the Court, she voted in some sixty-seven cases dealing directly and specifically with the rights of racial and other minorities. Of these, twenty-six cases were decided either unanimously (thirteen), by 8-1 votes (five) or by 7-2 votes (eight), with forty-one sharply split racial decisions.

Putting aside for the moment the twenty-six decisions decided by unanimous, 8-1, or 7-2 votes, where she voted for minorities sixteen times, Justice O'Connor voted against the minority litigant in thirty-nine of the forty-one close cases involving race. These cases dealt with almost every legal issue related to racial justice, including voting rights, employment, school desegregation, affirmative action, the scope of enforcement for federal civil rights statutes, jury selection, and capital punishment. In recent years the Court has taken very few race cases, but her votes and opinions have continued to show a consistent hostility to the aspirations of minority claimants.[3]

There is one significant break in this pattern: the 2003 decision upholding individualized racial preferences for minority law students at the University of Michigan in *Grutter v. Bollinger*. In essence, she adopted the approach taken by Justice Lewis Powell in the 1978 *Regents of University of California v. Bakke* case, where he laid out a road map for universities to follow: Race could be considered a plus factor so long as others factors like background, personal history, and other achievements were also considered in a system that analyzed each application individually.

The same day the Court decided another University of Michigan case, *Gratz v. Bollinger*, which involved a point system used by the undergraduate colleges at Michigan in which minority status was given twenty points out of 150. In that case, she reverted to form and voted against the program because it was not individualized enough.[4]

The law school case, *Grutter*, is immensely important, because it preserved significant opportunities for racial and ethnic minorities to obtain a graduate education and will probably not be difficult for universities to abide by. Its impact in other contexts like government contracts and employment is quite uncertain, however, since the case for diversity in both *Bakke* and *Grutter* was linked to the academic setting. A Court sympathetic to racial minorities would find *Grutter* useful for these other settings, but neither this Court nor Justice O'Connor have shown such sympathy for racial minorities in other contexts.

Moreover, the two rulings do little to make educational affirmative action more acceptable to the courts than it is now— they merely keep the status quo. In the undergraduate case, *Gratz*, they made it very difficult to use a point system, and insisted on individualized decision-making. This may be quite feasible for schools of higher education, but it is impossible to apply in elementary and secondary schools. Children have not done much at these young ages, even at the high school entry level, except to get grades. Federal judges have struck down affirmative action plans for magnet schools in Maryland and Virginia, the Boston Latin School and elsewhere. Such schools will not be helped by the Court's rulings, which will continue to make even a limited amount of elementary and secondary school desegregation very difficult.[5]

In other areas, O'Connor has been equally conservative. She has been a solidly reliable member of the 5-4 bloc led by Rehnquist that has elevated the long-discredited "the King can do no wrong" doctrine into a superconstitutional principle to block suits by disabled, elderly, and other people whose rights have been violated by state governments; she has voted against allowing legal services lawyers to challenge unconstitutional or otherwise illegal welfare statutes and to obtain attorney's fees even when they win; she has also led in the movement on the Court to deny habeas corpus access to federal courts for state prisoners who want to challenge constitutional violations in their conviction. She has set so low a standard for appointed counsel that the level of representation allowed in these cases—including the many death penalty cases from Texas, Florida, and elsewhere—is a national scandal. She has also worked consistently to undermine the protections provided under the Constitution by the Warren Court to the criminally accused in the *Miranda* and *Mapp* cases.[6]

The one area where O'Connor has consistently supported individual rights is where women have suffered discrimination. When she graduated from Stanford Law School in 1952 near the top of her class, the future Supreme Court Justice was offered jobs only as a legal secretary. Whether it was that or other factors, her rulings on the Court have been consistently and strongly in favor of women in discrimination cases, including an effort to require supporters of laws that disadvantage women to provide "an exceedingly persuasive justification for those laws."

Nevertheless, with this overall record, it is hardly surprising that the Justice with whom she has voted most often is William Rehnquist, hardly a centrist on anything. Except perhaps for her 1992 vote in the *Casey* abortion decision that preserved a woman's right to choose to have an abortion but allowed states to throw up numerous obstacles to the exercise of that right, the Reagan campaign to tilt the courts to the right has been substantially advanced by O'Connor.[7]

The ideological screening system was designed not only to find the ideologically acceptable but also to screen out the ideologically impure. Interviews with candidates were designed to smoke out their views and judicial philosophy, and many highly qualified candidates were rejected because they were not sufficiently committed. According to political scientist David O'Brien, "the questions asked at these interviews have stirred considerable controversy. Some who made it to the bench and others who didn't, say they were asked for their views on abortion, affirmative action, and criminal justice." National Public Radio's Nina Totenberg reported that several women candidates "were asked directly about their views on abortion," and one female state court judge was quoted as saying, "I guess most of us have accepted that we're not going to get these judgeships unless we're willing to commit to a particular position which we think would be improper." As Sheldon Goldman observes, "the Reagan administration did not proceed with any judicial nomination, particularly to the appeals courts, unless it felt assured that the nominee shared the administration's judicial philosophy."[8]

Even when the administration concluded that a candidate was acceptable, outside right-wingers exercised a veto over those whom they found insufficiently pure. Early on, the White House proposed Judith Whittaker, the daughter-in-law of former Supreme Court Justice Charles Evans Whittaker. An associate general counsel of Hallmark Cards in Kansas City, Missouri, she had solid credentials as a Republican, was a highly respected lawyer, and a trustee of Brown University and of the University of Missouri at Kansas City. In early 1981, the White House decided to nominate her for a vacancy on the Court of Appeals for the Eighth Circuit. Unfortunately for her, she had supported the Equal Rights Amendment, which deeply offended local right-wingers. In a harbinger of things to come, they launched a campaign against her, accusing her—falsely in all respects—of being a closet Democrat, against business, in favor of abortion, a "strong feminist," a "liberal Democrat," "a member of a women's caucus at Hallmark Cards which took fairly liberal stands on abortion and the ERA," and an opponent of a "curb on pornography" in Kansas City. They initiated a massive letter-writing campaign against her, and the White House soon folded.[9]

Andrew Frey was another White House choice who had served the conservative cause but upset the hard-liners because he had strayed from the true faith in a few instances. Frey was a deputy solicitor general when he was recommended for appointment to the Court of Appeals for the D.C. Circuit. The Solicitor General's office, which argues on behalf of the United States in the Supreme Court and controls federal appeals in the lower courts, is probably the most elite group of lawyers in the United States. Frey was not just another elite government lawyer, however. He headed the Solicitor General's criminal section and was the chief Supreme Court advocate for the United States in criminal cases. He had earned numerous honors, including the Presidential Award for Meritorious Service from Reagan, and the Attorney General's Distinguished Service Award. When he left in April 1986 he had argued fifty-five cases in the Supreme Court and had written more than 200 briefs. His many victories included several landmark decisions. During his time in the Solicitor General's office, he had probably done more to limit restraints on police and prosecution authority than any other lawyer in the country.

In summer 1984, a slot opened on the D.C. Court of Appeals. A District of Columbia selection panel proposed Frey and two others, and Reagan selected Frey. The nomination caused concern among some of the district's civil rights groups, for much of that court's business is criminal, and they feared that Frey would be predisposed to favor the prosecution.

That is not where Andrew Frey's troubles came from, however. He had made a few small contributions to a gun-control group and to Planned Parenthood, and had successfully defended a conviction under the gun-control law. The National Rifle Association and anti-abortion groups immediately began to lobby against Frey, even though it was very unlikely that he would ever hear a gun-control case—there are very few such cases anywhere—and he wasn't much more likely to hear abortion issues.

Right-wing Republican senators, including Jeremiah Denton of Alabama and Jesse Helms of North Carolina, wrote Reagan that they considered Frey's "political and judicial philosophy . . . very much at odds with your own philosophy and the public positions you have taken" (even though Reagan himself apparently did not think so), and they would have "no choice but to oppose" the nomination.[10]

The pressure worked. A few weeks after receiving the senators' letter, the White House withdrew the nomination, the first time a president had ever turned down a D.C. panel's recommendation.

Because federal law is made primarily at the appellate level and because the Supreme Court reviews so few federal appellate decisions, the Reagan forces focused their efforts at the appellate level. Also, the tradition that presidents defer to home-state senators from the president's party on District Court nominations made it harder for the White House to control those choices though it often tried to.

Richard Posner was one of Reagan's earliest and most prominent appellate court appointments. A summa cum laude graduate of Yale and first in his class at Harvard Law School, Posner has been the high priest of the law-and-economics movement. He has written numerous books and articles applying economic theory to all human problems, from antitrust regulation, where it clearly has a place, to such unlikely contexts as criminal law, social benefit distribution, family law, adoption of babies, abortion, ethics, literature, democracy, court administration, privacy, and almost every other facet of human life. To Posner, the economic perspective can be used to understand "utilitarian and Kantian ethics, the social and legal arrangements of primitive and ancient societies and the concept and law of privacy." In his world, human beings function as rational, wealth-maximizing, calculating machines in all areas of life. They act according to inexorable working economic principles in so-called free markets that, if left to themselves, according to Posner, work out the best possible social solution. To him, these principles are not only useful to society but define what is moral.[11]

Posner's theories have always ignored inconvenient realities, such as that even in a truly free market, which starting point rarely exists, how one succeeds depends on how much one starts with. To ignore that is to legitimize unhappy outcomes for poor people who don't have much to put into the market. This, however, has apparently never troubled him.

His theories also produce some startling policies and results. Posner's conception of human nature is reflected in his suggestion that child adoption should be subject to auction. He calculates that most babies would cost about $3,000 (in 1978 dollars), and they would be better off if allocated by an auction because "the more costly a purchase, the more care a purchaser will lavish on it." He thinks that a prisoner blinded by negligent prison doctors should find a lawyer on the open market, even though anyone who has had any contact with prison and prisoners knows it is almost impossible for the typical inmate to find a lawyer. For Posner, if there were no unions, there would be no discrimination against blacks—racial segregation can be cured by the free market, and the government should enforce real estate agreements that discriminate against blacks and Jews. Discrimination by trade unions may be prohibited but not discrimination by private business.[12]

When Richard Posner's name came before the Senate in November 1981 as one of Reagan's first Court of Appeals nominees, most members of the Senate had no idea who he was or what his ideas were. His confirmation hearing took place on a Friday afternoon in a joint session with four other nominees, with just two senators present. It lasted a few minutes. Although few realized it, the Reagan-Meese court-packing campaign had begun, and the model Reagan nominee had just been displayed: a young, intellectually strong academic having little trial or other legal experience, with ultraconservative views based on an economic model, who was often quite far from the mainstream of American legal thought.

This model was followed in other appellate court nominations during the first Reagan term; only the youth factor was sometimes sacrificed for ideological reliability. Among those nominated and promptly confirmed were:

- Robert Bork, 54, who had spent most of his professional life as an antitrust and constitutional law teacher at Yale (though he had left the school six months earlier to work with a Washington law firm), nominated to the District of Columbia Circuit in January 1982;
- Ralph Winter, 46, a Yale professor specializing in corporate and election law, nominated to the Second Circuit in New York in December 1981;
- Antonin Scalia, 46, from the University of Chicago, a specialist in administrative law, who later went to the Supreme Court, nominated to the District of Columbia Circuit in 1982;
- J. Harvey Wilkinson, 39, a law professor at the University of Virginia and former editorial-page editor of the *Norfolk Virginian-Pilot*, nominated to the Fourth Circuit in 1983;

- Pasco Bowman II, 50, dean of the law school at the University of Missouri at Kansas City and formerly dean at Wake Forest Law School, a corporate and international trade specialist, nominated to the Eighth Circuit in 1983.

The focus on such ideologically oriented academics enabled the administration to be sure of what it was getting. Each of these men had expressed himself on a variety of issues before being chosen, and there were few surprises in their decisions and opinions. Also, the hallmark of the academic role is to criticize. There is usually little respect for precedent in academia and not much for stability, regardless of the lip service invariably given to judicial restraint at confirmation hearings. By choosing very conservative academics, the administration ensured an aggressive, uncompromising conservatism that was willing to shake up and overturn settled issues.

And it was not disappointed. At the end of Reagan's first term, a former high Justice Department official involved in the judicial selection process said that the administration was "tremendously pleased," particularly with its judges from academia, who had "fully met our expectations of being people committed to the president's judicial philosophy."

In only one case during Reagan's first term did his nominee have serious confirmation problems: J. Harvey Wilkinson, the 39-year-old Virginian nominated to the Fourth Circuit in 1983.

Wilkinson's résumé was quite impressive except for one thing: Not only was he only 39, twelve years younger than even Reagan's average appellate nominee, but he had almost no experience as a lawyer, despite having graduated from law school in 1972. At that time, American Bar Association rules required judicial nominees to have twelve years of post–law school experience as a lawyer. Wilkinson had been a newspaper editorial-page writer and editor for six years, a law clerk to Supreme Court Justice Lewis F. Powell, who was his godfather, and had taught law for about six years. His only involvement with any form of law practice was one year in the Justice Department where his inexperience and ignorance of court procedure caused the department to be fined for missing a court deadline; such a fine on the government is almost unheard of. He was not a member of the bar of either the Fourth Circuit Court of Appeals or of any of the District Courts supervised by the court to which he was nominated. And at 39, he was hardly the age at which someone has acquired the experience of life that one normally assumes a judge should have, particularly a judge who reviews the work of others for what could be many years.

Wilkinson's lack of experience resulted in an initial determination by the ABA circuit representative that he was "not qualified." A second ABA representative was then brought in and he came up with a "qualified" recommendation, the lowest level of eligibility. Such a second chance is very rare, although Kenneth Starr's lack of experience when he was appointed also earned him a "not qualified" rating. The ABA committee thereupon voted 10-4 to give Wilkinson a "qualified" rating, despite its twelve-years-of-experience rule.[13]

Wilkinson had, however, written books, articles, and editorials on school desegregation, affirmative action, bilingual education, abolition of capital punishment, and gay and lesbian rights. He was against them all. At the Justice Department he had played an important role in blocking effective remedies for proven civil rights violations, and in keeping black parents who insisted on more effective remedies than the Justice Department out of desegregation suits. According to one former civil rights division lawyer, for Wilkinson "the bottom line would always be the most restrictive interpretation possible, one that would afford the people that we were supposed to be representing the least rights possible." As a result, the NAACP and other groups came out against him.[14]

In the Senate, Wilkinson's inexperience became the focus of controversy, especially because of his editorials for the *Norfolk Virginian-Pilot*. In a 1979 editorial probably written by Wilkinson and certainly approved by him, the paper praised Virginia Senator Harry Byrd and the Virginia Bar Association for insisting on "merit" and refusing to bow to Carter's insistence that blacks and women be on Byrd's recommendation lists. His former employer, the *Norfolk Virginian-Pilot*, opposed his nomination, concluding, "Obviously he is a bright young man in a hurry, but what's the rush?" Wilkinson's willingness to abandon positions when they became inconvenient was exhibited again some twenty years later, when he supported Senator Jesse Helms in blocking African-American Clinton nominees to the Fourth Circuit, on the grounds that no more judges were needed. Wilkinson did not speak out on this issue and refused to allow African-American nominees to be confirmed a few years later when President George W. Bush started to fill the four seats left vacant by Helms.[15]

Shortly after Wilkinson's Senate hearing, in February 1984, it was learned that the ABA's 10-4 vote in early November 1983 had not been taken in monastic isolation. Not only had there been the second vote, but committee members had been heavily lobbied by Wilkinson's friends, including Supreme Court Justice Lewis Powell, a former ABA president and Wilkinson's godfather and mentor. Powell had called a friend on the committee after being contacted—improperly—by a worried Justice Department official who had learned in confidence from an ABA committee member that the nomination was in trouble. Powell's opinion of Wilkinson had already been made known to the committee twice before, so the call could hardly have been considered informational. High Justice Department representatives called at least three other committee members, including the chairman.[16]

Wilkinson did not depend only on others to promote his cause. Between November 5, the day after the unfavorable ABA report appeared, and November 7, the day before the ABA vote, Wilkinson made at least sixty calls and contacted fourteen influential people, including law school deans and a newspaper publisher, who in turn contacted at least eight of the fourteen committee-members. The bar committee members were startled to learn of Wilkinson's massive lobbying campaign, and many senators were dismayed. Nevertheless, it made the difference. Wilkinson was confirmed a week after the Judiciary Committee hearing, with thirty-six votes against him.[17]

Reagan chose wisely. In Wilkinson's twenty years on the Fourth Circuit Court of Appeals, he has helped make that court probably the most conservative federal appellate court in the nation. In a 2003 study of six names on George W. Bush's short list for Supreme Court appointments, Wilkinson was ranked the most conservative. *The Legal Times* described him as "A Soft Face On the Hard Line." [18]

Soon after Reagan took office, a little-noticed event took place: Four conservative law students at the University of Chicago, Yale, and—later—Harvard formed the Federalist Society. The organization quickly drew support from prominent conservatives like Orrin Hatch, Theodore Olson, and C. Boyden Gray, and began holding forums and recruiting members. With the help of the Reagan administration, right-wing funders and Chief Justice Warren Burger provided the Society with funds for so-called nonpartisan discussions and debates. At the panels, the discussion invariably featured an even number of liberals and conservatives moderated by a conservative, and an audience of virtually nothing but conservative students, making the event primarily an occasion for recruiting and organizational development. Prominent conservative judges, lawyers, and other public officials participated in these meetings, mingling with the students. The primary goal of the meetings and of the organization was to provide opportunities for right-wing students to get jobs in executive, legislative, and judicial offices. The society became very skilled at this, and within a few years, many Federalist Society members held important positions in the Reagan administration and as law clerks with prominent Republican judges like Scalia, Bork, and others. Soon, Federalist Society members came to play a particularly important role in the Republican judicial selection process in the Reagan and the two Bush administrations.

By the end of Reagan's first term, he had made 129 appointments to the District Courts, and thirty-one appointments to the thirteen Courts of Appeals. He had appointed nine women to the District Courts but only one to the Courts of Appeals. Seven Hispanics and one black were appointed to the District Courts, and one black and one Hispanic to the appeals courts. This was the worst record on the judicial appointment of minorities since Eisenhower, who appointed none. A total of 20 percent of the appellate nominees were academics, a modern record.[19]

Despite the Reagan administration's plans to stack the courts with ideological appointees, during Reagan's first term there were only a handful of such appointments to the Courts of Appeals. Although the administration was pleased with how its nominees had performed, the emphasis during the first four years was on legislative and constitutional changes. Existing civil rights laws were to be rolled back, the federal courts were to be stripped of authority over school desegregation and related cases, and the school-prayer decisions were to be overturned, by a constitutional amendment if necessary. *Roe v. Wade* would be either overturned by an amendment or undermined by statute.

These efforts all failed. The amendment to overturn the school-prayer decisions did not even get out of committee. Instead of being rolled back, in 1982 the civil rights laws were augmented by an amendment to the Voting Rights Act that extended and expanded it.

In view of those failures, the administration apparently decided to concentrate on changing the judiciary, and a 1984 law adding twenty-four new appellate judgeships and sixty-four District Court judges gave Reagan the opening. The new judgeships, plus the normal forty per year from attrition, gave him the opportunity during his eight years in office to appoint more than half of the federal judiciary, something no president had done since Franklin D. Roosevelt in his twelve years as president. In addition, five of the nine Supreme Court justices were over 75 and might not last out Reagan's second term.[20]

To fight this, coalitions of civil rights, environment, labor, and similar groups organized to resist the Reagan campaign. The Alliance for Justice, led by Nan Aron, and People for the American Way, founded by Norman Lear, led the way. The rejection of Andrew Frey, together with the veto of William E. Hellerstein, a distinguished New York lawyer who was supported by leaders of the New York Bar, including numerous Republicans, worried Democratic senators. When a few extreme-right Republicans led by Senator Orrin Hatch of Utah, who was to become a central figure in the judgeship wars of the Clinton and George W. Bush administrations, tried unsuccessfully to block Joseph Rodriguez, a New Jersey lawyer supported by Republican Governor Thomas Kean, from a district judgeship, the Senate Democrats woke up to what was happening, as did many others. As the *Los Angeles Times* lamented in October 1985, a few months after Rodriguez was confirmed, "The ideological screening that is taking place is demonstrated by the administration's dismal record on appointing minorities and women to the federal judiciary. Among his appointments so far, the president has managed only one black and thirteen women. He cannot find blacks and women who believe that abortion should be illegal, school prayer should be allowed, access to the courts should be restricted, Congress should leave civil rights to the states, the rights of criminal defendants should be cut back and gun control should be outlawed." [21]

Even Professor Philip Kurland of the University of Chicago, a caustic critic of both the Warren and Burger Courts, complained, "Judges are being appointed in the expectation that they will rewrite laws and the Constitution to the administration's liking." And traditional conservatives like former Attorneys General Herbert Brownell and Edward Levi, who served Presidents Eisenhower and Ford, respectively, called the situation "shocking" (Brownell) and "badly politicized" (Levi). [22]

None of this stopped the Reagan administration. During the next three years there were fifteen staunchly conservative nominees, all but three on the appellate level, many of whom were law professors.

Most of these nominees had no trouble getting confirmed. Senators are normally very reluctant to oppose a lower court nominee because of judicial or political philosophy, and there were no challenges to such conservative selections as Frank Easterbrook, nominated to the Seventh Circuit, a brilliant colleague of Posner's at the University of Chicago, and so extreme in his views as to be to Posner's right; John Noonan, a Berkeley law professor, one of the leading theorists of the anti-abortion movement (Ninth Circuit), who has since harshly condemned the Rehnquist Court's decisions narrowing federal power; J. Daniel Mahoney, founder of the New York State Conservative

Party (Second Circuit); and Bobby Ray Baldock, whose performance as a Reagan-appointed district judge led one attorney to call him "death on wheels for civil liberties" for the Tenth Circuit.

The District of Columbia Circuit Court of Appeals was a particular target for the administration's ideological efforts, partly because it shapes the nation's regulatory law (one of the administration's top priorities was deregulating business), and partly because so many vacancies became available. In 1986–87, the Senate quickly confirmed such market zealots as Douglas Ginsburg, a Harvard Law School professor and assistant attorney general for antitrust, later to be unsuccessfully nominated to the Supreme Court under President Reagan, and former Senator James L. Buckley, brother of William F. Buckley of *National Review* fame. Stephen Williams, a Colorado law professor, was also appointed.

Williams's primary goal on the court was to revive the nondelegation doctrine. This doctrine seeks to limit the scope of what Congress can delegate to the administrative and other agencies by requiring that Congress set explicit criteria for agency action. Until Williams used it to strike down an environmental law involving air pollution, the doctrine had not been used since 1935, when it was invoked by the pre–New Deal judiciary; it had not been used before and has not been used since. Although Williams got the other conservatives on the D.C. Court of Appeals to go along with him, the Supreme Court reversed the ruling. Had the doctrine survived, it would have threatened the survival of numerous environmental, worker safety, and other governmental agencies and actions.[23]

David Sentelle was a more effective judge. A protégé of Jesse Helms, he was first appointed to the District Court in 1985 and elevated by Reagan to the D.C. Circuit in 1987. Rehnquist chose him to sit on the Special Court of Appeals that appointed the Independent Counsel in the investigation of President Clinton's role in the Whitewater case. Shortly before that court removed the highly respected Robert Fiske and appointed Kenneth Starr as Independent Counsel, Sentelle met with North Carolina Senators Jesse Helms and Lauch Faircloth for lunch; Faircloth and other Republicans had been agitating to remove Fiske. Although Sentelle has always denied that there was any discussion of the Independent Counsel, the day after that lunch Starr, who had considered filing a brief in support of Paula Jones's case against Clinton, was appointed.[24]

Sentelle also "distinguished" himself in the Iran/*contra* investigation. He joined Judge Lawrence Silberman in setting aside the convictions of both Oliver North and John Poindexter. In *Firewall*, Judge Laurence Walsh's book on his experiences as Independent Counsel in the investigation, Walsh reports that Sentelle, who was appointed by Rehnquist to be chairman of the Special Court of Appeals that supervised Walsh (replacing another judge), was continually hostile to Walsh and obstructed the investigation at every turn. "This meant that we could no longer count on the division's support," wrote Walsh. "Having sided against us in the North and Poindexter cases, having actively badgered our lawyer in the Poindexter oral arguments, and having voted to narrow the interpretation of the statute that prohibited the obstruction of congressional investigations, Judge Sentelle had to be presumed hostile."[25]

Laurence Silberman was soon to become a more notorious appointment. As US ambassador to Yugoslavia in the Ford administration, he publicly warred with President Tito and other Yugoslav officials over the jailing of an American citizen, much to the discomfiture of some State Department career officers. When a Tito supporter wrote him a critical letter, Silberman replied: "I have received your letter of Aug. 4th. Kiss my ass. Sincerely." In a speech to the Federalist Society he referred to "the wicked witch of the airwaves," which was universally assumed to refer to NPR's Nina Totenberg. In an affirmative action case, he and Abner Mikva were on opposite sides. As they were taking off their robes, Silberman growled at Mikva, "If you were ten years younger, I'd punch you out." Silberman later denied that he had threatened Mikva, because he prefaced his statement with "if you were ten years younger," and Mikva was not ten years younger.[26]

Like most Reagan appellate appointees, Silberman was intellectually strong and on the far right of the political spectrum. His nomination ran into a few snags when it turned out that while he was executive vice president and general counsel of the Crocker National Bank, the bank had been fined more than $2 million for not reporting a $3.98 billion cash transaction. Silberman, an able and experienced lawyer, claimed he had not known about the bank's omission. The *Washington Post* reported at the time of Silberman's hearing that "the Treasury Department said that the transactions appeared to involve large-scale laundering of drug money, a charge sharply disputed by Crocker officials." Silberman had also belonged to an all-male club and resigned only when told by the committee he had to.[27]

Silberman was also accused by David Brock, a self-described hit man for the Right who reformed and recanted, as having been crucially involved in the savaging of Anita Hill in the Clarence Thomas confirmation fight during the first Bush administration, and in trying to bring down President Bill Clinton in the Paula Jones case. Brock's credibility is of course questionable, and Silberman refused to respond to questions by a reporter about Brock's charges.

Silberman joined with Sentelle to help stymie Judge Laurence Walsh's Iran/*Contra* investigation by consistently ruling against Walsh and by being so aggressively hostile toward

Walsh and his staff in court that according to Walsh, they had difficulty presenting a coherent argument. Silberman and Sentelle joined in two 2-1 decisions freeing Oliver North and John Poindexter; the North decision effectively granted North immunity from prosecution.

Silberman led the largely successful drive against implementation of recommendations by a task force on race and gender bias in the D.C. Circuit. He also claimed credit for advising Antonin Scalia not to answer any questions at the latter's hearing on his nomination to the Supreme Court, even if he were asked about *Marbury v. Madison*. Had Scalia displayed his true colors at that time, it is almost certain that he would not have gotten a 98-0 vote, and he might have been in some trouble.

Even the current Supreme Court is not conservative enough for Silberman. In a speech on November 16, 2002, at a Federalist Society celebration in Washington, he lambasted the Court for its handful of liberal opinions. Silberman charged that the Supreme Court ignored the Constitution, dodged tough cases and had a secret plan to end capital punishment. His timing about the Court's attitude toward the death penalty was peculiar—the month before, the Court had again approved the death penalty for 16-year-olds. In language echoing his former colleague Antonin Scalia, Silberman charged that "the Court's policy choices masquerading as constitutional law are generally accepted so long as they are well received by elites. Ironically, the Supreme Court has become what the framers envisioned for the role of the Senate. I think elite public opinion is the primary guide to the Supreme Court." He also accused the Court of having a secret plan to declare the death penalty unconstitutional.[28]

By mid-1986, the D.C. Circuit had a solid right-wing majority. As a harbinger of things to come, Judiciary Committee chairman Strom Thurmond, the former segregationist and

Dixiecrat candidate for president, speeded up the confirmation process to allow little time to investigate candidates for these life-time appointments. When Senator Edward M. Kennedy was Judiciary Committee chairman in 1979–80, the average time between a nomination and the committee's hearing was sixty-five days, and Kennedy readily acceded to requests by Senator Hatch and other Republicans for more time, even when there was no good reason for the delay. Under Thurmond that period dropped to twenty-three days, and votes were scheduled an average of ten days after the hearing, twice as fast as under Kennedy.

The administration also paid attention to the District Courts. Perhaps the most disturbing District Court nominee was Sid Fitzwater, a thirty-two-year-old Texas state judge. At his hearing in November 1985, it was revealed that three years earlier, he had posted Republican signs in three minority precincts that warned in big red and black letters that it was a crime for which "you can be imprisoned . . . if you influence or try to influence a voter how to vote." This is obviously untrue. The Justice Department even under William Bradford Reynolds told the Dallas County Election Commissioner's office that "we are concerned that no nonracial justification has been offered for placing most of the signs at minority precincts." Texas election officials agreed to make sure there would be no more such signs.[29]

Despite opposition from black and Hispanic civil rights groups, the Judiciary Committee approved Fitzwater 10-5, and after a brief filibuster, he was confirmed by a narrow 52-43 vote.

Jefferson B. Sessions III was another Southern nominee who had tried to keep black voters from the polls, but much more egregiously and more frequently. This time, the administration went too far.

Sessions had been the US Attorney in Mobile, Alabama. He had made his mark by prosecuting black civil rights activists on voting fraud charges. This was part of a campaign by the Justice Department against black civil rights activists that an appeals court later found was targeted at "those counties where blacks since 1980 had come to control some part of the county government." Sessions obtained only one conviction, and even that was later overturned when the appellate court concluded that the prosecution was racially and politically motivated.[30]

When Sessions was nominated, a detailed NAACP Legal Defense and Education Fund report revealed that Sessions had called the NAACP an "un-American" and "Communist-inspired" organization that was "trying to force civil rights down the throats of the people." He had also called a white lawyer who represented civil rights workers "a disgrace to his race," and has said he thought that the Ku Klux Klan was "OK until I learned they smoked pot."[31]

Sessions's testimony was so filled with inconsistencies and alterations that the very conservative Senator Howell Heflin from Sessions's own state of Alabama concluded that Sessions's "admissions, explanations, partial admissions [and] statements about [racially insensitive] jokes" led him to harbor "reasonable doubts about his ability to be fair and impartial." Heflin voted against Sessions, and the nomination failed in committee 10-8, as two Republicans, Specter and Mathias, joined the eight Democrats in opposition.[32]

The Sessions defeat was to haunt the Democrats later. In 1996, Sessions was elected to the Senate. It was payback time. He was appointed to the Judiciary Committee where he used his position to become one of the leaders in the Republican campaign to block Clinton nominees from being voted upon or even getting hearings.

The Reagan administration continued to turn down moderate Republicans. Perhaps the most prominent was Philip Lacovara. A brilliant lawyer, Lacovara was the senior Republican in the

Watergate special prosecutor's office in 1973–74. He had always considered himself a conservative Republican. In 1964 he co-chaired the Columbia University Students for Goldwater. During the Nixon administration, he was one of a handful of registered Republicans living in Washington who supported Ronald Reagan in 1980 and 1984. He even passed the administration's litmus test on abortion. In 1981 Reagan appointed him as his representative on a panel that screens candidates for the president to name to District of Columbia local courts.

Despite this background, the Justice Department viewed Lacovara as "too liberal" and "not politically reliable" because of his membership in the Washington Lawyers Committee for Civil Rights Under Law and the ABA Section on Individual Rights and Responsibilities, two nonpartisan, solidly establishment groups. At least equally sinful in conservative eyes, he had made it clear that he did not agree with the administration's policy that made ideology the primary qualification. "Unique to our nation's history," he had written, "the current Justice Department has been processing judicial candidates through a series of officials whose primary duty is to assess the candidate's ideological purity." Such heresy was clearly unacceptable.[33]

David Doty's sin involved his wife. Although both were life-long Republicans, Mrs. Doty had worked for John Anderson in 1980 and was the Republican chairman of the Gender Gap Coalition, a bipartisan group formed to evaluate the impact of Reagan administration budget cuts affecting women. To Marlene Reid, vice chairman of the Minnesota Republican Party, Mrs. Doty's activities were "unforgivable" and showed that Mr. Doty was not fit to be a judge. Although Doty said that he did in fact have political differences with his wife, the nomination languished and ultimately died.

The bitterest fight before Robert Bork was over Clarence Manion, a nominee to the Seventh Circuit Court of Appeals.

The most important thing about Daniel A. Manion, an obscure forty-four-year-old South Bend, Indiana, lawyer, was his name. He was the son of Clarence Manion, a founder of the John Birch Society, who had once accused the Eisenhower administration of "creeping socialism." In 1954 Clarence Manion founded the Manion Forum, which turned out an avalanche of ultraconservative written and broadcast material. His son Daniel was a trustee of the Manion Forum and participated with his father in its weekly radio and television broadcasts.

Though equally conservative, Manion differed from most Reagan appellate nominees in one important respect: He was a mediocre lawyer. His briefs were filled with weak arguments; inadequate expression, and grammatical, syntactical, and other errors. He had a small personal and commercial practice with virtually no experience in federal issues. Although the ABA had made an especially poor investigation, he was still only able to get a split "qualified" rating in his favor; the Chicago Council of Lawyers, which studied his briefs closely, concluded that he was not qualified because he "would not be able to deal adequately with the difficult legal issues which are routinely presented to the Seventh Circuit." [34]

But his ideological position was sound, and apparently that was enough for the administration. Though the ideological issue may have been a ticklish one for many senators, such as ranking Judiciary Committee Democrat Joseph Biden, Manion's patently inadequate intellectual credentials were something else. Forty-four law school deans, and almost every major law school, opposed Manion, as did more than two hundred other law school professors. Newspapers all over the country also opposed him.

Reagan did not back down, and the first round ended in a victory for Manion. At its meeting in early May 1986, the committee divided evenly, which would normally kill a nomination. "But then," as the London *Economist* put it, "alarmed at the precedent they were creating, members voted to pass Mr. Manion's nomination on to the full Senate." There the battle resumed, on June 26.[35]

It is likely that no one will ever know what really happened on the floor that day, but charges of deceit, doublecrossing, political vote trading, and chicanery filled the air. In the end, with Vice President George H.W. Bush in the chair and eligible to vote because of a 47-47 tie, Manion won 48-47. A later motion for reconsideration failed 49-41.

The news was not all bad for the administration's opponents, however. In addition to defeating Sessions, they managed to force the administration to withdraw a few nominations without a fight:

- William Harvey. Harvey had been nominated to be chair of the Legal Services Corporation's board of directors in March 1982. He immediately set out to end the corporation's law reform and class action activities, and an irate Senate committee refused to confirm him. Shortly thereafter, evidence came to light raising serious questions about expenses and other allowances he claimed from the corporation. The administration nominated him to the Seventh Circuit, but he could not get even a "qualified" rating from the normally generous ABA.[36]

- Michael J. Horowitz. A former general counsel to the Office of Management and Budget, Horowitz had earned a reputation for being abrasive, abusive, and intolerant. He had insulted business executives, colleagues, and adversaries, often alienating his own allies with temper tantrums and insults. While at OMB, Horowitz promoted measures to weaken public-interest advocacy and litigation groups. Many of these measures turned out to be legally and technically flawed. When word got out that the administration planned to nominate him to the District of Columbia Circuit Court of Appeals, his opponents prepared a twenty-two-page report documenting his failings. Horowitz decided to withdraw before being formally nominated.[37]

• Marion Harrison. A Washington, D.C., lawyer who was counsel to presidential candidate Rev. Marion "Pat" Robertson in 1987, Harrison was also considered for the D.C. Circuit. His name was linked to the milk industry's illegal contributions to Nixon's 1972 campaign, however, and though he was never charged with any wrongdoing, his name appeared frequently in press accounts of the matter. Harrison's name was quietly dropped.[38]

• Lino A. Graglia. Graglia is a Texas law professor who opposed judicial review on principle, especially in civil rights cases. An outspoken foe of busing for desegregation, he urged Austin, Texas, residents to defy a federal court busing order, telling a crowd of 1,800 in 1979 that "you are under no obligation to go along with this." Graglia also argued that white parents in Louisiana should be allowed to evade federal court orders by sham custody arrangements, referred in his class to black children as "pickaninnies," and condemned judicially created constitutional safeguards for individual rights as "just bad ideas."

Despite the obviously intense opposition Graglia was going to face, Meese pushed him for a Fifth Circuit Court of Appeals judgeship. The ABA twice found him "not qualified," and the nomination finally died in the Senate in late spring 1986.[39]

The nomination of William H. Rehnquist to be chief justice of the United States when Warren Burger retired in May 1986 at first seemed to be the culmination of the conservative court-packing. On a conservative Court dominated by Justices appointed by Presidents Nixon, Ford, and Reagan, Rehnquist was frequently off by himself in dissent from all eight of the other Justices, particularly in major civil rights, First Amendment, and criminal procedure cases. This happened so often—approximately fifty-four times, a record—that one year his law clerks presented him with a Lone Ranger doll.[40]

For example, Rehnquist alone voted to:

- give tax breaks to segregated private schools;
- allow states to force pregnant teachers to take unpaid leave five months before their due date, regardless of their ability to work;
- make servicewomen meet higher standards for obtaining support allotments from their spouses than servicemen;
- allow Maricopa County, Arizona, to deny vital medical care to new residents;
- allow the federal government to deny food stamps to households in which one of the members is not a blood relative of the others;
- allow Arkansas to leave in place some of the worst prison conditions in modern history;
- allow Texas to deny a Buddhist prisoner a reasonable opportunity to practice his religion;
- allow Indiana to deny unemployment benefits to a Jehovah's Witness who refused to work on armaments for religious reasons;
- allow Northern school districts to maintain segregated schools;

and more, much more.[41]

Rehnquist also developed unique theories limiting individual freedoms that no other Justice adopted. He was the only
member of the Court, for example, to take the position that the
courts may scrutinize official discrimination closely only when
it is against blacks and perhaps other ethnic groups. Not surprisingly, in a dozen cases he had not voted once in favor of
aliens when they were discriminated against with respect to
civil service jobs as typists or janitors, or denied the right to
become lawyers or even notaries public; the Court upheld such
claims eight out of twelve times. Rehnquist refused to lift special burdens on out-of-wedlock children, such as denying them
the right to financial support from their fathers, to inherit
equally with other children, to share in their father's workmen's
compensation recoveries, and to obtain child welfare and
parental disability benefits; Rehnquist was often the lone dissenter when the Court lifted some of these burdens. He also
voted often against women's rights.[42]

Only where Congress had passed a statute unmistakably
granting a right did Rehnquist vote to uphold it, and even then
he tried to narrow it. When the Court split on interpreting
such a statute, Rehnquist voted to sustain the claim in only
three of eighty-one cases, whereas the Court voted for the
plaintiff in thirty-five such cases.[43]

Finally, Rehnquist was the only justice to advance the theory
that the First Amendment imposes lesser obligations on states
than on the federal government. This would produce a multitude
of problems, for it would require the Court to work out a dividing
line between what the states can do and what the federal government can do, which would enable states to get away with much
more suppression of free speech and expression than they do
today.[44]

Witnesses opposing Rehnquist's confirmation again

appeared, charging that in the early 1960s Rehnquist had intimidated minority voters in Phoenix by challenging their eligibility, this time including James Brosnahan, a former FBI agent and later a distinguished trial lawyer who had flown in from San Francisco.[45]

Working in Rehnquist's favor was a failure to realize the power of the chief justice's position. Many senators, knowing the limited *judicial* powers of the chief justice, thought it not worthwhile to fight the nomination and to risk being criticized for voting on ideological grounds. But who is chief justice is very important in many subtle and not-so-subtle ways.

First of all, there is the obvious symbolism of the choice. The Court had come to be seen, in Justice Lewis Powell's words, as a leader in the nation's effort to afford "protection [to] . . . the constitutional rights and liberties of individual citizens and minority groups against oppressive or discriminatory government action." To elevate to leadership someone like Rehnquist, who was so hostile to this fundamental mission of the court, was to mock and disparage that mission.[46]

There are also more tangible considerations. The chief justice assigns the writing of opinions when he is in the majority. Like his predecessors, Rehnquist probably would (and did) write the most important opinions himself, and probably a large number of them. (He reportedly writes easily and quickly.) In the past, when he has spoken for the Court in a decision restricting someone's rights, he has used sweeping and often vague language, the scope and ramifications of which are difficult to confine. Conversely, on the rare occasions when Rehnquist has joined his colleagues and written an opinion upholding someone's rights—and invariably these have been decisions in which the other eight are unanimous—he has defined the right narrowly, as in a case involving the rights of out-of-wedlock children to child support, and in the recent decision refusing to overturn the *Miranda* decision.[47]

Finally, the chief justice heads the vast administrative apparatus that runs the federal judiciary. He designates the members of special courts and panels, including the panel that appoints independent counsel, the Temporary Emergency Court of Appeals, and the secret Foreign Intelligence Surveillance Act (FISA) court and its appellate section, which pass judgments on national-security wiretapping, an especially critical matter today. The importance of who appoints the FISA court and its appellate panel was underscored a year after the September 11 events. Under FISA, which was enacted in 1978 after years of controversy, electronic and other surveillances for investigations not aimed at criminal prosecutions but to gather intelligence about terrorism and foreign agents, are brought by the FBI to a special court that meets in secret and decides on the applications for the surveillances and secret intrusions into the home. The standards for issuing FISA warrants are much looser than those applied to search warrants for criminal investigations. In order to enforce the distinction, criminal investigators were not allowed to have anything to do with the intelligence or counterintelligence investigations, for otherwise they would try to use the looser FISA standard to evade the stiffer criminal justice standards. In November 2002, an appellate panel made up of Reagan appointees—Laurence Silberman, Ralph Guy, and Edward Leavy—reversed the lower FISA court and ruled that the separation between the two kinds of investigations was set aside by the USA PATRIOT Act and that the two could henceforth be mingled. The lower court had held otherwise and in the course of its opinion reported that the FBI had filed affidavits containing numerous misrepresentations to justify some seventy-five FISA orders. Prosecutors can now use the much lower FISA standards to make criminal cases and evade the more stringent criminal rules.[48]

The chief justice also presides over the Judicial Conference, a policymaking body that proposes and evaluates rules and substantive legislation affecting the federal courts. He appoints the staff of the conference and the membership of all its twenty judicial committees. These groups play a significant role in the administration of justice in this country, for they deal with matters such as class-action rules and pretrial discovery. The importance of this authority is magnified by the chief justice's role as the spokesman to Congress on these and other legislative matters affecting court administration, which can affect substantive legislation like the Violence Against Women Act which the judges opposed.

Republican control of the Senate and the reluctance to impugn a sitting justice combined to gain Rehnquist confirmation by a 65-33 vote, the largest vote against a chief justice in history. One journalist commented that if the information that emerged about Rehnquist's past had been available in 1971, he would not have been confirmed at that time. But the then-Judiciary Committee chairman, James O. Eastland of Mississippi, had refused to order a full investigation, and Rehnquist's 1971 opponents were stymied.[50]

To fill Rehnquist's associate justice slot, Reagan named Judge Antonin Scalia of the D.C. Circuit Court of Appeals; both names went up simultaneously.

Antonin Scalia was, if anything, even more radical than Rehnquist about rolling back and overturning the liberal decisions of the previous era. One wag commented that whereas Rehnquist was a statist, Scalia was a monarchist. That was probably not so apparent during Scalia's few years on the D.C. Circuit, because most of an appellate court's cases are noncontroversial or not well-known. Once Scalia was on the Supreme Court, however, he not infrequently took positions to the right of Rehnquist.[51]

Scalia's philosophical position is a religiously based strict authoritarianism. In an address to the University of Chicago Divinity School in January 2002, he drew on St. Paul's pronouncement about "the powers that be are ordained by God." Scalia elaborated this saying "The Lord repaid—did justice—through His minister, the State." He went on to say that democracy went counter to this and that "the reaction of people of faith to this tendency of democracy to obscure the divine authority behind government should not be resignation to it, but the resolution to combat it as effectively as possible." Given this attitude, it is hardly surprising that in numerous opinions and other contexts he has expressed profound contempt for members of Congress and other legislators.[52]

Equally noteworthy is his writing style. Although a very skillful writer with a vigorous style, he has used it to excoriate those he disagrees with, both on the Court and off, with sarcasm, charges of "elitism," "tak[ing] sides in the culture wars," "having signed on to the so-called homosexual agenda," and similar epithets.[53]

Although he remains personally charming and affable, his influence on the Court may be limited because of his abrasive opinions. Although he seemed to be quite influential with Justice Anthony Kennedy, a jogging partner and law school contemporary, during the latter's early years, his only reliable ally now seems to be Justice Thomas.

Nevertheless, the losing fight over the Rehnquist nominations had exhausted the Democrats. Following Silberman's advice, Scalia refused to answer any questions about his views, he was not pressed, and his record on the Court of Appeals was not closely examined. He was confirmed unanimously without a fight.

When Justice Powell retired in spring 1987 and Reagan nominated Robert Bork, Jerry Falwell exulted. But a crucial change had occurred—the Senate had returned to the Democrats, so Thurmond could not rush the Bork nomination through. Although Democratic chairman Joseph Biden was not eager for a fight, he had no choice given Bork's record.

Much has been written about the Bork nomination, including some by this author, and there is no point repeating the story. But it is worth noting a few things that have gotten lost in the rewriting of history that Bork's defenders have promoted.

Before turning to these, however, it is important to note that the key factor was that Robert Bork was a hard-right extremist, not a moderate conservative as some of his supporters urged. A Reagan aide described Bork as a "right-wing zealot." As conservative commentator Bruce Fein conceded, Bork was nominated for the express purpose of giving "the entire docket of the Court . . . a conservative hue," particularly on "the fighting issues—abortion, affirmative action, free speech, church-state," where the normally conservative Powell had voted with the liberals.[54] For example:

- *Privacy*. Bork opposed not only the abortion decision but also the 1965 *Griswold v. Connecticut* case allowing married couples the right to use contraceptives. This was a position that even the Reagan administration's Solicitor General Charles Fried was unwilling to push.[55]
- *Equality*. Bork condemned the Fourteenth Amendment's Equal Protection Clause decisions outlawing the poll tax (to him it was just "a very small tax"), the decisions establishing the one-person, one-vote principle, abolishing school segregation in the District of Columbia, barring courts from enforcing racially restrictive housing covenants, preventing a state from sterilizing certain criminals or interfering with the

right to travel, and prohibiting discrimination against out-of-wedlock children. As late as June 1987, he declared, "I do think the Equal Protection Clause probably should have been kept to things like race and ethnicity." Bork's hostility to governmental action on behalf of minorities did not stop with his critique of court action. In 1963 he criticized a section of the proposed Civil Rights Act of 1964 that required white businesses to serve blacks as resting on a principle of "unsurpassed ugliness."[56]

- *Free Speech.* In 1971, Bork wrote that the First Amendment should protect only "explicitly political" speech, which he defined as limited to "criticisms of public officials and policies, proposals for the adoption or repeal of legislation or constitutional provisions and speech addressed to the conduct of any governmental unit in the county." In later years he expanded the protected class to include scientific or moral discourse that "directly feed[s] the democratic process," but as late as June 1987 he did not think "courts ought to throw protection around . . . art and literature."[57]

In 1982 Bork was appointed to the Court of Appeals in Washington, D.C. There he quickly established a reputation for ingenuity in denying litigants access to the courts and for excessive deference to executive authority.

When the nomination was announced, Bork supporters went to work. Bill Roberts of the Dolphin Group in California, who had led the successful recall campaign against California Chief Justice Rose Bird in California in 1986 and was a former Reagan campaign manager, was brought in to raise $2.5 million for an advertising campaign, and to target some twelve senators who seemed important. Jerry Falwell's Moral Majority delivered 22,200 postcards to the Senate Judiciary Committee on Bork's behalf, and senators were continually bombarded with orchestrated pro-Bork mail and phone calls.

But Bork faced a torrent of opposition. His own colleagues in the academy and on the bar were against him. More than 2,000 law teachers, more than 40 percent of the total at accredited law schools, signed letters against him, including the deans of Harvard, New York University, Michigan, Georgetown, Northwestern, and many other schools. The normally very conservative Philip Kurland of the University of Chicago wrote that "Bork's entire current constitutional jurisprudential theory [is] directed to a diminution of minority and individual rights."[58]

Most important, five of the fifteen members of the American Bar Association committee on the federal judiciary refused to give Bork a "qualified" rating—the first time the ABA had not been unanimous in favor of a Supreme Court nominee since it began evaluating candidates during the Eisenhower administration—and four ruled him "not qualified."

The hearings began on September 15, 1987, and lasted four days and thirty hours. Bork performed badly. Never before had a candidate responded to so many questions on so wide a range of issues. Unfortunately for him, his performance on the issues did not match his willingness to discuss them. Trying to moderate his conservatism and explain away his conservatism, he expressed numerous "confirmation conversions." Describing himself as neither a "conservative" nor a "liberal," he backed off from some of his more extreme positions on equal protection and free speech, leaving many senators dubious about his candor. This was apparently a strategic decision, for Washington lawyer Lloyd Cutler, one of his strategists, had predicted at the beginning of the fight that "the confirmation will turn on whether Judge Bork is able to satisfy the members of the Senate and the general public that he is not, in fact, a right-wing ide-

ologue, but is, in fact, a judge much closer to the center and . . .
Justice Powell, than he is to the justices over on the right."
Bork failed to do that because he could not do so—nobody
could have, given his views and his frequently reiterated public
positions.[58]

Polls indicated that Bork lost support with his performance
at his hearing. Before the hearing, 12 percent of the public
were unfavorable, 11 percent were favorable, and 77 percent
were undecided or had no opinion. After the hearing, his unfa-
vorables more than doubled to 26 percent, his favorables rose
to 16 percent, and 57 percent were undecided or had no
opinion.[59]

The vote against him was overwhelming. The Judiciary
Committee voted against him 9-5, and when Reagan insisted
on a floor vote, Bork lost 58-42.

Bork did not lose because of an unfair public relations campaign. The ads and public statements of the Bork opponents
were in fact occasionally guilty of hyperbole, but that is hardly
unusual in any highly contested public issue. Opinion surveys
showed that the ads played a very minor role in the public
mind. It was how Bork had come across at his hearing that was
decisive.

Nor was he rejected, as he bitterly complained, because he
had been falsely painted as "a racist, a sexist, and probably a
fascist." All the senators and the many law professors who
opposed him, many of whom knew him personally, certainly
did not believe that. It was his narrow view of the Constitution
and the role of the judiciary in protecting constitutional rights
that caused his downfall.[60]

Bork's defeat did not dampen Reagan's eagerness to find a
candidate who would tilt the Courts sharply to the right.
Accordingly to Mitchell E. Daniels, a former White House
political director, Reagan and Meese were looking for

"someone close enough to Bork's philosophy to keep faith with his supporters but perhaps someone obscure enough to be immune from caricature." Washington D.C. Court of Appeals Judge Douglas Ginsburg, seemed to fit the bill. Although an ardent free-marketeer who had written on almost nothing outside economic regulation and antitrust issues, the Justice Department was nevertheless sure he was "one of us," a "son of Bork," as Patrick Buchanan happily dubbed him. One judge on their court commented that Ginsburg followed Bork "like a Saint Bernard." Ginsburg was also Jewish, and according to one administration official, this might be a selling point to neutralize Jewish liberal opposition. Jesse Helms, Orrin Hatch, and other conservative senators rallied behind Ginsburg, as well as the martyred Bork. It was not to be.[61]

Ginsburg had never practiced law, had been a judge for only a year during which time he sat on very few cases and wrote no important opinions, had briefly held only three middle-level jobs in the Reagan administration, and had not been a particularly distinguished scholar at Harvard. This would normally have provided ammunition for his natural opponents on the Left. It was the Right that did him in, however.

A week after Ginsburg was nominated, on Thursday, November 5, 1987, National Public Radio reported that Ginsburg had smoked marijuana several times, most recently in 1979 while a law professor. Conservative senators were stunned and outraged. The Reagan administration, particularly Mrs. Reagan, was on an antidrug crusade, using every opportunity to urge people to "Just say no."

The president's first instinct was to defend the nominee. A "youthful indiscretion," Reagan called it, in marked contrast to his normally less tolerant judgment on those who had used drugs in the 1960s. To no avail, on Saturday, nine days after the nomination was announced, Ginsburg withdrew.

The last word went to the *Wall Street Journal*. Under the headline THE GINSBURG MARIJUANA MUDBALL, the *Journal* bitterly condemned those at Harvard who had breached Ginsburg's "privacy" by asking about his drug use, and concluded: "Washington, D.C. is a city of lying in the gutter, wallowing in hypocrisy. It has become a bizarre sinkhole of character assassination and smirking self-righteousness. It will eagerly cast not only the first stone, but any other rocks it can lay its hands on." How the Babylon of the Potomac wound up responsible for the conservative reaction to Ginsburg's indiscretions was not made clear.[62]

When Bork was defeated, presidential Chief of Staff Howard Baker had tried to promote a more moderate, more confirmable nominee, but Reagan had wanted another Bork and chose Douglas Ginsburg. Now Reagan decided he had to settle. Baker proposed 51-year-old Ninth Circuit Court of Appeals Judge Anthony Kennedy, who had a reputation for pragmatism and moderation. Initially, Meese, Helms, Hatch, and Meese's lieutenants, Assistant Attorney General for Civil Rights William Bradford Reynolds and Reynold's assistant Charles Cooper, strongly opposed the nomination. Kennedy had indicated some sympathy for homosexuals fired by the Navy and had even suggested there might be a constitutional right to privacy for intimate relations.[63]

Now Reagan and Meese felt they had no choice. Further delay might jeopardize their chance to get someone on the Court. Four days after Douglas Ginsburg withdrew, a chastened president nominated Anthony Kennedy, saying, "The experience of the last several months has made all of us a bit wiser."

The Judiciary Committee, pleased that Kennedy did not come across as an ideological zealot and fearful of another nasty fight, "played pattycake with him," in Washington lawyer Joseph Rauh's words, and asked him very few probing questions. It also scheduled the hearings to take place very quickly, before much work could be done on his record. On February 3, 1988, Kennedy was unanimously confirmed.[64]

During his eight years, Reagan appointed one female and two new male Supreme Court justices, including one chief justice, and seventy-seven whites, one Hispanic, and one black to the appeals courts, including four women. On the District Courts, he appointed 268 whites, fourteen Hispanics and six blacks, among whom were twenty-four women. Reagan's record for appointing black judges was the lowest since Eisenhower; Reagan appointed only twenty-nine women in contrast to Carter's forty.[65]

Conservatives were quite satisfied with the Reagan appointees. As early as 1984, a writer in the right-wing magazine *Benchmark* wrote: "Of the sixty-two judges evaluated in this study under the standards specified [adherence to the Republican Platform of 1980] . . . thirty-one judges exercised restraint in all of their significant cases without exception . . . sixteen exercised restraint in nearly all their significant opinions . . . nine . . . exercised restraint in no more than half of their significant cases . . . and six published no [pertinent] opinions. . . . The conclusion is inescapable that a Reagan judiciary, so far, has lived up to expectations."[66]

Nevertheless, the Reagan-Meese strategy could not pay off in a substantially changed constitutional and legal picture. Because Brennan, Marshall, Blackmun, Stevens, and Powell were still on the Court through 1987, there were only sporadic successes. Access to the federal courts for public interest suits was reduced a bit; civil rights were cut back somewhat, though affirmative action seemed established in education, employment, and government contracts, albeit with certain limitations; the wall of church-state separation was still high, though some cracks had begun to appear; abortion remained a fundamental right; and a judicial attack on federal power had been beaten back. The Court continued to shrink protections for criminal defendants, but that had preceded Reagan as had the severe weakening of the antitrust laws.

In one area, however, the Court fully realized the right wing's hopes: In 1986, in *Bowers* v. *Hardwick*, a 5-4 majority of the Court ruled that states could criminalize homosexual activity, a decision widely condemned by many. *Bowers* stayed on the books until June 2003, when the Court finally overturned it in an eloquent and passionate opinion by Kennedy, *Lawrence* v. *Texas*. By then, however, the *Bowers* decision had done a great deal of damage, serving as the basis for the denial of employment, licensing, custody, and many other rights, as well as being part of the justification for the military's "don't ask, don't tell" policy of the 1990s.[67]

• • •

1. Sheldon Goldman, *Picking Federal Judges* (Yale U. Press, 1997), pp. 297-98 (Goldman 1997).
2. Ibid.
3. Id. At 337. The full story is in Herman Schwartz, "O'Connor As A 'Centrist.' Not When Minorities are Involved," *Los Angeles Times*, (April 12, 1998).
4. *Grutter* v. *Bollinger*, 123 S. Ct. 2325 (2003); *Gratz* v. *Bollinger*, 123 S. Ct. 2411 (2003); *Regents of University of California* v. *Bakke*, 438 U.S. 912 (1978).
5. See cases cited at p. 14 n. 10
6. *Miranda* v. *Arizona*, 396 U.S. 868 (1969); *Mapp* v. *Ohio*, 367 U.S. 643 (1961).
7. See generally, Herman Schwartz, Book Review of Sandra Day O'Connor, "The Majesty of the Law," *The Nation*, August 11, 2003, p 55; *Planned Parenthood of Southeastern Pennsylvania* v. *Casey*, 505 U.S. 1833 (1992).
8. David M. O'Brien, *Judicial Roulette: Report of the 20th Century Fund Task Force on Judicial Selection*, (1988), p. 62; Nina Totenberg, National Public Radio, April 1, 1985; Goldman 1997, p. 305.
9. Fred Barbash, "Protesters Deny Woman Judgeship," *The Washington Post* (December 23, 1981).
10. A letter from thirteen Republican senators indicating their intention to oppose the nomination is reported in *The Washington Post* (March 23, 1985).
11. Richard Posner, *The Economics of Justice* (Cambridge, Mass.: Harvard University Press, 1981)
12. The baby sales figures and analysis are from Posner and Landes, "*The Economics of Baby Shortage*," 7 J. *Legal Studies* 323 (1978). See also Press and McDaniel, "Free Market Jurist," *Newsweek* (June 10, 1985). Discrimination is discussed in Posner, n. 11 pp. 351-407 and Posner, *Economic Analysis of Law*, 2nd ed. (Boston: Little, Brown, 1977), p. 525-534.
13. The ABA's rating of Wilkinsen is explored in Hearings Before The U.S. Senate Judi-

ciary Committee on Federal Appointments, 98th *Cong., 2nd Sess.* pp. 229, 245, 318-23, 376-77 (1984).

14. Quoted in 130 *Congressional Record* S 9276 (July 26, 1984).

15. The Virginian-Pilot is quoted in David Margolick, "Critics Question Experience of Reagan's Choice for Judgeship," *The New York Times* (April 1, 1984).

16. The Powell calls and the calls by two high-ranking Justice Department officials are discussed in *Hearings,* n.13 at p. 290. Deputy Attorney General Edward Schmults and Assistant Attorney General Jonathan Rose are discussed on pp 272-292 of the *Hearings.*

17. *Hearings* n.13, p. 368.

18. The description is a subheading in Shannon P. Duffy, Mike McKee, Mary Alice Robbins, Jonathan Groner, Tony Mauro "The Six on Bush's High Court Short List," *Legal Times* (March 3, 2003), p.11.

19. Sheldon Goldman, "Reorganizing the Judiciary: The First Term Appointments," 68 *Judicature* 313, 319, 325 (1985); see also O'Brien, p. 97.

20. The legislation creating the new judgeships is the Federal Judgeship Act of 1984, P.L. 98-353.

21. Editorial, *Los Angeles Times* (October, 1985).

22. Philip Kurland is quoted in *U.S. News & World Report* (October 14, 1985) p. 65.

23. Whitman v. American Trucking Ass'ns, Inc., 531 U.S. 457 (2001).

24. Howard Schneider, "Judge Met Sen. Faircloth Before Fiske Was Ousted; Sentelle Says Special Counsel Wasn't Discussed," *Washington Post,* August 12, 1994, p. A1.

25. Lawrence Walsh, *"Firewall: The Iran-Contra Conspiracy and Cover-Up,"* p. 477 (1997).

26. The Yugoslav matter is reported in Philip Smith and Al Kamen, Silberman Backed for Appeals Court; Reagan Expected to Name Ex-Envoy, *Washington Post* January 15, 1985, p. B1. The outburst at Mikva is reported in Ann Pelham, Silberman Dogged by Story, Provides Details of Outburst, *Legal Times,* March 11, 1991, p. 7 and in Michael Winerip, Ken Starr Would Not Be Denied, *New York Times,* September 6, 1998, p. A36.

27. Sandra Sugawara, "Vote Stalled on Nominee for Judicial Post in D.C.," *The Washington Post,* October 11, 1985.

28. *Houston Chronicle,* November 17, 2002; Adam Cohen, Hell Hath No Fury Like A Conservative Who Is Victorious, *New York Times,* November 24, 2002, p. A12.

29. Hearings Before the U.S. Senate Judiciary Committee on Federal Appointments, 99th *Cong. 2nd Sess.* P. 53 (February 5, 1985).

30. The appellate decision is described in *The Washington Post* (July 4, 1987). The cases are discussed throughout Hearings Before The U.S. Senate Judiciary Committee on the Nomination of Jefferson B. Sessions, III, 99th *Cong. 2nd Sess.* (1986) especially pages 181-299.

31. Id. pp.3, 28-30.

32. Senator Heflin's comments are in *Cong. Q.* 1297 (June 7, 1986).

33. Philip Lacovara, "The Wrong Way to Pick Judges," *The New York Times* (October 3, 1986).

34. The Chicago Counsel of Lawyers' letter appears in Hearings Before the U.S. Senate Judiciary Committee on Federal Appointments, 99th *Cong. 2nd Sess.* pp. 205-6 (1986)

35. *The Economist,* (May 17, 1986), pp. 24-25.

36. *Indianapolis Star,* June 20, 1986; *The Wall Street Journal,* October 21, 1985.

37. Judicial Selection Project letter to American Bar Association Standing Committee on the Federal Judiciary (January 10, 1986), in author's files.

38. *Legal Times,* June 15, 1987.

39. Lino Graglia's record is summarized in editorial, "Strict Constructionist" *Los Angeles Times,* November 8, 1985; an ad signed by Graglia appears in Austin American Statesman, December 7, 1979; the Louisiana incident is reported in U.S. NEWS & WORLD REPORT, January 19, 1981, p.8.

40. "Reagan's Mr. Right," *Time* (June 30, 1986), p. 24.

41. Bob Jones University v. United States, 461 U.S. 754 (1983) (segregated private schools); Cleveland Beard of Education v. LaFleur, 414 U.S. 632 (1974) (pregnancy leave); Frontiero v. Richardson, 411 U.S. 677 (1973) (servicewomen); Memorial Hospital v. Maricopa County, 415 U.S. 250 (1974) (medical care and residency); U.S. Department of Agriculture v. Murry, 413 U.S. 508 (1974) (food stamps); Hutto

v. Finney, 437 U.S. 678 (1978) (prison conditions); Cruz v. Beto, 405 U.S. 319 (1972) (Buddhist prisoner); Thomas v. Review Board, 450 U.S. 707 (1981) (Jehovah's Witness); Keyes v. School Dist. No. 1, Denver, Colo., 413 U.S. 189 (1973) (school desegregation).

42. Sugarman v. Dougall, 413 U.S. 634 (1973) (aliens); Trimble v. Gordon, 430 U.S. 762 (1977) (out-of-wedlock children); Frontiero v. Richardson, 411 U.S. 677 (1973) (women); but see Meritor Savings Bank v. Vinson, 106 S. Ct. 2399 (1986) (sexual harassment under Title VII).

43. Memorandum of the AFL-CIO with Respect to the Nomination of Justice William Rehnquist to Be Chief Justice of the United States, (September 9, 1986), pp. 3-4

44. First National Bank v. Bellotti, 435 U.S. 765, 823 (1978) (Rehnquist, J., dissenting); Buckley v. Valeo, 424 U.S. 1,291 (1976) (Rehnquist, J., concurring and dissenting).

45. Rehnquist's change of heart is in Hearings Before the U.S. Senate Judiciary Committee on the Judiciary on the Nomination of William H. Rehnquist and Lewis F. Powell, Jr., 92nd Cong., 1st Sess. p. 70 (1971).

46. The Powell statement is in United States v. Richardson, 418 U.S. 166, 192 (1974) (Powell, J. concurring).

47. Dickerson v. United States, 530 U.S. 428 (2000).

48. 310 F.3d 717 (For. Int. Surv. Ct. Rev. 2002); Dan Eggen, "FBI Applies New Rules to Surveillance," Washington Post, December 15, 2003, p. A1.

49. Morrison and Stenhouse, "The Chief Justice of the United States: More Than Just the Highest Ranking Judge," 1 Const. Comm. 57 (1984).

50. The comment was made by Professor Stephen Wermiel, then of the Wall Street Journal on Washington Week in Review, National Public Radio (August 1, 1986).

51. See Virginia Military Institute v. U.S., 508 U.S. 946 (1993); Nevada Department of Human Resources v. Hibbs, 123 S. Ct. 1972 (2003).

52. Antonin Scalia, "God's Justice and Our's," First Things, J. Religion and Public Life (May 2002).

53. Planned Parenthood of Southeastern Pennsylvania v. Casey, 505 U.S. 833 (1992) (sarcasm); Romer v. Evans, 517 U.S. 620, 652 (1996) (taking sides); Lawrence v. Texas, 123 S. Ct. 2472, 2496 (2003) (homosexual agenda).

54. Bruce Fein comments were in a Voice of America Broadcast (July 31, 1989) and in Newsweek (September 14, 1989) p.24.

55. The criticism of the contraception decision is reported in The New York Times (September 13, 1989). The limited judicial role in enforcing equality is set forth in Robert Bork, 41 Ind. L.J. 12; the June 1987 is in Report of the Senate Judiciary Committee on the Judiciary on the Nomination of Robert H. Bork, 100th Cong. 1st sess. p. 46; The 1963 criticism of the Public Accommodations Act is in Bork, "Civil Rights—A Challenge," New Republic (August 31, 1963) p.21.

56. The 1971 discussion of free speech is in Robert Bork, "Neutral Principles and some First Amendment Problems," 41 Ind. L.J. 20 (1971), the 1987 comment was made in a United States Information Agency program (June 10, 1987), quoted in Report, n. 56.

57. The Kurland comment was in "Bork: The Transformation Of A Conservative Constitutionalist," Chicago Tribune (August 18, 1987).

58. Bork's descriptions of himself as neither "conservative" nor "liberal" are reported in Stuart Taylor, "No Big Critic of the Court; Nominee's Answers Contrast With Bork's" The New York Times (September 17, 1987). Cutler's comments were broadcast on Voice of America (July 31, 1987).

59. The results of the poll are reported in The New York Times. Shenon, Philip, "The Bork Hearings; Poll Finds Public Opposition to Bork is Growing," The New York Times (September 23, 1987).

60. Bork's comments were reported in The Washington Post (December 15, 1989).

61. Mitchell Daniels is quoted in Steven V. Roberts, "Washington Talk: The White House; Picking Another Nominee: Lessons From Bork," The New York Times (October 28, 1987), p. B8; the comments on Ginsburg are in Kenneth Karpay, "In Search of Judge Ginsburg; Bork Helped Win Nomination For His D.C. Circuit Protégé," The Legal Times, (November 2, 1987) p. 1. The anonymous judge on Bork's court is quoted in Legal Times (November 2, 1987) p. 14. The Jewish factor is noted in Stephen Wermiel, "Ginsburg's Sparse Record May Result in a Confirmation Process Unlike Bork's," The Wall Street Journal, (November 2, 1987).

62. Editorial, "The Ginsburg Marijuana Mudball," The Wall Street Journal, (November

9, 1987). *The Wall Street Journal,* November 9, 1987.
63. *Beller v. Middendorf,* 632 F.2d 788, 819 (9th Cir. 1980).
64. Joseph Rauh's comments appear in Hearings Before the U.S. Senate Judiciary Committee on the Nomination of Anthony M. Kennedy to Be an Associate Justice of the Supreme Court, 100th *Cong. 1st Sess.* pp. 145-146 (December 16, 1987) (daily ed).
65. 1997 Goldman, p. 350.
66. Craig Stern, 1 Benchmark 1, 2-3 (1984).
67. *Bowers v. Hardwick,* 478 U.S. 186 (1986); Lawrence v. Texas, 123 S. Ct. 2472 (2003).

Chapter 3

George H. W. Bush's Judges, 1989–1992

President George H. W. Bush's four years saw the culmination of the Reagan court-packing strategy and the beginning of the full-scale conservative counterrevolution. By the time Bush left office, Republican judges comprised 80 percent of all federal judges and 75 percent of the appellate bench. Eleven of the thirteen Courts of Appeals were dominated by Republican judges.

The impact of the Reagan Supreme Court appointments, particularly the appointment of Anthony Kennedy to replace Lewis F. Powell, was felt shortly after Reagan left office, especially with respect to civil rights and the conservative crusade against federal power.

When nominated, Kennedy was largely an unknown quantity. In most respects, Reagan did better than he expected. Kennedy—who turned out to be a far more conservative judge than Lewis Powell—has become a reliable member of the five-member majority that has dominated the Court since the arrival of Bush appointee Clarence Thomas. In fact, Kennedy made a quite solid five-member conservative majority in civil rights cases even before Thomas arrived. This was not too surprising because his record on race, gender, and disability cases had aroused considerable anxiety among liberals. He showed some sympathy for affirmative action at his confirmation hearing, but has been a vigorous opponent of such programs from his first year on the Court, starting with the 1989 *Croson* case. In his first full year on the Court, (1988–89), he joined Rehnquist and the other conservatives in some six key decisions that severely weakened Title VII, the employment discrimination provision of the Civil Rights Act of 1964. All the decisions were overturned by a bipartisan coalition in Congress in the Civil Rights Restoration Act of 1991, over the vigorous opposition of the Bush administration. Kennedy also showed himself to be no friend of labor.[1]

Once Thomas was on the Court, the Court had an even more solid conservative majority, and Kennedy was a reliable member of this bloc. There were, however, several very important exceptions in Kennedy's record. He broke with the conservative bloc and made a five-member majority striking down a state law imposing term limits on federal legislators. Also in his first full year on the Court, he seemed to be with Rehnquist and Scalia on abortion, joining Rehnquist in an opinion that would have eviscerated *Roe*. But he shocked his erstwhile allies and many others two years later when he joined O'Connor and Souter in the *Casey* abortion decision preserving a woman's right to an abortion. Most notable, he was the author of the Court's two decisions favoring gay rights. In the first, in 1996, he wrote for the Court in a 6-3 decision—O'Connor joined him—striking down a Colorado constitutional amendment that excluded gays from any state or local antidiscrimination legislation or regulation. And in 2003, in one of the most important decisions of recent years, he authored an eloquent opinion for a five-member majority striking down laws criminalizing homosexual and heterosexual sodomy, overturning the 1986 *Bowers v. Hardwick* decision. O'Connor agreed only

with the result and wrote a separate opinion on equal protection grounds, which, had it been adopted by a majority, would
have made it easy to keep the *Bowers* case in force.[2]

Kennedy has also been one of the Court's staunchest supporters of free speech, one example of which was one of the
most surprising results of the Kennedy and Scalia appointments. In 1989, a 5-4 majority of the Court struck down a
Texas law penalizing flag-burning when the burning is for the
purpose of expression. Included in the five were both Kennedy
and Scalia. Although Scalia simply joined the Brennan opinion,
his vote was obviously based on the statute having penalized
only dissent, a violation of the principle that the state may not
take sides, a principle on which Scalia had always insisted. It is
almost certain that if Burger had been on the Court instead of
Scalia, the vote would have been 5-4 the other way.[3]

On the other hand, the Reagan Supreme Court legacy was
felt in religion cases, where the appointment of Kennedy and
Scalia made a difference in the most important freedom of religion case in the past fifty years. In that case, *Employment Division v. Smith*, another 5-4 majority, again including Scalia and
Kennedy, this time in a Scalia opinion, declared that the Constitution did not require any exemption for religious reasons to
laws that applied to all in general. In the *Smith* case, the Court
ruled that a law penalizing the use of peyote did not have to
allow an exemption for those who used it only for religious
purposes. Had Powell still been on the Court, the Court would
probably not have adopted such a position.[4]

The same can be said for many of the church-state separation cases, where the wall of separation has been steadily low-
ered. Kennedy and Scalia have consistently voted against the
separationist position, winning many though losing a few.
Here, too, Powell's absence has been felt, for he frequently supported the separationist position.

Reagan's impact was also seen in the tentative beginning of what is the major campaign for the right wing today: the assault on the federal government's welfare and regulatory roles. Rehnquist fired the first shot in 1976 when he managed to pull together five votes to set aside the applicability of the federal Fair Labor Standards Act to state and local government employees. That lasted only nine years, however, and was overruled in the 1985 *Garcia* case, as discussed earlier.

Now the conservative drive resumed. The opening gun was fired in a little-noticed case about whether the federal Age Discrimination in Employment Act barred the forcible retirement of state judges. In an O'Connor opinion singing the praises of the states and adopting many of the arguments against federal power unsuccessfully made by the dissenters (including herself) in the *Garcia* case noted earlier, a 5-4 majority ruled that the act didn't apply to state judges; Kennedy and Scalia, who came on the Court after *Garcia*, were two of the five, and Bush's first appointment, David Souter, a former state judge (as was O'Connor) in his first year on the Court following Brennan's retirement, was the fifth. Souter would soon abandon the conservatives on federalism issues and write very strong opinions in support of federal authority.[6]

David Souter, whose nomination and confirmation will be discussed later, was one of the few mistakes made by the Bush administration in its court-packing efforts. The administration's success with its other nominees was largely due to two people: C. Boyden Gray, Bush's White House counsel, and his deputy, Lee Liberman, one of the three student founders of the Federalist Society. In pursuance of his goal of "shift[ing] the federal courts in a more conservative direction," Gray made the counsel's office a "bastion of conservatism," and staffed it with Federalist Society members and others who were well on the right. Gray, an heir to the R.J. Reynolds tobacco fortune, was also a close personal friend of Bush and had been his lawyer since Bush's vice presidency. He became one of the most powerful Counsels to the president in history, with a finger in almost all domestic matters. Described by one Bush administration official as "the true believer," he continued to fight very hard against the bipartisan efforts to overturn the 1989 civil rights cases discussed earlier, even after losing. For example, when the Leadership Conference on Civil Rights and others began to negotiate on a compromise bill with the Business Roundtable, which includes the chief executives of most major American corporations, Gray telephoned members of the roundtable, and demanded that they break off the negotiations, which they did. Then, after a bill was passed, on the eve of the signing, and without consulting with Bush or anyone else, Gray issued a proposed directive to end all federal affirmative-action programs. The directive overturned a twenty-five-year-old policy that had survived Nixon and Reagan, and produced such a political uproar that the White House quickly withdrew it.[7]

Lee Liberman was Gray's chief assistant. A University of Chicago Law School graduate, where she had joined two other law students to found the Federalist Society, and an associate deputy attorney general in the Reagan administration, Liberman was appointed associate White House counsel and Gray's chief assistant in judicial selection. It was her job to analyze opinions and other writings of judicial nominees to ensure that they were sufficiently conservative. She, in turn, was supported by a group of bright young conservatives from the Federalist Society, including former law clerks to Rehnquist, Scalia, Silberman, and other conservative judges.

Gray's task was made easier by the concentration of the judicial selection process in the White House, diminishing the role of the scandal-tarnished Meese Justice Department. Gray, Liberman, and their staff succeeded in putting candidates on the bench who were as conservative as the Reagan appointees, particularly on the Courts of Appeals.

With the help of eighty-five new judgeships, and the normal attrition of forty per year, in his four years Bush was able to appoint 187 judges: 148 to the District Courts and thirty-seven to the Courts of Appeal. Although he could have nominated many more, the insistence on ideological purity and a fight over the Senate Judiciary Committee's right to see FBI reports slowed the process considerably. When Bush left office, he had failed to submit nominations for forty-two district and five appellate court vacancies. Because so many new judgeships were created, the Committee was swamped with nominees and also failed to act on fifty-three nominations, leaving 100 vacancies (fifteen at the appellate level and eighty-five at the trial level) when Bush left office; many of these nominations were made at the end of 1991 and a few in 1992. These included Sidney Fitzwater, who had been put on the District Court in Dallas at the age of thirty-two, after having posted signs in minority precincts which were found to have an intimidating effect on minority voters. Also stalled were John Roberts, a brilliant conservative lawyer, who had taken several positions very hostile to abortion rights as a high-level department official and was nominated to Clarence Thomas's seat on the D.C. Circuit; and Terence Boyle, a district judge from North Carolina who was a protégé of Jesse Helms. Roberts and Boyle would be nominated again by George W. Bush, and would gain confirmation, Boyle to the Fourth Circuit. Nevertheless, the Democratic-controlled Senate under the chairmanship of Joseph Biden confirmed sixty-three nominations in 1992 (ten appellate and fifty-three district nominees), which was and remains a record for a presidential election year when the opposition party controls the Senate.[8]

The Bush nominees were largely white, male, and wealthy.

In his invaluable analyses of the demographic and other aspects of federal judges, Sheldon Goldman found that more than 40 percent of Bush's appellate court nominees were millionaires, and two-thirds had a net worth of more than a half-million dollars. Well over half of the District Court appointees were worth over $500,000 and over a quarter of those judges were millionaires. Not surprisingly, in light of these proportions, "the Bush appointees set a modern record with the highest proportion of judges recruited from large law firms."[9]

They were also very young. Goldman found that at the time, Bush's nominees were the youngest of any administration going back to Lyndon Johnson's, outdoing the Reagan-Meese record. Bush's appellate nominees averaged 48.7 years old, the lowest of the six previous administrations studied by Goldman, and even younger than Reagan's nominees for these lifetime seats.

Perhaps because of the presence of Lee Liberman and other women in the counsel's office, Bush appointed a substantial number of women—almost 20 percent. His record on blacks was only 6 percent, however, and even worse on Hispanics, barely 4 percent.

Most significant, his appointees were as conservative as Reagan's, thanks to Gray and Liberman. In 1991, Meese commented, "Bush has done an excellent job . . . The results are the same as in the Reagan administration." Clint Bolick, one of the chief strategists for the far right in the judgeship wars, said with satisfaction, "There is no area in which conservatives are more happy with George Bush than in judicial nominations." Bush's appellate court nominees were considered by Thomas Jipping, another arch-conservative, "as good as or better on the whole than Ronald Reagan's." The result was that Bush put on the bench some of the most conservative judges in the entire federal judiciary. Yet, except for a few particularly publicized cases—Clarence Thomas, Kenneth L. Ryskamp, Edward

Carnes, and a few others—the Democrats let almost all of them through without even a recorded vote. In 1991, they confirmed every one of Bush's nominees on voice votes except for Ryskamp. When Clarence Thomas was nominated to the Court of Appeals in 1990, only two senators voted against him in a voice vote; Souter went through with a 90-9 vote.[10]

The reasons for this Democratic passivity are not altogether clear. One reason may be that Bush did not nominate law professors and others who had helped create and promote the right-wing agenda, like Reagan appointees Rehnquist, Scalia, Bork, Wilkinson, William Harvey, Daniel Manion, and Bernard Siegan. Bush was also helped by his legislative liaison with the Judiciary Committee, William Barr, who later became Attorney General, and with whom Committee chairman Biden and the other Democrats got along well.

For their part, the Democrats were not eager for more fights over judges. Republicans had turned their defeat on Bork into a weapon with which to bludgeon the Democrats. For his part, Bush obviously did not want a repeat of the Bork bloodletting. Moreover, the Democrats never really wanted fights over judgeships, and this was particularly true for Judiciary Committee chairman Joseph Biden. Biden had built his career on ostentatiously separating himself from liberals like Kennedy and Howard Metzenbaum though he often voted with them. Biden also had presidential aspirations, and was particularly reluctant to get into noisy liberal/conservative fights. Also, Democrats mistakenly considered Bush less of an ideologue than Reagan. Bush and Gray were in fact less openly confrontational than Reagan and Meese. Still another factor may have been that many of his appellate nominees were district judges who had already been approved by the committee. It was harder for committee members to challenge an appellate nomination if they had already approved the nominee for a district judgeship. For the District

Courts, Bush nominated a substantial number of state judges and federal magistrates, more than Reagan or Carter. Since many of those nominees had records that could be assessed, it was possible to weed out those who would set off fights. The best example of this was the nomination of the "stealth candidate," David Souter.

When Justice William J. Brennan retired in 1990, the Bush administration saw a chance to begin rebuilding a relationship with the conservative wing of the Republican Party, which was angry about Bush's going back on his "Read my lips: No new taxes" pledge. Replacing a liberal like Brennan with a solid conservative would go a long way toward shoring up Bush's conservative base. On the other hand, Bush was afraid to risk another Bork, especially so early in his term. David Souter seemed to be the answer.

When nominated, Souter was a 50-year-old recent appointee to the First Circuit Court of Appeals from the New Hampshire Supreme Court. A quiet, solitary bachelor, almost ascetic in appearance, he was unknown to almost everyone. On the hot-button federal issues like abortion, affirmative action, church-state separation, and federalism issues, he had no judicial record to speak of, since his Supreme Court nomination came within weeks after the arguments in his first cases on the First Circuit Court of Appeals. Nevertheless, Bush's Chief of Staff, former New Hampshire Governor John Sununu, who had appointed Souter to the New Hampshire Supreme Court, pushed Souter's nomination over the very conservative and younger 41-year-old Edith Jones of the Fifth Circuit, assuring nervous conservatives that Souter would be a "home run" for their cause. Before Souter's hearings, Sununu told the *New York Times*, "I was looking for someone who would be a strict constructionist, consistent with basic conservative attitudes, and that's what I got." A hint that Sununu may have been claiming more than he knew came from Republican Senator Warren Rudman of New Hampshire who complained, "I told Ronald Reagan about him, I pushed him for the Circuit Court job and I urged Bush to choose him this time. He's not Sununu's man." [11]

But there was in fact a basis for Sununu's confidence. While Souter was New Hampshire Attorney General, he had described abortion as the killing of unborn children, had argued that Congress couldn't bar state literacy tests for voting, and taken other conservative positions. He was described by a fellow New Hampshire State Supreme Court judge as a "status quo, stare decisis conservative," and Souter inscribed a photograph he gave one of his law clerks on that court "from David, still a conservative." [12]

Liberals were of course concerned, and despite Sununu's assurances, Souter's nearly blank record on abortion and other controversial issues deeply troubled prominent conservatives. The day before Souter's hearings opened, right-wing columnist George F. Will lamented that Souter's nomination "indicates that the rejection of Bork has resulted in the institutionalizing of anti-intellectualism. One reason Souter was nominated is that for 30 years he has walked across the sands of adulthood without leaving intellectual footprints." But this "stealth nominee" strategy also gave liberal opponents little ammunition with which to oppose him, especially after he refused to say anything about Roe v. Wade at his hearing. Kate Michelman of the National Abortion Rights Action League could only complain, "We're at too critical an historic juncture to see a justice confirmed whose views are not clear, who is not willing to tell us his views, and who has no record." Together with the Planned Parenthood Action Fund, NARAL came out against him, but other elements of the anti-Bork coalition, such as the Alliance for Justice and People for the American Way, only expressed concern. Writing just before the hearings, Linda Greenhouse noted that the anti-Bork coalition was broken: "The mood among these groups is one of wariness and frustration." [13]

The hearings were a triumph for Souter. He displayed a keen legal mind, seemed open to discussing every legal issue that was raised except *Roe*, on which he avoided expressing an opinion, and expressed compassion for people in trouble. As the *New York Times* television critic summarized it,

> Seated alone at a big table covered with a red cloth, he quietly took over. He was careful yet responsive, mild yet firm, well briefed yet conversational, consistently intelligent yet never off-puttingly brilliant. The second day, unfortunately, he showed that he would outtalk even a senator. [14]

After the hearings, many senators remained puzzled. Conservatives were troubled by his answers, and liberals did not know what to think. To questions inviting condemnation of the Warren Court's criminal procedure decisions, he responded with a defense of the rulings, particularly *Miranda v. Arizona* (1966), which he described "as a 'pragmatic' effort by the Supreme Court to protect the pre-existing right against involuntary confessions." He seemed to support a Supreme Court decision that authorized federal judges to order local tax increases to pay for school segregation remedies. He dismayed Republican Senators Charles Grassley of Iowa and Arlen Specter of Pennsylvania when he insisted that when the legislature leaves a "vacuum," judges "have an obligation to come down with practical decrees that implement rights," citing *Brown v. Board of Education* and *Miranda*; when asked if he could think of any case in which the Court had "improperly created new rights," he said "No." He rejected specific historical intent as a touchstone for constitutional interpretation, especially the very narrow view supported by Scalia and Rehnquist.

He supported affirmative action, and said he considered the Ninth Amendment an indication that courts sometimes needed to go beyond the text and the specific intent of the Framers. He shocked Senator Thurmond's states-rights' soul with a comment that "the Tenth Amendment [which reserves to the states the powers not delegated to the federal government] is something we can't look at through the eyes of the people who wrote it . . . [given] constitutional developments outside the framework of the Tenth Amendment which would have astonished the Framers." He repudiated positions he had taken as New Hampshire Attorney General, saying he had then been an advocate and not the "me of now." [15]

In hindsight, a significant hint of his judicial philosophy was his praise of Justice Brennan, who, he declared, "is going to be remembered as one of the most fearlessly principled guardians of the American Constitution that it has ever had and ever will have." When he joined the Court he became very close to the retired Justice, so much so that it was he who gave the Court's eulogy at Brennan's funeral. And since joining the Court, he has been a mainstay of the liberal minority.[16]

Yet, his answers were sufficiently general that once on the Court, he could still prove quite conservative. There was the example of Anthony Kennedy, who had turned out to be far more conservative than some of his answers at his hearing seemed to indicate. At the end of the Souter hearings, Senator Paul Simon of Illinois summed up the mood of many senators when he said, "We're all worried. I don't think there's anyone who feels completely comfortable."

Souter's appointment to the Court turned out to be a substantial disappointment to conservatives who soon realized that he was no "home run" for their cause. But not right away. In his first term, 1991–92, he generally lined up with the conservatives, particularly O'Connor. This was particularly true in the criminal justice area, where he provided a crucial fifth vote for 5-4 majorities in seven important cases that cut back significantly on defendants' rights. Had Brennan remained on the Court, those cases would have gone the other way. Souter is still tough on criminal defendants. That same year, he joined the conservatives in *Rust v. Sullivan*, which allowed the government to stop those who received federal family planning moneys from even mentioning the word "abortion" when dispensing family planning advice. But Souter's conservatism did not last very long. The following year, he joined O'Connor and Kennedy in the *Casey* abortion decision, and from then on, he has aligned himself quite consistently with the Court's liberals.[17]

No such surprises confounded the Bush administration's lower court choices. Their appeals court nominees included some of the most conservative judges on the federal bench today. Yet all of them breezed through their nominations with hardly a murmur from the Democrats and almost always just by a voice vote, often with enthusiastic support from Democratic senators. Samuel Alito (Third Circuit), Michael Luttig (Fourth Circuit), Emilio Garza (Fifth Circuit), A. Raymond Randolph (D.C. Circuit), and Andrew Kleinfeld (Ninth Circuit) are good examples.

Michael Luttig is probably the best-known of the Bush appellate judges, and probably the most outspoken and controversial to this day. Even on the Fourth Circuit, considered by most observers the most right-wing of all the circuits, he is thought to be the most extreme, though there are indications that Chief Judge J. Harvie Wilkinson may be even more so. His nomination drew only mixed reviews from the American Bar Association, a majority funding him "qualified"; and a minority finding him "unqualified"; the ABA's highest ranking is "well qualified."

Luttig is typical of many Bush/Reagan judges in several

respects. He clerked for Scalia when the latter was on the D.C. Court of Appeals and then moved along the usual Federalist Society track to a clerkship with Chief Justice Warren Burger. He was an Assistant Attorney General in the Bush administration, and was deeply involved in the Clarence Thomas struggle. Anthony Lewis of the *New York Times* reported that Luttig and Boyden Gray devised the strategy of destroying Anita Hill's character and attacking the committee by having Thomas charge the Democrats with racism, a charge Republicans would use again in 2003 when Democrats opposed Janice Rogers Brown for a seat on the D.C. Circuit. Even after Luttig was confirmed for the Fourth Circuit Court of Appeals but before he was sworn in, he continued to play a key role in the nomination fight, resulting in charges by the *New York Times* and others that he had violated the spirit if not the letter of the Code of Judicial Conduct which prohibits judges from engaging in partisan politics. The walls of Luttig's chambers are adorned with pictures of Thomas, one of which is inscribed "This would not have been possible without you. Thanks so much buddy."[18]

Also like many Reagan/Bush judges, Luttig is very bright, an excellent writer, extremely young when appointed (36), and on the far right of the judicial spectrum. He is hostile to abortion, the rights of minorities and women, and to affirmative action, habeas corpus, defendants' rights, and environmental protection, to mention but some of the many contentious matters that come before the federal judiciary today. In some eleven years on the bench, he has never voted to overturn a death sentence. Luttig is a fervent crusader against federal power. He wrote the lower court decision overturning the Violence Against Women Act, which the Supreme Court affirmed 5-4; he has narrowly construed the Federal Disabilities Act; he dissented from one of the few times that the Fourth Circuit has upheld an environmental protection action, an application of the Endangered Species Act to red wolves; he was a member of a panel that severely undermined the federal courts' ability to enforce the Federal Surface Mining Act in a West Virginia case where mountaintop mining was alleged to have "decapitate[d] the State's mountains and dump[ed] the resulting waste in nearby valleys, burying hundreds of miles of headwaters of West Virginia's streams"; he wrote a decision upholding a state law barring so-called "partial births," which was annulled by a later Supreme Court decision. Clint Bolick has described Luttig admiringly as "a conservative's conservative." He too was confirmed by voice vote, without any opposition.[19]

On the other hand, Luttig is not entirely predictable. He has come down with some liberal decisions, often disagreeing with Wilkinson.[20]

Luttig is now on George W. Bush's short list for Supreme Court appointments.

Judge Samuel Alito of the Third Circuit is also a typical Reagan/Bush judge. A bright young veteran of the Meese Justice Department (40 when nominated), he has been nicknamed by some lawyers "Scalito," meaning "little Scalia," on whom he seems to be modeling himself in outlook though not in expression— unlike Scalia, he is polite and respectful. Also mentioned as a possible Supreme Court nominee, in his thirteen years on the Third Circuit he has put together so consistent a conservative record that lawyers who practice before the Third Circuit say that his vote in sensitive cases is highly predictable. He was the only dissenter from the Third Circuit's ruling in the *Casey* abortion case striking down the Pennsylvania provision requiring women to notify their husbands before getting an abortion, the only abortion regulation invalidated by the Supreme Court in that case, and the only regulation invalidated by the Supreme Court since then, other than the "partial birth" abortion case. He was the lone dissenter in an 11-1 decision in a 1996 sex-discrimination case that allowed a discrimination case to go to a jury when the female employee managed to cast some doubt on the reason the employer gave for firing her. Once the jury got the case, they found that she had been wrongly discharged. And in an alien deportation case, he was again the dissenter in a case allowing the deportee to file a habeas corpus petition in federal court to challenge the deportation, a right the Supreme Court upheld a year later.[21]

Unlike Luttig and Alito, Emilio Garza was a Texas District Court judge when Bush nominated him to the Fifth Circuit in 1991, having been appointed by Reagan to the District Court in San Antonio in 1988. When appointed to the District Court, he was the youngest federal judge in the country. He thus had a judicial track record when nominated for the Court of Appeals, but district judges do not get much of an opportunity to make law, and since the Democrats confirmed him in 1988, when they controlled the Senate, they apparently found it difficult to oppose him for the Circuit. One of the few Hispanic appellate judges, Garza is considered "solidly conservative"; one appellate litigator in Dallas commented that Garza and Edith Jones, one of the most conservative of the Reagan/Bush federal judges, rarely differ. He too had no trouble with his confirmation.[21]

In 1991, Garza came close to being nominated for the Supreme Court as the first Hispanic Justice when Thurgood Marshall retired at the end of June 1991. Although Bush claimed that he chose Clarence Thomas because he had been impressed with Thomas's "seasoning" on the D.C. Court of Appeals, where he had been for about fifteen months, and believed him to be "the best person at the right time," it is likely that the choice obviously had more to do with Thomas's race. Although Garza is still mentioned as a possible Supreme

Court nominee, he has one glaring problem: He has severely criticized both *Roe v. Wade* and the 1965 *Griswold v. Connecticut* decision that established the right to privacy and allowed a married couple to use contraceptives, respectively. He has also expressed approval for *Bowers v. Hardwick*, the now-overruled and discredited gay-rights case. Were Garza nominated to the High Court, these views would probably produce such a firestorm, including a filibuster, that his nomination is unlikely.[22]

Karen Williams is another hard-right conservative whom Bush appointed. She holds the dubious distinction of having written two of the rare decisions in which the Rehnquist Court reversed the Fourth Circuit: the circuit's effort to overturn *Miranda v. Arizona* and to strike down the Driver Privacy Protection Act. She was also the only dissenter from an en banc decision in which the rest of the ultraconservative Fourth Circuit found that a female employee had been subjected to sexual harassment by the pornographic actions of the male employees. Williams thought this was merely "vulgar talk." Among her other decisions was a ruling that the Americans with Disabilities Act does not generally cover an individual who is infected with HIV but has no harmful symptoms. She too was confirmed by voice vote.[23]

Other "solidly conservative" judges like Paul Niemeyer of the Fourth Circuit, Andrew Kleinfeld and Pamela Rymer of the Ninth Circuit, and Raymond Randolph of the D.C. Circuit also breezed through without recorded votes. There were, however, some lower court controversies, and in one of them, a nominee was actually voted down by the Judiciary Committee, the only one dealt such a fate during Bush's four years.

Kenneth Ryskamp was a 58-year-old federal district judge in Miami, Florida, in April 1990 when Bush nominated him to the Eleventh Circuit, which covers Georgia, Florida, and

Alabama; he was appointed to the District Court bench by Reagan in 1986. When nominated to the Eleventh Circuit, he had belonged for some twenty-three years to a club that excluded blacks and Jews. Membership in clubs that discriminate against African-Americans, Jews, or women had become a serious issue, and many nominees resigned when they became serious judgeship candidates, like Anthony Kennedy. While the appellate nomination was pending, the club changed its policy. When the Judiciary Committee decided to look into the matter further, the nomination was caught in the year-end slowdown. Bush renominated him in early 1991. Until the Ryskamp nomination the Senate had approved seventy-six Bush nominees without a murmur.

On the eve of Ryskamp's hearings in March 1991, he resigned from the club. When pressed about the reason he had waited so long, he said he had believed the club did not discriminate and learned of it only when some Jewish friends told him about it. This was ludicrous on its face and Jewish leaders told the committee that the exclusionary policy was well-known. Indeed, when Ryskamp joined the club in 1967, the *Miami Herald* was already carrying articles about the club's exclusion of blacks and Jews, and had done so for years. Despite the 1990 change in policy, at the time of the hearing, the club still had no black members and insisted that its members speak only English because, as Ryskamp explained, members wanted a place "where we didn't have to hear Spanish." A week before the hearings, he told a Judiciary Committee staff member that Miami was "like a foreign city." He also complained that his wife could no longer find many food items at the grocery where she shopped because it stocked mainly items typical of Spanish-speaking countries, and she was annoyed that the clerks spoke mainly Spanish.

There were many more such insensitive and impolitic remarks

at the hearing. The administration had worked for weeks to polish him and to teach him how to answer the senators' questions without getting into trouble, but it had made little impression. He finally told the committee members that he would resign from any club the committee wanted him to, leading Senator Howard Metzenbaum of Ohio to say "You seem to be missing the point entirely. . . . It is not enough for a judge to resign at the point of confirmation."

He had also made some shocking comments from the bench. In one case, a suit was brought against the police department by victims of badly supervised police dogs. Among the plaintiffs were two black men who were admitted thieves. They had been badly mauled by the police dogs, and one of the two had his testicles ripped out. During the trial, Ryskamp commented that in some countries the two men could have had their hands cut off. "It might not be inappropriate to carry around a few scars to remind you of your wrongdoing in the past, assuming the person has done wrong," he said. The jury found for the plaintiffs against the city and its police chief, but Ryskamp set aside its finding. The Court of Appeals, however, reversed him and reinstated the jury's findings.[24]

To explain his apparent callousness, Ryskamp said he was only musing on "a certain irony" that thieves might "feel vindicated" by an award of damages and would then return to a life of crime. "I thought that would have the opposite result that I would like to see, because I would like to make sure that he would straighten out his life and go on. I did not say he was justified in being bitten." [25]

Other decisions he had issued also raised concern. The Eleventh Circuit had reversed him seventeen times in his four years as a judge, eight times in cases involving the civil rights of minorities, the elderly, and other disadvantaged groups, as well as on other constitutional issues. He was also frequently reversed for setting aside jury verdicts for the plaintiff, as in the police dog case, even when there was no evidence in the record to support the defendant. In a case involving an Egyptian doctor who sued a hospital for firing him because of his ethnicity, the appeals court criticized Ryskamp for having "ignored" the standard for over-riding a jury verdict when he threw out the $135,000 damages award. "Once the jury found in [the doctor's] favor, the district court was not free to reweigh the evidence," the appeals court admonished him. In another case involving a bus driver who claimed he was fired because he was 66, Ryskamp took the unusual step of finding that age was a "bona fide occupational qualification" for the job even though the school had not made that argument. The appeals court reversed this ruling too, saying there was no proof to support that defense.

Committee Democrats did not want to turn Ryskamp down, and sent up easy questions offering him many opportunities to say the right thing. For example, Democratic Senator Howell Heflin, whose state of Alabama falls within the jurisdiction of the Eleventh Circuit, asked, "Should you be confirmed, could you share with the committee what you perceive your role would be on this appellate court?" Ryskamp started out by saying he would "earnestly seek the facts and apply the law to the facts as I see them," which is not the primary role of an appellate court—fact-finding is the trial court's job. He then dug a deeper hole for himself. Continuing with a discussion of sensitivity and sympathy, he said "I am not always sure what people mean when they say you have got to be sensitive. Some-times people say you have got to be sympathetic. As you know, we always instruct a jury you should not decide this case based on sympathy. So it would be a violation of the oath that I take to be sympathetic to one side and not the other." Biden unsuc-cessfully tried repeatedly to get Ryskamp to admit that his comment to the black men who'd been bitten by the police dogs was a mistake, saying, "that is all I am trying to get from you and you are making it very hard for me." Ryskamp refused. As one commentator put it, Ryskamp was "clueless." [26]

Thirty-five civil rights, labor, and Jewish organizations joined fifty Florida groups in opposing Ryskamp. When the vote was taken, all the Republicans on the committee supported him, but the Democratic majority voted him down 8-6. An effort to send the nomination to the floor without a recommendation failed on a tie vote.

The other major lower-court battle of the Bush administration was over another Eleventh Circuit nomination. This one the Democrats lost, and badly.

In fall 1991, Eleventh Circuit Judge Frank M. Johnson of Alabama, one of the most revered figures of the civil rights revolution, retired from active service. To succeed him, President Bush nominated 41-year-old Alabama Assistant Attorney General Edward E. Carnes, chief of the Capital Litigation Division in the Alabama Attorney General's office; service with the Attorney General was the only job he had ever had since graduating from Harvard Law School.

Carnes, an avid supporter of the death penalty, was called "Mr. Death Penalty." At 30, he wrote the Alabama death penalty statute that allowed judges to impose a death sentence even if the jury recommends life imprisonment. At the time of Carnes's nomination, one-fourth of Alabama's death row inmates were there because the judge had overridden a jury's recommendation for a lesser sentence. Carnes was also responsible for eight of the nine executions during his tenure. The other controversial aspect of the law was that it did not prevent prosecutors from trying to select jurors based on race, a not uncommon practice in Alabama. When asked about this, Carnes told the Senate Judiciary Committee that the exclusion of jurors on the basis of race was not necessarily unfair, despite the Supreme Court's 1986 decision in *Batson v. Kentucky*. He also said that he did not believe that racial discrimination influenced application of the death penalty in Alabama or elsewhere, and insisted that in Alabama "capital defendants receive excellent representation." [27]

Carnes's zeal for the death penalty extended beyond writing the statute. He apparently worked to get other prosecutors to support efforts to curtail federal habeas-corpus relief for state prisoners who challenged unconstitutional aspects of their convictions or sentences. Also, the *Atlanta Journal & Constitution* reported that as head of the capital prosecution unit, he had "blocked Alabama from contributing support to the federally funded resource center that gives legal help to indigent murder defendants in Alabama. Alabama is the only state in the 11th circuit not to provide such funding." In 1989, Carnes sent glossy color pictures of a murder scene to federal appeals judges even before the case went before their court. [28]

Carnes's defense of the systematic exclusion of black jurors from capital cases, both at his hearing and in the appellate courtroom, became one of the main bones of contention between his opponents and his supporters. In one of these cases, the prosecutor had been able to remove twenty-six blacks to make sure the jury would be all white. The jury list itself was set up under the categories "strong, medium, weak, and black." Carnes had not challenged this practice, which led Biden to question "the depth of Mr. Carnes' commitment to equal justice," and to charge that Carnes was a "nonfeasor" for defending such practices.

Carnes's opponents included the civil rights organizations, as well as leaders like Coretta Scott King, Julius Chambers, and Jesse Jackson. His supporters, however, included not only nineteen Democratic attorneys general but also Morris Dees of the Southern Poverty Law Center in Montgomery, Alabama, one of the leading Southern civil rights lawyers, as well as several black lawyers and judges, and some other civil rights lawyers, including a former law clerk to Johnson who had handled capital cases against Carnes. Dees in particular lobbied heavily for Carnes, writing Senator Heflin, Carnes's sponsor, that "besides distorting Ed's role in the capital case process and failing to give him credit for his work against racial discrimination in jury selection, Ed's critics have failed to acknowledge other aspects of Ed's professional and personal life that demonstrate a commitment to equal justice." Dees noted that Carnes had prosecuted nineteen sitting judges, including two who made racially disparaging remarks from the bench, and had successfully litigated a case against the Ku Klux Klan. And in a letter to the *Atlanta Journal & Constitution*, which had called the Carnes nomination "shameful," Dees stressed that Carnes had promptly turned over to the defendant exculpatory material that he had found hidden in prosecutors' files, resulting in some convicted murderers getting new trials and arousing the ire of some prosecutors. He had adopted an open file policy making available to the defense everything in the prosecution files, one of the few prosecutors to do so. Also, he successfully represented the state on appeal against a member of the Ku Klux Klan convicted of killing the four young black girls in the notorious Baptist church bombing in Birmingham.[29]

Carnes's opponents asked majority leader George Mitchell not to bring up the nomination, which would have killed it. The fight lasted eight months, and by the time it was ready for a Senate vote it was already September and would have died. Both Democratic senators from Alabama, Heflin and Richard Shelby (who has since switched to the Republicans) pressed hard for a vote, however, and Mitchell acquiesced. The opponents tried to filibuster the nomination but lost on a cloture petition to cut off debate 66-33. On September 9, 1992, Carnes was confirmed, 62-36.

Dees may not have been far wrong. The 2002 Judicial Almanac reported that although many lawyers consider Carnes quite conservative, a list of some of his notable decisions shows more than a few with which conservatives could not be very happy.[30]

The Carnes controversy was of course dwarfed by the Clarence Thomas fight, in which both Democrats and Republicans hit bottom—the Republicans in dirty tricks and the Democrats in spinelessness. When the smoke cleared, one of the strangest and most controversial figures ever to sit on the Supreme Court was confirmed by a 52-48 vote, the highest number of votes ever recorded against a Supreme Court nominee.

The most complete study of the nomination is by Jane Mayer and Jill Abramson, *Strange Justice: The Selling of Clarence Thomas*, published in 1994. No more than a relatively brief account drawing primarily from the Mayer-Abramson book seems necessary here.

Even before Souter began to show a liberal streak, conservatives like Thomas Jipping of the Free Congress Foundation, a key figure in Republican judicial nominations during the recent Republican administrations, and Paul Weyrich, founder of the Free Congress Foundation, were furious with Souter's answers at his hearing. To appease them and to shore up Bush's right flank, a defensive Sununu promised them "a knockdown, drag-out, bloody-knuckles, grassroots fight" to get a true conservative on the Supreme Court at the next opportunity. And Bush came through.[31]

When Thurgood Marshall retired, it was almost immediately evident that the right-wing favorite was Clarence Thomas, then an undistinguished judge on the District of Columbia Court of Appeals whom Bush had appointed in 1990. Thomas had also been chairman of the Equal Employment Opportunity Commission under Reagan and an aide to a powerful Republican Senator from Missouri, John Danforth. As EEOC chairman,

Thomas had drawn fire for his lax enforcement of employment discrimination law, and was known to his associates to be very conservative. But he was obviously an affirmative action nominee and difficult for Democrats to challenge.

The Democrats' dilemma was compounded by Thomas's personal history, as described at the confirmation hearing. He was born in harsh poverty in Pin Point, Georgia, a tiny rural town of a few dozen black families fifteen miles from Savannah. His father deserted Thomas's mother and three small children a few years after Clarence was born. Things changed radically however, when Thomas was 6. Unable to manage on her own, Thomas's mother asked her father, who lived in Savannah, for help. Thomas's grandfather, an uneducated man of intelligence and determination, had built himself a successful coal, ice, and oil delivery business, and was modestly well-off. He reluctantly agreed to take the boys, leaving Thomas's sister to fend for herself, which she did poorly; she ultimately had to go on welfare, after giving birth to four children.

The grandfather, a stern taskmaster, had converted to Catholicism, partly so his grandsons could attend parochial school at reduced tuition. Consequently, as Mayer and Abramson point out,

> The subsequent portrait of Thomas as a self-made man, single-handedly escaping the depths of deprivation, would therefore rankle some of those who knew him earlier. "It's a myth to say those boys were poor," said Roy Allen, a Georgia state senator and a supporter of Thomas who was a classmate of his at St. Benedict the Moor, a black parochial grammar school . . . Thomas "always had pocket money and never went without anything. . . . I mean, how many kid's fathers ran a coal and oil business?"

• • •

Another man who knew the family well and watched Clarence grow up, commented, "Thomas's was a select, pampered development that wasn't the experience of the vast majority of blacks," adding, "except for his earliest exposures, all of his experience was in white groups. He was in a very elite and ideal situation." [32]

The parochial school that Thomas attended was strict, and he did well. This was followed by a scholarship at Holy Cross College in Worcester, Massachusetts, in honor of Martin Luther King Jr., an instance of the affirmative action that Thomas subsequently disdained, and from which, according to the Holy Cross president, Thomas "certainly" benefited. He then went to Yale Law School, again because of affirmative action. Both at Holy Cross and at Yale, he apparently resented this status deeply, and later denied he had gained admission to Yale because of a racial preference, despite the clear evidence to the contrary.

At Yale, Thomas was known not only for the extreme crudity of his sexual talk, but also for avidly watching pornographic films and reading pornographic magazines, which he would describe to friends in lurid detail. When Anita Hill accused Thomas of talking crudely to her about sexual matters, some of Thomas's schoolmates were struck by the familiarity of the behavior she described, and did not believe his professions of "horror" at "this kind of grotesque language" during the hearings. He apparently limited this kind of talk to blacks, however, and whites never knew about this side of him.

After graduating from Yale, he went to work for John Danforth, who was then the Missouri Attorney General. While in that office, Thomas abandoned his longtime Democratic Party leanings and became a Republican. According to friends, he saw more opportunities as a black Republican, then a rare species, than as another black Democrat. His instincts, however, were already quite conservative, and he probably felt more at home among Republicans. When Reagan won in 1980, Thomas joined the administration and ten years later was appointed by Bush to the D.C. Court of Appeals.

When the White House settled on Thomas to succeed Thurgood Marshall, it was faced with several problems in trying to back up Bush's ludicrous claim that he had chosen "the best qualified man." Thomas's record was hardly distinguished, especially not for the nation's highest Court. Also, Thomas had made no secret of his views, and they were sure to draw a great deal of fire. Thomas had attacked Congress as incompetent, praised Louis Farrakhan, criticized Thurgood Marshall, and characterized the civil rights leadership as doing nothing but "bitch, bitch, bitch, moan and moan, whine and whine." He had also endorsed Oliver North, Ayn Rand, Thomas Sowell, Lewis Lehrman, and the far-right journal *Lincoln Review* (the only journal on whose board he had served). There was, in addition, the uncertainty about his views on constitutional issues like *Roe v. Wade*.[33]

The solution devised by Gray, Liberman, and Attorney General Richard Thornburgh was simple: Disavow the views, avoid saying anything about constitutional questions, and focus on his "deprived" background, as appropriately reconstructed. Thomas was elaborately coached on what to say and what not to say, which he later denied. And just in case there were substantive constitutional questions, Michael Luttig, who had already been confirmed for a seat on the Fourth Circuit but had not yet been sworn in, tried to prep him on the law.

Christian fundamentalists, right-wing activists like Gary Bauer, Paul Weyrich, and Ralph Reed of the Christian Coalition, White House operatives like William Kristol, who was Vice President Dan Quayle's Chief of Staff, and other conservatives organized groups with names like the African-American

Freedom Alliance and the Coalition for the Restoration of the Black Family and Society. Large amounts of money were raised and efforts were made to obtain support from the black community despite Thomas's record of hostility to what most blacks wanted and believed.

At the hearing, Thomas disavowed all the right-wing statements he had earlier made, saying that now that he had been a judge for some sixteen months, he no longer held such views because his role was different. He claimed he had never thought about *Roe v. Wade*, even though it was decided while he was in law school. No one really believed this, especially after Leahy pointed out to Thomas that:

> You have participated in a working group that criticized *Roe*. You cited *Roe* in a footnote to your article on the privileges and immunity clauses. You have referred to Lewis Lehrman's article on the meaning of the right to life. You specifically referred to abortion in a column in the *Chicago Defender*. [34]

Former Harvard dean Erwin Griswold, 90 years old, came to testify that Thomas had not shown "any clear intellectual or professional distinctions." [35]

But the Pin Point strategy worked. Thomas was treated as if he were Abe Lincoln. Pennsylvania Senator Arlen Specter declared, "his character is shown more by his roots than by his writings," and Biden gushed similarly. Republican Alan Simpson of Wyoming was impressed at how Thomas "came though the crucible of a life described as we know it now." Many blacks, especially in the South, were eager to see another black lawyer replace Marshall, and Southern Democratic senators were not inclined to vote against a black candidate whom some of their black constituents supported, no matter what his views. [36]

And then Anita Hill came along. Also a Yale Law School graduate, and an Oklahoma Law School professor in 1991, she had worked for Thomas as special assistant at both the Department of Education, Thomas's first post in the Reagan administration, and at the EEOC. At first reluctant to testify, she was finally persuaded to come forward with a story of how Thomas had continually harassed her sexually. It began at the Department of Education, subsided for a while, then resumed at the EEOC until she finally quit. The story contained many lurid details about pubic hair on a Coke can, about a "Long Dong Silver," and about similar matters; others recalled seeing Thomas at porno shops where he was apparently a regular customer, renting graphic videos. None of this came as a surprise to those who had known Thomas at Holy Cross and Yale. As a friend at Holy Cross put it, "I didn't know what to think until I heard the Coke can story. When I heard that, I knew he'd say stuff like that." And a Yale friend said that when Hill quoted Thomas, the friend thought, "That's my boy . . . that's him talking." [37]

Hill had confided this story to several close friends over the years and by the time of the hearings, it reached Nan Aron, head of the Alliance for Justice, one of the two leading liberal groups focusing on the judgeship issue (the other was People for the American Way, founded by Norman Lear), and she passed it along to Ohio Senator Howard Metzenbaum's staff. The Democrats were, however, very reluctant to get into the matter. Kennedy was compromised by his involvement with the rape trial of his nephew Willie Smith; Biden had been attacked by Republican ads about his plagiarism in the 1988 presidential campaign; Metzenbaum was reluctant to get into sexual issues and would soon be attacked by a false claim that his staff had leaked an FBI report. And they still faced the original dilemma: how to attack a black affirmative-action candidate who seemed to have widespread black support, at least according to what turned out to be somewhat skewed polls.

Biden and the Democrats ultimately realized they had no choice and contacted the FBI to interview Hill. The FBI report was circulated to Judiciary Committee members on September 27, 1991, the morning of the vote. To widespread public amazement, for the report was held confidential, the committee deadlocked 7-7, and the committee decided to send the nomination to the floor without a recommendation. A floor vote was scheduled for October 8. No explanation for the tie vote was given, but it was clear that something strange was going on.

After several days, the story gradually emerged, and became public on Sunday, October 6. Hill and those who supported her were deluged with threats and hate calls. Democratic majority leader Mitchell was urged to delay the vote, and though he was at first reluctant, he ultimately did so and new hearings were called.

The administration and Senate Republicans panicked. But not for long. Gray, Luttig, and Danforth devised another simple strategy, with Bush's approval: Thomas would deny everything and Judiciary Committee Republicans would destroy Hill.

The plan worked perfectly. Hill was accused of being a "fantasizer," a "spurned woman," sick with something committee Republicans called "erotomania." Senator Alan Simpson of Wyoming, who has always covered up a fierce partisanship with a veneer of folksiness, claimed that he was receiving information "over the transom" about Anita Hill's character. "I've got letters hanging out of my pockets . . . I've got statements saying . . . watch out for this woman!" No one asked him to take the letters out of his pockets. In an attempt to confer legitimacy on the new Supreme Court justice the charges were later expanded upon in *The Real Anita Hill*, a full-scale defense of Thomas concocted largely out of whole cloth by David Brock at the behest of the Right; after Thomas's confirmation, Brock, who said he had in fact believed Hill, would later recant and write, "In their treatment of Anita Hill, the Senate Republicans set a new low in the threshold for public discourse in the Capitol, and I would go lower still, checking whatever independence I had at the door." The always sanctimonious Orrin Hatch charged that Hill had got the pubic hair idea from the novel *The Exorcist* and the reference to "Long Dong Silver" from a court case. Specter, eager to rehabilitate himself after his vote against Bork, charged Hill with "flat-out perjury," though only after he got out of the hearing room. Commenting on all this, the respected former federal District Judge Marvin Frankel said that the attack by Hatch and Specter represents "a fantastic, far-out approach that really has nothing to do with the issues." Specter's perjury accusation in particular "hit a low level. . . . The idea of a former prosecutor who said he has tried perjury cases taking a supposed difference between what somebody said in the morning and what they said in the afternoon to say they committed perjury is really below the belt. He has to know that nobody would ever begin to place a perjury charge on that sort of testimony." [38]

Nevertheless, the strategy worked. The charges cowed the Democrats, who made almost no attempt to defend Hill. Biden was on the defensive, as criticism began mounting about his handling of Hill's charges, and he decided that Democrats should take a neutral stance. Yet, he inexplicably failed to call a corroborating witness, who had still a third witness. Hatch falsely accused Metzenbaum of leaking FBI documents, which effectively intimidated the Ohio Senator. Alabama Senator Howell Heflin was not about to attack a black nominee. Arizona Senator Dennis DeConcini, implicated in the Keating Five scandal, was in no position to attack Thomas for unethical behavior, and Kennedy, who would soon be testifying at his nephew's rape trial, was worried that his defense of Hill might do her more harm than good. [39]

The public opinion polls went decisively against Hill. When

the vote was taken, Thomas was confirmed by the barest of margins, 52-48. To avoid any further problems, the White House hastily scheduled his swearing-in on October 23. That day, *Washington Post* reporters found evidence corroborating Hill. It was too late.[40]

Simpson later apologized for his attacks, after being jeered by students at a football game in Wyoming; Specter faced a tough re-election fight and found it necessary to also apologize. Since then, public opinion has swung decisively in favor of Hill, as more and more evidence about Thomas has been revealed.

Once on the bench, Thomas fulfilled his supporters' wildest hopes, going even farther to the right than Scalia, whom he has usually followed faithfully.

The Thomas nomination did not end the judgeship fights. An affidavit by Anita Hill to the FBI had been leaked and the Senate launched a four-month investigation. Nothing ever turned up. Judiciary staff was suspected, and Bush announced that only certain senators would be allowed to see FBI reports. This was obviously unacceptable to the Democrats, who refused to process any further nominations. After several months of acrimony, in July 1992 Bush backed down. By then, an already large backlog was made even greater, a situation made worse by a hold on all nominations by the then-Democrat Richard Shelby of Alabama, and by an unidentified Republican on several female nominees.

By the end of Bush's four years, approximately 75 percent of the federal judiciary consisted of Republican judges, and the federal courts had been tilted sharply to the right. After twelve Republican years, and despite the creation of many new judgeships, the number of African-Americans on the federal courts dropped—from forty-nine in 1981 to forty-three in 1992.

None of this did any good, however, and he lost to Arkansas Governor Bill Clinton in 1992. It would be up to Clinton to restore balance, and conservatives geared up to fight him. In early 1993 Robert Bork sent out a fundraising letter for the Free Company Foundation, Thomas Jipping's organization to "monitor" the Clinton nominees.

• • •

1. Herman Schwartz, *Packing the Courts: The Conservative Campaign to Rewrite the Constitution* (New York: Scribner, 1988), p. 223 n. 64; 97. *Richmond v. J.A. Croson Co.*, 488 U.S. 469 (1989)

2. *Webster v. Reproductive Health Services*, 492 U.S. 490 (1989); *Planned Parenthood v. Casey*, 505 U.S. 833 (1992); *Romer v. Evans*, 517 U.S. 620 (1996); *Bowers v. Hardwick*, 478 U.S. 186 (1986); *Lawrence v. Texas*, 123 S. Ct. 2472 (2003)

3. *Texas v. Johnson*, 491 U.S. 397 (1989)

4. Employment Div., *Dep't of Human Resources v. Smith*, 485 U.S. 600 (1988)

5. For the earlier discussion of *Garcia*, see p. 37; *Gregory v. Ashcroft*, 501 U.S. 452 (1991)

7. Neil A. Lewis, "Bush Picking the Kind of Judges Reagan Favored," *The New York Times*, April 10, 1990, p. 1; John E. Yang, Sharon LaFraniere, "Role Differs From Predecessors'; Counsel at Forefront On Domestic Policy" *The Washington Post*, November 22, 1991, p. A14; Gary Lee, Sharon LaFraniere, "Business Coalition Pulls Out of Civil Rights Talks," *The Washington Post*, April 20, 1991, p. A1; Opinion Editorial, "The Revoked Proclamation," *The Washington Post*, November 22, 1991, p. A24; Ann Devroy, "President Signs Civil Rights Bill; White House Disavows Proposed Directive to End Affirmative Action," *The Washington Post*, November 22, 1991, p. A1.

8. Sheldon Goldman, Bush's Judicial Legacy: The Final Imprint, 76 *Judicature* 282, 284 (1993).

9. Id. p. 294 Table 4; Ibid. p. 286

10. The Bolick and Jipping statements are in Ruth Marcus, "Bush Quietly Fosters Conservative Trend in Courts" *The Washington Post*, February 18, 1991, p. A1.

11. Jane Mayer & Jill Abramson, "Strange Justice: the Selling of Clarence Thomas" (New York: Houghton Mifflin Co., 1994); *The New York Times*, 4, p.12; Apple, R.W., Jr. "Bush's Court Choice: Sununu tells How and Why He Pushed for the Court" , *The New York Times*, July 25, 1990, p.12.

12. David J. Garrow, "Justice Souter Emerges," *NY Times Magazine*, Sept. 2, 1944, p. 36.

13. George F. Will, "Let's Hear from Judge Souter," *The Washington Post*, September 13, 1990, p. A23; Steven Holmes, "A Window to Souter's Way of Life," *The Washington Post*, September 13, 1990; Linda Greenhouse "Opponents Find Judge Souter is a Hard Choice to Oppose," *The New York Times*, September 9, 1990, sec. 4 p.4; Ibid.

14. Walter Goodman "TV Critic's Notebook; The Judge's Image Grew and Grew," *The New York Times*, September 15, 1990 sec. 4 p. 4.

15. Ruth Marcus "Senators Left Wondering After Hearing: Which is the Real David Souter?," *The Washington Post*, September 23, 1990, p. A4; Linda Greenhouse "Souter Tacks Over Shoals; Bork's Defeat Echoes as Questioning Starts," *The New York Times*, September 14, 1990, p. A1.

16. Souter's statement on Brennan is quoted in Neil A. Lewis, "Souter Seems Sure to Win Approval, Key Senators Say," *The New York Times*, September 15, 1990, sec. 1 p. 1.

17. Scott P. Johnson, Souter's First Term on the Supreme Court: The Impact of a New Justice, 75 *Judicature* 238 (1992); Rust v. Sullivan, 500 U.S. 173 (1991).

18. Anthony Lewis "Abroad at Home; Slash and Burn," *The New York Times*, October

18, 1991, sec. A p. 31; "Thomas Role Questioned," *The Washington Post,* October 22, 1991, p. A19; Deborah Sontag, ("The Power of the Fourth") *The New York Times Magazine,* March 9, 2003, sec. 6, p. 40.

19. *Bragg v. W. Va. Coal Ass'n,* 248 F.3d 275, 285 (45h Circ. 2001); Jeffrey Rosen "The Next Court," *The New York Times,* October 22, 2000, sec. 6, p. 74.

20. Shannon P. Duffy, McKee, Mary Alice Robbins, Jonathan Groner, Anthony Mauro "The Six on Bush's High Court Short List. Possible Nominees Include A Black Woman, Two Hispanic Men, Two 4th Circuit Jurists, And A Judge Dubbed Scalito," *The Legal Times,* March 3, 2003, p.11.

21. Id. at 11; Sheridan v. E.I. Dupont de Nemours & Co., 100 F.3d 1061 (3d Cir. 1996); Sandoval v. Reno, 166 F.3d 225 (3d Cir. 1999) aff'd; INS v. St. Cyr, 533 U.S. 289 (2001).

22. Shannon Duffy, n. 20

23. Dickerson v. United States, 530 U.S. 428 (2000), overruling, F.3d (4th Cir. 19); Reno v. Condon, U.S. 528 U.S. 141 (2000) (driver privacy).

24. Ryskamp's comments appear in Editorial, "Proud Tradition. Threatened," *The New York Times,* March 26, 1991, p. A22; Neil A. Lewis "Committee Rejects Bush Nominee To Key Appellate Court in South," *The New York Times,* April 12, 1991, p. A1; Tony Mauro "Judicial Nominee Has Rocky First Day," *USA Today,* March 20, 1991 p. 3A.

25. Editorial Desk "Proud Tradition. Threatened," *The New York Times,* March 26, 1991, p. A22.

26. Anne Kornhauser, "Unvarnished, Unimpressive; Ryskamp Goes His Own Way—To Senate Trouble," *The Legal Times,* March 25, 1991, p.2; Terence Moran "Kenneth Ryskamp: Just Not Good Enough," *The Legal Times,* March 25, 1991, p. 23.

27. Tyrone Brooks, "It's time for America to end policy of a racial exclusion in federal judiciary," *The Atlanta Journal and Constitution, July 23, 1992, p. A15.* Batson v. Kentucky, *476 U.S. 79 (1986).*

28. *Nat Hentoff,* "Shameful Judicial Appointment," *The Washington Post,* March 7, 1992, p. A23.

29. Lynn Duke "Vote slated Today on Controversial Judicial Nominees; But Filibuster, Also Possible, Could Kill Chances for Carnes," *The Washington Post,* September 9, 1992, p. A19; Editorial "Release Edward Carnes," *The Washington Times,* June 24, 1992, p. G2.

30. 2 *Almanac* of the Federal Judiciary, 11th Circuit, pp. 10-12 (2003).

31. Mayer and Abramson p. 13.

32. Id. at 40-41

33. Gary Wills, "Thomas's Confirmation: The True Story," *New York Review of Books,* Feb. 2, 1995, P. 36.

34. Id.

35. Mayer and Abramson, p. 219

36. Wills, p. 41

37. Mayer and Abramson p. 107; Id. at 106; Wills p. 40.

38. Mayer and Abramson pp. 310-11; David Brock *The Real Anita Hill: The Untold Story* (New York: Free Press, 1993); David Brock *Blinded by the Right: The Conscience of an Ex-Conservative* (New York: Three Rivers Press, 2002), p. 104; Ibid. p. 103; Andrew Rosenthal "The Thomas Nomination: White House Role in Thomas Defense," *The New York Times,* October 14, 1991, p. A1.

39. Mayer and Abramson, pp. 303-304; Id. at 300, 204, 233.

40. Id. at 350.

Chapter 4
The Clinton Years, 1993–2000

Not so very long ago, Senate confirmation of lower court judgeships was routine, even when the president and the Senate were from opposing parties. Delays and stoppages in an election year were of course common, but rarely a confirmation battle. As late as the Reagan administration, relatively few of Reagan's lower court nominees were blocked by the Democrats, and only a few nominations produced a fight—Manion, Sessions, and Wilkinson. George H.W. Bush was also the beneficiary of such restraint except for Carnes and Ryskamp. After the Gingrich revolution in 1994 and the Republican takeover of the Senate, that restraint began to fade, and by 1996, an election year, it had entirely disappeared. From that time until today, a substantial number of lower court nominations, particularly to the Courts of Appeals, have become almost as contentious as Supreme Court nominees. Many nominations still go through routinely, particularly during George W. Bush's tenure in 2001–03, even though Democrats controlled the Senate from July 2001 until November 2002. This was also true for a few years during the Clinton administration, but between 1995 and 2000, the Republican Senate blocked Clinton's nominees or delayed them for many years.[1]

When William Jefferson Clinton took the oath of office as president, the federal court was overwhelmingly Republican. All thirteen appellate courts were dominated by Republican appointees, with eleven controlled by Reagan-Bush appointees. Four-fifths of all the trial courts and only a quarter of the appeals court judges were Democratic appointees.

By July 1993, the 100 vacancies left by Bush had grown to 113 because of attrition, retirement, and other factors. Many of these seats had been vacant for more than eighteen months, and the Administrative Office of the US Courts, which administers the federal courts, had classified them as "judicial emergencies." These many vacancies, a Judicial Conference recommendation of a new judgeship bill creating fifty-three more judgeships, and the presence of a Democratic Senate presented Clinton with a great opportunity to reshape the courts. Many liberals, dismayed and angered by the Reagan-Bush judgeship strategy, hoped that the first Democratic administration in twelve years, and only the second in twenty-four, would nominate strong liberals to bring a more even balance to the federal courts.

They had the wrong man. According to Deputy Attorney General Jamie Gorelick, Clinton is "quite a conservative person," though with strong feelings about racial injustice and equality for women, as he showed in his judicial selections and otherwise. Except for a brief, apparently atypical liberal flurry during his first term as governor of Arkansas in 1981–82, Clinton has usually situated himself on the Democratic right. He is a founding member of the Democratic Leadership Conference, which represents the conservative wing of the Democratic Party. As Dave Maraniss described him,

> The notion that Bill Clinton began his political career as a radical and moved inexorably rightward over the decades is

misleading. He was a cautious defender of the establishment during his student politics days at Georgetown. In his Oxford and Yale years, he was in the moderate wing of the antiwar movement. From the beginning of his ascent in Arkansas, he would attack organized labor and court corporate interests when it served his political purposes. He had supported the death penalty since his 1976 race for attorney general. As early as his 1980 speech at the Democratic National Convention in New York, he was turning away from traditional liberal demo-cratic rhetoric. The sphere in which his movement from left to right seemed most apparent was foreign policy. . . .[2]

Moreover, Clinton did not consider judicial nominations an important political instrument, even when challenged by the Republicans after the 1994 Congressional elections. In his eyes, judicial selection was not worth expending any of his political capital, especially after Whitewater and other contro-versies weakened his presidency.

It is not surprising, therefore, that, as Assistant Attorney General for the Office of Policy Development Eleanor D. Acheson (the Justice Department official who headed the judge-picking for the Department) stressed, the administra-tion avoided ideological tests, and focused instead on intel-lect and judicial temperament. Clinton's primary goal was to reduce white male dominance on the federal bench, and his success in doing so became one of the signal achievements of his eight years.[3]

1993–94

The Clinton nomination process started out as it usually does with a new administration—very slowly. The delays were prob-ably compounded by Clinton's difficulty in finding an Attorney General after his first two choices—Attorney General Counsel

Zoe Baird and New York District Judge Kimba Wood—did not work out. Finally, Janet Reno was named and confirmed in April 1993. The judicial selection process included high-level White House staff, as usual, and an Assistant Attorney General. For the latter post, Clinton nominated Acheson in late April 1993, but she was not confirmed until August 2, slowing the process further.

In October 1993, when the administration was finally ready to send up nominations, storm signals from the Republicans appeared. The Bork and Thomas fights still rankled. Senator Orrin Hatch announced that Republicans would ensure that the Clinton nominees were not "'starry-eyed' about the death penalty . . . Where the death penalty is warranted, we don't need judges who look for excuses not to carry it out." In Republican sights on this issue were two women: Tennessee Supreme Court Justice Martha Daughtry, nominated to the Sixth Circuit, and Florida Supreme Court Chief Justice Rosemary Barkett, nominated to the Eleventh Circuit. Thomas Jipping of the Free Congress Foundation (now on Hatch's staff) issued a report on Daughtry criticizing her rulings in death penalty cases, but it was immediately refuted by her supporters. She was easily confirmed in November 1993, three and half months after being nominated.[4]

Barkett, born in Mexico of Syrian descent, a former nun and schoolteacher, had received the highest ABA rating. She was nevertheless opposed by both antiabortion forces and by the National Rifle Association as soft on crime. Her record showed that she was indeed sympathetic to people in trouble, including some criminal defendants, but the attack on her focused primarily on charges that she had avoided imposing the death penalty. In response, she distributed data showing her support for the death penalty in more than 200 cases. She was also supported by both Florida senators including Republican Connie

Mack, and had won the election for chief justice by some 62 percent of the vote. A Hatch request produced a delay of six months, but in April 1994, two months after she finally got her hearing, and after a cloture petition was filed to break a filibuster, she was easily confirmed.

The death penalty issue actually offered little traction to the Republicans. Clinton supported capital punishment and had allowed it to take place in Arkansas several times. Indeed, during the 1992 presidential campaign he had made his support for the death penalty very clear by allowing a mentally retarded man to be executed.

Liberal groups did not automatically rubber-stamp Clinton's choices. Three potential nominations drew liberal criticism, particularly Gary Gaentner, a judge on the Missouri Court of Appeals, who was recommended for a Missouri district judgeship by Democratic House leader Richard Gephardt. The Alliance for Justice and People for the American Way accused Gaentner of insensitivity to the rights of criminal defendants, homosexuals, and women. Two other men considered for District Court possibilities, William Downes of Wyoming and Thomas Whalen of Albany, New York, were charged with being against abortion rights. As mayor of Albany, Whalen had blocked the placement of a Planned Parenthood clinic in Albany, and Downes was said to have called abortion-rights activists "bra burners," which he denied. Clinton did not nominate Gaentner and Whalen, but he did nominate Downes, who was confirmed.

Liberals were troubled not only by the nominations of Gaentner, Downes, and Whalen, but by the general reluctance of the administration to try to tilt the balance back from the rightward shift produced by the Reagan-Bush appointees. Judge Stephen Reinhardt of the Ninth Circuit, a particularly sharp critic of the administration, wrote a strong letter to the

Assistant Attorney General Acheson in February 1995 protesting the Clinton policy. In his letter, Reinhardt wrote,

> Who in the world is not for judges with "judicial temperament"? Who is not for "productivity"? Who is opposed to judges with "energy", "integrity", or mental "agility"? . . . To say, as you do, that the Clinton administration willingly accepts the Reagan-Bush administrations' successes in changing the philosophy of the federal courts so radically, and that it has no desire to redress the current judicial imbalance or to try to restore any glimmer of liberal representation to the courts is to abdicate, or more accurately repudiate, your historic responsibilities.[5]

Despite his innate conservatism, in these first two years Clinton had three lasting achievements. He appointed two Supreme Court Justices who were to become reliable members of the four-member liberal minority of the next decade—Ruth Bader Ginsburg in 1993 and Stephen G. Breyer in 1994—and he made a significant dent in white male dominance among federal judges.

There is little to say about these two Supreme Court nominations, for both were uneventful, and neither nominee faced any significant opposition. When named, Ginsburg was a sixty-year-old former Columbia Law School professor whom Carter had appointed to the D.C. Circuit in 1979. Referred to by some as the Thurgood Marshall of the women's movement, Ginsburg had argued six sex-discrimination cases before the Supreme Court and a seventh as an *amicus curiae*.

During her thirteen years on the D.C. Circuit, she developed a reputation as a cautious liberal, who voted most often on economic and regulatory matters with Kenneth Starr, Laurence Silberman, and Judge Robert Bork. Indeed, when she was nominated in June 1993, after a difficult three-month search by Clinton, the *New York Times*'s Richard Berke commented that it was "debatable just how much she is either liberal or conservative." To add to the uncertainty, she had criticized the *Roe v. Wade* decision as unnecessarily sweeping, dismaying some of her natural allies. At one point in her hearing, she told the committee that her favorite Justice was the second Justice Harlan, a conservative judge who is widely respected for his principled and reasoned approach to judging.[6]

Like Souter, Ginsburg gave signs that she would not be a passive justice. Answering a questionnaire from the Judiciary Committee, Ginsburg emphasized that judges who take over public school districts to enforce desegregation rulings or order mental hospitals or prisons to insure patients' and prisoners' rights, do so with great reluctance. "Had State and Federal legislatures and administrators assumed the implementation burden," she wrote, "the managerial jobs the courts took on, generally with reluctance and misgivings, could have been avoided or at least substantially curtailed." Commenting on judicial activism, she added that "in a representative democracy, important policy questions should be confronted, debated, and resolved by elected officials." But if they fail to do so, she said, judges have to fill in the gaps, and become vulnerable to criticism that they are using excessive power.[7]

She encountered opposition only from antiabortion groups and far-right conservatives like Thomas Jipping, who called her a "radical feminist." In the Democratic-controlled Senate she was easily confirmed by a 96-3 vote in August 1993.

Also like Souter, Ginsburg's record on the Supreme Court is more liberal than her prior record would indicate. She has been an eloquent voice not only for women, which was expected, but for liberal causes in general, particularly civil rights, equal protection, and the environment. In the environmental area, she wrote a landmark opinion allowing citizen groups to recover for environmental law violations even if the violator complies after a lawsuit is filed.[8]

Stephen Breyer's road to a Supreme Court nomination was rockier. Also a former law professor, from Harvard, and chief judge of the First Circuit when nominated, he was initially considered for the seat ultimately given to Ginsburg. After pulling Breyer out of a hospital bed where he was recuperating from a bicycle accident, Clinton decided that Breyer had over-sold himself and lacked a "big heart." When Justice Harry Blackmun retired in 1994, however, Clinton again turned to a consideration of Breyer and this time concluded that his heart was big enough.[9]

Breyer was a regulatory law specialist who had championed environmental and other deregulation; he was the architect of airline deregulation. He had also served as a former Senate Judiciary Committee chief counsel under Senator Edward Kennedy, and worked for a criminal code revision that the ACLU and others opposed. Some saw him as a "technocrat lawyer," a "perennial defender of corporate interests," and Ralph Nader charged that he would be a "corporate judge, not a people's judge." Indeed, conservative activist Clint Bolick was "very supportive" of the nomination, approving of Breyer's "skepticism toward government power—particularly economic regulation." The opposition had little support, and Breyer was easily confirmed, 87-9.[10]

On the Court, Breyer has not been a surprise. He too has been a reliable member of the four-member liberal minority though less so than Ginsburg. His opinions tend to be calm and tightly reasoned. Some of his votes have been characterized as probusiness, but while he is sympathetic to economic approaches to antitrust and other regulatory matters, he has refused to line up with the Chicago School of Economics approach used by Scalia and other conservatives in antitrust cases. Despite the criticism in his writings about the regulatory process, he has supported environmental measures. Some of his votes have disappointed liberals, especially in drug case where he has lined up with the conservatives to make narrow majorities. His vote in the 2003 University of Michigan affirmative action case that struck down the point system used by the undergraduate college was also puzzling. Without explanation, he concurred in the Court's judgment, while also concurring with a crucial part of Ginsburg's eloquent dissent.[11]

The other lasting achievement of Clinton's first two years was to make a start on improving racial and gender diversity in the courts. Although he could accomplish only a limited amount in the two years of Democratic Senate control, especially after the slow start, Clinton's efforts paid off. Sixty percent of his nominees were minorities and women, whom political scientists Elliot Slotnick and Sheldon Goldman call "nontraditional" nominees, a record number for each. These included District Court appointments for thirty-four women and thirty-eight minorities, including seven minority women and five minority appointments to the Courts of Appeals, including one woman. Most of them had judicial or prosecutorial experience, in contrast with the white males.

The quality of Clinton's nominees was high, their ABA ratings surpassing those of the Reagan, Bush, and Carter administrations. Sixty-two percent of all Clinton nominees received the highest ABA ratings, a record, including many of the "nontraditional" appointees.[12]

Overall, 129 nominees were confirmed, filling 75 percent of the vacancies, a major achievement. The Alliance for Justice concluded its 1994 report by urging the president "to continue to make the type of choices he has made all along." Nevertheless, almost three-quarters of the federal bench was still occupied by

Reagan-Bush and Nixon appointees, and the Republican appointees still held a majority on twelve of the thirteen circuits, including the Federal Circuit.[13]

1995–1996

"Judge-Pickers' Last Waltz" is how the *Legal Times*, a Washington weekly for lawyers, headed its first story after the November 1994 Congressional election. "It's definitely the dawn of a new day," said Clint Bolick. "I think the Republicans have chafed under Democratic control of the [Senate] Judiciary Committee, and that the tables very much will be turned."[14]

A week later, Hatch told Fred Graham how the election would actually help Clinton. "Now, I think he's going to have to move to the center on judicial nominations, on criminal law, and on a lot of other issues. And if he does, he's going to be much more popular than he is now." Most objective observers thought Clinton was already solidly in the center.

Not enough, as Clinton apparently saw it, for he acted on Hatch's advice. In an unprecedented move, described by one observer as "unthinkable in recent administrations," Clinton made Hatch part of the nominating process. Potentially controversial nominees were either avoided or dropped after Republican objection. A key member of the administration team defended Clinton's unorthodox policy saying, "neither side is running an ideology shop. Neither of us considers ourselves to be the guardians of some kind of flame . . . . [T]his is not a do or die fight for American culture. This is an attempt to get . . . highly competent lawyers on the federal bench so they can resolve disputes." For his part, Hatch worked with the administration to push through nominees on whom he and the administration agreed. After months of working together, each side lavished praise on the other. "We've been together hours and hours and hours, regularly, each week," Hatch gushed. "They keep running them by us. I have worked with countless people on judges—from various White Houses, Republican and Democrat—and I have yet to work with anyone who is as straight-up as Vicki Radd, Ab Mikva, and Eldie Acheson," Clinton's judge-pickers. Hatch "has been very cooperative and very supportive of the idea that we need to fill as many vacancies as possible," said White House Counsel Abner Mikva. As a result, in the 1995 Congressional session, ten out of thirteen Court of Appeals nominees were confirmed. The Senate also confirmed fifty-four district judges, leaving thirteen either temporarily or—as it turned out—permanently stranded, making a total of sixty-two judges confirmed in 1995. On the average, they went through quickly, even faster than in Clinton's first two years.[15]

Some observers praised both the White House and Hatch for this approach. "You have to give the administration credit," said Elliot Mincberg, legal director of the liberal People for the American Way. "They have substantially reduced the number of vacancies. They have improved diversity. They have kept quality high. And they have depoliticized the process." Thomas Jipping, however, was unhappy. Hatch's "kind of back-of-the-hand approach is a joke," he complained. "It makes a total mockery of representative democracy and of the most significant job the Senate has—advice and consent on the appointment of federal judges."[16]

Liberals were not pleased either, particularly about Clinton's decision to withdraw nominations that drew conservative fire. Three such instances caused particular concern. Samuel Paz, a Mexican-American civil rights lawyer, and Judith McConnell, a municipal court judge, were both nominated to District Courts in California, and both were attacked by Republicans. Clinton also decided not to submit prominent liberal activist Peter Edelman for a D.C. Circuit slot. These three nominees—a minority, a woman, and a liberal—were typical of nominees opposed by the Republicans throughout Clinton's administration.

Samuel Paz was a 50-year-old Alhambra, California, lawyer who specialized in police brutality suits. He had obtained a $5.5 million settlement for a Los Angeles groundskeeper who had been shot by a Los Angeles policeman, and a six-figure settlement for a prisoner who died of an embolism after being strapped to a jail infirmary cot for six days; police brutality suits accounted for about a third of his practice. He had also been president of the Southern California ACLU as well as a lecturer to Latino children on the importance of education. He received strong support from the *Los Angeles Times* who praised his "passionate defense of humble clients." With the approval of both California senators, Clinton nominated Paz in March 1994. He had an uneventful hearing at the end of August, was approved by the committee, and everyone, including Paz, assumed that he would be easily confirmed; it seemed so certain that he gave up his law practice.[17]

It was not to be. After the hearing and committee approval, five police organizations, a conservative think tank, and the *Washington Times* came out against him, charging him with filing baseless suits and "making his fortune off our backs." Clinton did not push the nomination with the Democratic-controlled Senate in the waning days of the session. When the Republicans took over the Senate in January 1995, they made it clear that Clinton would have to fight for Paz. Clinton promptly pulled the nomination, in sharp contrast with the approach taken by Reagan and the two Bushes when confronted with opposition from a Democratic-controlled Senate.[18]

Judith McConnell was also dropped by Clinton after Republican opposition developed. McConnell, a 50-year-old Superior Court judge in San Diego, was nominated in April 1994. Her problem arose out of a custody fight over a 16-year-old boy.

Some years back, a gay father was awarded custody of a boy by a judge other than McConnell. The father died in 1987, and the boy, then sixteen, wanted to continue living with the father's male partner. The mother sought custody of the boy, and the partner challenged her fitness. Basing her decision on confidential reports about the mother, McConnell agreed with the partner about the mother's lack of fitness and turned the boy over to him, saying:

> It would be detrimental to give custody to the boy's mother. She has consistently interfered with his education, interfered with his need for therapy, and interfered with his attempt to make independent decisions. Despite all this, the boy has turned out remarkably well.[19]

The *Washington Times* obtained the story and used it to lead a conservative assault on her. In January Clinton withdrew her nomination without giving her a chance to explain to the Committee her reasons for the decision.

Peter Edelman was the most prominent of these cases. A fifty-six-year-old Georgetown Law School professor who was a counselor to Health and Human Services Secretary Donna B. Shalala when nominated, he had been one of Senator Robert Kennedy's principal aides, a former vice president of the University of Massachusetts, and director of New York State's Division for Youth. Together with his wife Marian Wright Edelman, head of the Children's Defense Fund (of which Hillary Clinton was a former chair), he was a longtime friend of the Clintons, and had cochaired Clinton's 1992 Department of Justice transition team.

In late 1994 it was reported that Clinton planned to nominate Edelman to a slot on the D.C. Circuit Court of Appeals. Conservative columnist George Will immediately sprang to the attack. His target was a 1987 law review article Edelman wrote advocating a federal constitutional right to a minimum income. This was a purely theoretical exercise, reiterating an idea that had been urged and abandoned in the late 1960s, and it had no chance of being adopted. The *Wall Street Journal* charged Edelman with being a "radical" liberal on welfare, accusing him also of being someone who favored "coddling" criminals. For evidence of the latter, it charged that

> as Director of New York State's Division for Youth in 1978, Mr. Edelman ordered a one-week furlough for a 17-year-old who had knifed a girl during a robbery. While on his furlough, this juvenile Willie Horton was arrested for raping, robbing, and trying to electrocute a 63-year-old woman.[20]

As the *New York Times*'s Anthony Lewis wrote,

> that charge is completely false. Mr. Edelman had nothing to do with furloughing the 17-year-old. When a judge told him the youth was dangerous, he ordered a bar on any home visits— but one had already been approved by the director of the facility where he was.

For the next eight months, the issue stayed in the papers. At one point, Hatch indicated that he might accept a district judgeship for Edelman. Clinton, however, decided that even that would produce a fight. Unwilling to use any political capital on judgeships, Clinton turned down Hatch's offer. By late summer 1995, Clinton decided not to nominate Edelman. Peter Edelman's name again made the newspapers in 1996 when he resigned his post as HHS Assistant Secretary in protest against the 1996 welfare bill that Clinton supported.

A few years later, Edelman commented, "it's been his philosophy from the beginning of his presidency that appointments weren't important to him, whether it's unsuccessful Justice

Department civil rights nominee Lani Guinier [Clinton's first choice for Assistant Attorney General for Civil Rights, whom Clinton promptly dropped when opposition developed over her writings] or a judge." [21]

Many liberals were angered by these retreats. Paz and McConnell "were two excellent nominees, and the administration wouldn't stand up for them," complained Judge Reinhardt. "They are clearly people that an administration with principles would have stood up for. There was no legitimate beef against them." Paul Simon, an Illinois Democrat on the Judiciary Committee, lamented "we're giving up on fights too easily." I think it is important that we stand up and fight for people who are nominated." Nan Aron of the Alliance for Justice was more muted, though also disappointed: "My concern with the administration is its reluctance to engage the public in any debates about judgeships," Aron said. "Win or lose, it's good for the country to hear what the president thinks about the courts." [22]

One of the casualties of Clinton's accomodationist approach may have been a greater degree of diversity on the federal bench than he did in fact achieve, significant as that achievement turned out to be. According to the Alliance for Justice, in 1993 and 1994, 25 percent and 35.5 percent of Clinton's appointments to the bench, respectively, were people of color. In 1995, despite Hatch's "cooperation," only 15 percent of Clinton's appointments to the bench (eight out of fifty-three) were people of color. The statistics were even more striking for African-Americans: 21.4 percent of appointments to the federal courts in 1993 and 25 percent of the appointments in 1994 were African-American. In 1995, only 9.4 percent of the appointed federal judges (five out of fifty-three) were African-American. Similarly, 3.8 percent of Clinton's appointments in 1995 were Hispanic (two out of fifty-three), down from 9.9

percent of the 1994 appointments. The Alliance also noted that the appointment of Asian-Americans had been consistently low: Only one was appointed in each of 1994 and 1995. The Fourth, Seventh, and Federal Circuits still lacked any minority members. The appointment of women remained at roughly a third. And in a sign of things to come, no nominees were confirmed between August and the end of the session.

The presidential election year 1996 was a different story from 1995. With a president wounded by the massive Republican victory in the '94 elections, and the possibility of the Republicans recapturing the White House, the judgeship wars resumed. Cooperative bipartisanship faded quickly as presidential politics took over.

During 1995, some of the Republican conservatives, unhappy with Hatch's cooperativeness, had revived the perennial campaign to split the Ninth Circuit, the largest of the circuits. The circuit was large, but neither the judges nor the lawyers complained about that. The proposal was motivated in large part by an effort to split the Northwest off from what Republican Senator Slade Gorton of Washington, one of the primary sponsors of the bill, called the influence of "California judges and California judicial philosophy" over the Northwestern states. The Alliance for Justice suggested that the pressure for the split came from timber companies, unhappy with the environmentalism of California judges.[23]

The Republicans adopted another strategy, but this one has come back to haunt some of them: an effort to prevent Clinton from filling vacant seats by abolishing them. In August 1995 Iowa Republican Charles Grassley, later joined by Alabama Senator Jefferson B. Sessions III after the latter's election in 1996, launched a campaign to eliminate a D.C. circuit seat, charging that it was unnecessary. Earlier, Clinton had nominated Principal Associate Deputy Attorney General Merrick Garland for the only remaining vacancy on the D.C. Circuit. Supported by the ever-helpful D.C. Circuit Judge Laurence Silberman, Grassley argued that eleven judges were enough to do the work and that a twelfth was unnecessary. This was followed a few years later by an effort to reduce the number of judges of the Fourth Circuit, which covers Maryland, Virginia, West Virginia, and the Carolinas, where Jesse Helms blocked any African-American nominee. This time it was Fourth Circuit Judge J. Harvie Wilkinson who helped. He obligingly testified that the circuit could get along perfectly well with the judges it already had, and that more judges would interfere with collegiality. More judges, he added, would also provide more opportunities for federal intervention. Their arguments raised problems for Grassley, Sessions, and Wilkinson when George W. Bush was able to make the nominations, but consistency is not a prime virtue among politicians. At the time, the strategy and supporting statements helped to block and delay appointments to the two circuits. Garland, a thoroughly noncontroversial Justice Department official, who was considered by many to be a law-and-order candidate, was not confirmed until March 1997, eighteen months after he was first nominated.[24]

These strategies were soon eclipsed by a far more formidable and dangerous tactic: an assault on judicial independence, led by Republican presidential candidate Robert Dole.

The occasion was a drug case decision in March 1996 by New York Federal District Judge Harold Baer, a Clinton appointee and a former prosecutor. Baer ruled that a car search in which the police found seventy-five pounds of cocaine and four pounds of heroin was unconstitutional, and refused to allow the drugs into evidence. The case had to be dropped, and a firestorm erupted. Dole and other Republicans called for Baer's impeachment, and at first even Clinton joined in the chorus, but wiser heads in the White House prevailed, and

Clinton reversed himself. Other judges, including even Chief Justice Rehnquist (though very obliquely), criticized the assault on Baer as an attack on judicial independence. Within a few weeks, Baer reversed himself after hearing the case a second time.[25]

None of that stopped Dole or the other Republicans. In a major speech on April 20, Dole attacked Clinton as soft on crime and his judges as too liberal and lenient. They were "dismantling those guard rails that protect society from the predatory, the violent, and the anti-social elements in our midst," charged Dole. This was ludicrous, for it was generally agreed that Clinton's judges were not particularly liberal or lenient. An impartial study had found that the Clinton judges were closer in their decision-making to judges appointed by Gerald Ford than to those of any other recent president, and were significantly less liberal than Carter's appointees. Even some conservatives recognized that.[26]

The Republican target was so-called judicial activism, which, in the eyes of the conservative Republicans who had come to dominate the party, meant any form of liberalism. The "activist" label is of course just a form of name-calling, a dirty word for judges who issue decisions that the speaker does not like.[27]

Sophisticated observers know this. Nevertheless, Republican conservatives have used the epithet "judicial activists" so often that a digression on "judicial activism" may be appropriate here.

The conservative attack on liberal "judicial activists" is ironic. It has been taking place at a time when the Supreme Court's five conservatives are embarked on the most "activist" enterprise since the pre-1937 Court in order to further the right wing's counterrevolution. Unlike the Warren and Burger Courts, which almost always focused on *state* laws that violated constitutional rights under the Equal Protection Clause of the Fourteenth Amendment and other constitutional provisions including the First Amendment, the five conservatives are aiming their fire primarily at *federal* laws passed by a coordinate branch of government. In the past, the Supreme Court and the lower courts have paid great deference to Congress, for not only is it a coordinate and coequal branch, but it is periodically accountable to the voters, while the Supreme Court and the lower federal courts are not accountable at all. During its first 75 years, the Court struck down only two federal statutes. Since Rehnquist became Chief Justice, seventeen years ago, the Court has invalidated 37, nine on newly developed states'-rights-related theories.[28]

Today's conservatives are not so respectful. In the name of nebulous states'-rights conceptions based on theories of constitutional structure and state sovereignty, some of which are new and others, like state sovereign immunity, long discredited, they have hit at many of the have-nots of our society. They are quick to abandon their respect for states' rights, however, when they do not like what the states are doing, such as state legislative districting designed to help minorities, state and local affirmative action plans, and even areas traditionally subject to state law, like punitive damages in tort cases and state safety provisions. And history offers few examples of "judicial activism" to match the Right-Wing justices' taking over Florida election law in 2000 in *Bush v. Gore*. Election law is a quintessentially state matter, and those judges ignored all settled principles of the proper role of the federal courts in order to help George W. Bush win the 2000 elections.[29]

The fact is that all judges are "activist" to some extent at one time or another, and it is unavoidable. Our Constitution is written in very broad terms. It had to be, to survive for centuries. Courts therefore have to fill in the gaps. The result is that very little of what our Constitution prohibits and allows can be learned from examining just the text of the Constitution. To learn that, one must study the 500-plus volumes of Supreme Court decisions, and the thousands of volumes of lower court decisions. The same holds true, though to a lesser extent, for knowing what statutes require. Legislators cannot foresee the myriad situations to which their statutes will be applied, and in many cases they do not want to. The compromises necessary to get legislation passed are often possible only by obscuring differences and avoiding a definitive decision. Moreover, language is both too poor to catch all the relevant possibilities and too rich with possible meanings always to be a clear guide, as any dictionary demonstrates and as every writer knows. Judges must therefore fill in these statutory gaps and ambiguities as well. Few judges can avoid importing their life experiences and values into this process, some more than others. For these reasons, no judge can avoid some degree of "activism."

Dole's attack was not characteristic of him. He was not one of the name-callers. Although he strongly supported Clarence Thomas, he had little enthusiasm for Bork. He had also voted for 182 of 185 Clinton nominations. His own judicial recommendations were not conservatives of the kind favored by Jipping and Bolick. Rather, like Clinton, Dole looked for intellect and judicial qualities. Once on the bench, his selections were fair and nonideological. As one observer put it, "Dole has championed an unbroken series of well-qualified, establishment-oriented Republican moderates who have written their share of decisions upholding the constitutional rights of those accused of committing crimes."[30]

Dole's electoral strategy on judges drew so much fire and was of so little benefit to him that he soon dropped the issue. Once the election was over, however, the assault on judicial independence was resumed, as Texas Congressman Tom DeLay and his allies in the Senate and House tightened their hold on the Republican Party.

Dole's leadership of the Senate majority and his control of the Senate agenda offered a different approach that proved far more effective in blocking Clinton appointments: delaying or shutting down the confirmation process. By June, there were sixty-three vacancies; only three district judges had been confirmed and none of Clinton's appellate choices.[31]

In July, after Dole resigned his Senate seat, a deal was struck between the newly elected majority leader Mississippi Senator Trent Lott and minority leader Tom Daschle to allow twenty-three judges to be confirmed. But in a sign of things to come, Republicans allowed only seventeen more district judges to go through, leaving twenty-seven nominees not acted upon, including all the Clinton Circuit Court nominees; Clinton had also withdrawn an appellate nominee in May. This left some ninety unfilled seats, twenty-three of them open for more than eighteen months and hence "judicial emergencies" under the standard then in effect.[32]

Overall, in 1996 only seventeen judges were confirmed, the lowest in an election year in at least twenty years. They were all district judges—no Court of Appeals nominee was confirmed, which was also a record. The contrast with 1992, the last year of Bush's term, and with 1988, Reagan's last year, is striking. In 1992, Bush sent up seventy-five nominees and the Democratic-controlled Senate confirmed sixty-six, the highest number in any of the Bush years. In 1988, the Democratic-controlled Senate confirmed forty-two judges, and in 1984, when Republicans controlled the Senate, just forty-three. As a result of the 1996 shutdown on appellate nominees, the Reagan/Bush judges maintained their control of the appellate courts; overall they still accounted for more than half of the federal judiciary.

Clinton's reelection, together with a Judicial Conference call for a judgeship bill to add fifty-three new judges would normally have given Clinton another opportunity to reshape the federal judiciary and to add some balance, regardless of his concentration on middle-of-the-roaders. The Republicans, bolstered by a Senate margin increased to 55-45 and led by Trent Lott, had other ideas.

1997–1998

Shortly after Clinton's inauguration in January 1997, Republican conservatives began to work on taking over more control of the judge-selection process. They now included Bob Smith of New Hampshire, Jon Kyl of Arizona, Rick Santorum of Pennsylvania, and Jefferson B. Sessions of Alabama, who had been denied a district judgeship in 1986 by the Democrats because of his blatant hostility to civil rights workers and racist remarks. All but Sessions were among the House "Turks" who came over from the Newt Gingrich-run House and were very partisan and took over the Republican caucus with a very combative style. In February, Washington Senator Slade Gorton and Kyl came up with several schemes. The first involved allocating half the slots to Republicans. The second would have required the Republican majority to reject nominees whose philosophies they didn't like. Jesse Helms came up with a different idea: allowing every Republican senator from the states covered by a judicial circuit to deny a hearing and thereby veto a nominee to that circuit bench.

The allocation of half the slots to the Republicans had no chance, for it was too extreme to be official policy. The second Gorton-Kyl and the Helms proposal were brought before the GOP caucus in April. Both were turned down, primarily because they would have undermined the authority of Judiciary Committee chairman Hatch, which may not have been entirely unintentional. His cooperation with Clinton had irritated some conservatives, but the proposals threatened all committee chairmen and so had to be rebuffed. Nevertheless, anonymous "holds," whereby a senator could secretly block any action on a nominee, were respected by Lott and Hatch, and had the same effect as the Helms proposal. The second Gorton-Kyl proposal lost only narrowly, however, and the caucus agreed to get tough with Clinton's nominees, which they were doing anyway.[33]

The second assault, a cruder approach, came from the House of Representatives and continued the assault on sitting judges begun by Dole in the 1996 election. Texas Congressman Tom DeLay, then starting his rise to becoming the most powerful member of the House, called for the impeachment of liberal judges. In testimony before the House Judiciary Committee, he listed some of the judges and decisions that in his judgment warranted removal: judges who issued school desegregation orders that required tax increases (which had been approved by the conservative Supreme Court), and a judge who overturned California Proposition 209, which required the termination of all state-sponsored affirmative action. To charges that such talk might intimidate judges, he replied, "the judges need to be intimidated," and if they don't behave, he added, "we're going to go after them in a big way." DeLay naturally aimed his fire only on liberal opinions he did not like. As conservative observer Bruce Fein noted, he was apparently not troubled by New York District Judge John Sprizzo who, in a prosecution of two clergymen for illegally obstructing an abortion clinic, acquitted the defendants because they claimed that the clinic's operations offended their religious conscience. As Fein observed, religious conscience does not provide a license to break the law.[34]

Nor was DeLay the only one. Robert Bork weighed in with a proposal for a constitutional amendment that would allow a simple majority of either house of Congress to overrule any federal or state court decision, a proposal that even many of his usual allies rejected. Bork also joined a $1.4 million fundraising effort by Thomas Jipping's Judicial Selection Monitoring Project to fight Clinton nominees. It included a fifteen-minute videotape which recorded five Republican senators endorsing the anti-Clinton campaign, and described cases said to be typical of Clinton's choices. The chief culprit was Judge Stewart Dalzell of the federal District Court in Pennsylvania, who set free the accused killer of a young girl. The point was somewhat blunted when it was revealed that Judge Dalzell was a Bush appointee.

At the same time, conservatives came up with other approaches to curtail the federal courts in moves reminiscent of earlier court-stripping efforts by Helms and others: Republican Congressman Sonny Bono, one of California's many performers-turned-politicians, proposed requiring a three-judge court for reviewing voter initiatives and referenda; others suggested abandoning life tenure and requiring periodic elections; still another proposal would have allowed a dissatisfied litigant to remove a trial judge from a civil case. None of these had a chance and were obviously just political rhetoric to impress constituents.

These attacks on judicial independence drew fire from bar associations and others throughout the country, as well as from some conservatives like Bruce Fein. Despite his threats—which he knew could only be rhetorical—DeLay never moved to impeach any judge. But it is impossible to gauge the chilling effect on trial judges who aspired to become appellate judges, or judges who don't like controversy. Judge Baer, whose decision in the *Bayless* case provided the initial impetus for the Republican assault (though some other decision would probably have served Dole's purpose just as well), had quickly reversed himself. And an impartial observer like Johnny Killian of the Congressional Research Service, who was also a member of the ABA Committee on Judicial Independence, noted that though judges are protected by life tenure, the attacks would probably cause many "to look over their shoulder."[*]

The controversy may have produced one concrete victory for the Republicans. In disgust, Third Circuit Judge H. Lee Sarokin, who had survived a filibuster that the Republicans had mounted against him because of his role as a district judge in some tobacco litigation, resigned in 1996, against "those who have decided to Willie Hortonize the judiciary."[35]

The most powerful weapon at the conservatives' disposal lay in their now-enhanced control of the confirmation process. It provided all the benefits of a filibuster without drawing attention, and it avoided a floor vote, which because the arguments against a nominee were usually flimsy and drew only the most partisan votes, would usually go against them by top-heavy margins, as experience showed. Only one nominee was defeated in a floor vote during Clinton's two terms: Judge Ronnie White of the Missouri Supreme Court, an African-American. White

---

[*] There was probably a much greater impact on the state level, where most judges are elected. Conservatives had already begun to target state judges whose opinions displeased them, among whom Rose Bird, Chief Justice of California was probably the first victim. In 1996, Penny J. White, a Tennessee Supreme Court Judge was denied re-election because she had joined in a decision requiring a new hearing for someone sentenced to death; in Nebraska, in November 2002, supporters of term limits blocked the re-election of a judge who had ruled against the measure; in Florida, a Supreme Court judge was subjected to a nasty re-election campaign for dissenting from a death sentence, even though she had voted to impose the death penalty in some 200 other cases. She survived, but few state judges could have failed to get the message

In 2003, the Virginia General Assembly appointed a panel to interview judges up for reappointment. Republican legislators attacked three female judges for their decisions in custody cases and other sexual matters including homosexuality. As a result, one of the judges, the first African American female circuit judge in Virginia was not reappointed. (*Washington Post* January 2, 2003 B8).

The increasingly politicized nature of state elections for judges is also drawing large sums of money from the U.S. Chamber of Commerce, the Business Industry Political Action Committee and other groups. (Alexander Bolton, "K Street Enters Fray Over Bench" The Hill, October 8, 2003). The Supreme Court 5–4 decision in Republican Party of Minn. v. White, 536 U.S.765 (2002) which struck down a Minnesota law barring judicial candidates from arguing political and social issues in judicial elections, has made matters worse for now judicial elections are subject to openly partisan political combat.

was defeated in 1999 by a shameful campaign led by John Ashcroft, then a Missouri senator running for re-election, in a strict party-line vote.

Initially, the Republicans obtained unintended assistance from the Clinton administration. In the first six months of the second term, Clinton sent up relatively few judges, although in January, there were eighty-four vacancies, and by April there were almost 100, twenty-three of which were judicial emergencies. By August 7, there were 101, but by then Clinton had sent up fifty-two nominations.

The result was that judges were overwhelmed, and since criminal cases must be heard first, civil cases were put off. According to the Administrative Office of the US Courts, by September 1, 1997, 22,642 civil cases had been pending for three years or longer, an increase of 33 percent over 1996. The vacancy problem was most acute in the far West. In the Ninth Circuit by September 1997, ten of the twenty-eight judgeships were vacant, and there were fourteen empty seats at the district level. But the vacancies and backlogs were everywhere.[36]

Although the Clinton administration to some extent was at fault for this situation, it was not solely to blame. Between January and August Clinton nominated forty-six district judges, of which the Senate confirmed only eleven, and fifteen Circuit Court nominees, of which the Senate confirmed only three. Nominees were stalled or blocked, with many nominees denied any hearing at all, and some of those given hearings were not voted upon by the Judiciary Committee, while many of those who did get reported out never got a floor vote. The Republicans used anonymous "holds," in which a senator could block a floor vote on any nominee without identifying himself and certainly not his reason. They also used an occasional filibuster, but usually they just relied on majority leader Trent Lott not scheduling a vote.

All this, as Sheldon Goldman commented, was a "court-blocking strategy, unprecedented in its scope," an "unconscionable" effort to keep as many judgeships as possible open for the next president in hopes that he would be a Republican.[37]

In August the Administrative Office issued a report on the details of the twenty-five Circuit Court and seventy-four District Court vacancies; Attorney General Reno and American Bar Association President Jerome Shestack attacked the Republicans' delay tactics, as well as their proposals for impeachment and ending life tenure for "chilling judicial independence." The American Bar Association, joined by eight other bar associations, warned "of a looming crisis in the nation brought on by the extraordinary number of vacant federal judicial positions." "The injustice of this situation for all of society cannot be overstated," the associations wrote. "Dangerously crowded dockets, suspended civil case dockets, burgeoning criminal caseloads, overburdened judges, and chronically undermanned courts undermine our democracy and respect for the supremacy of the law."[38]

Hatch fired back in newspaper articles, including an op-ed in the *Wall Street Journal* titled "There's No Vacancy Crisis in the Federal Courts." Nevertheless, the Republicans were forced to relent slightly, and they began confirming some judges. By the end of 1997, the Senate had confirmed thirty-six judges, though only seven Court of Appeals nominees. Most of the appellate confirmations replaced judges appointed by Democratic presidents, leaving the appellate courts under the same Republican domination as before. During 1996–97, the Senate confirmed only fifty-three judges. Left over for the second session of the 105th Congress were forty-two nominations, including fourteen that had been pending for a year or more, the longest for about 973 days. Eight of these had not even received a hearing; seven of the eight were minorities, women, or, in one case, a minority woman.[39]

Among those left hanging at the end of 1996 and confirmed in 1997 was Christine A. Snyder, nominated to a California District

Court. First nominated in May 1996, she was not confirmed until
November 7, 1997, when Clinton renominated her after the 1996
election. The vote was an overwhelming 93-6. Her treatment at
the hands of the Judiciary Committee was indicative of what faced
nominees even if they got a hearing and moved forward.

Snyder had the misfortune of being among the earliest nominees to face the newly elected Senator Jefferson B. Sessions III
of Alabama. Sessions, it will be recalled, had been denied a federal judgeship eleven years earlier by a Democratic Senate
because of his racist comments and activities, which included
unfairly prosecuting civil rights workers trying to enforce
voting rights laws. After waiting eighteen months, Snyder
finally got a hearing on July 22, 1997. Sessions sharply questioned her about her pro bono activities in California and her
association with three organizations: Public Counsel, the
Western Center for Law and Poverty, and California Women
Lawyers. Democratic Senator Russ Feingold of Wisconsin commented on this line of questioning: "Let me just say that it is
kind of an irony when we get to the day where if you don't participate in pro bono activities, you are somehow in a situation
where your record is a little safer vis-à-vis being appointed to a
federal judgeship." Of course Snyder was doing only what
lawyers are supposed to do. The American Bar Association
Model Rules of Professional Conduct require all lawyers to try
to provide at least fifty hours of pro bono public legal services
per year, without a fee to those with limited means or to organizations that work with such people.

Sessions's attitude was also reflected in his comments on the
ACLU. When nominees who were members of the organization
or had worked with it came before him, he said, "they [the
ACLU] oppose the death penalty, they oppose the three-strikes
sentencing laws, they are in opposition to school vouchers for
sectarian schools, they oppose V-chips for television sets to limit

what is shown, opposition to voluntary labeling of albums, and support of the partial-birth abortion, support of the constitutionality of the issue of racial preferences, and the decriminalization of drugs." And he would then ask, "Well, do you agree with all of those views? Do you have any concern about them?" His press secretary suggested that "The senator may be troubled by association with certain organizations, and the ACLU would be one example. But more frequently, it's not the association with the organizations; it's the belief in certain ideas about American law. One could say that pro bono work is more likely to reflect passions that the individuals may have." [40]

Missouri Republican John Ashcroft also went after nominees over their ACLU affiliation. Susan Oki Mollway, a Hawaiian-American nominee for a district judgeship in Hawaii, was the first Asian-American woman nominated to the federal bench. Her sin in Ashcroft's eyes was that she had been on the board of directors of the Hawaii ACLU. After she successfully survived a hearing, Ashcroft had her return for a second hearing where he questioned her closely on how much she agreed or disagreed with ACLU policies on gay marriages, an ordinance banning sleeping in public parks overnight, community-notification provisions in pending sex-offender legislation, random and indiscriminate drug testing in the workplace, mandated HIV testing, elimination of mandatory minimum sentences, and other policies. Mollway had to wait two and a half years before being confirmed in May 1998.

By January 1998 one in ten seats on the federal bench were still vacant, and the court dockets were falling farther and farther behind. Chief Justice Rehnquist decided to do something about it. In his annual year-end report he delivered a startling rebuke to senators from his own party. While criticizing Clinton for his initial slowness in sending up nominations, Rehnquist aimed his primary criticism at the Republican-controlled

Senate. He first congratulated the Republican Congress for shrinking federal caseloads by eliminating opportunities for state prisoners to get into federal court to challenge unconstitutional convictions and by curtailing prisoners' rights to file suits challenging unconstitutionally severe prison conditions. But he then struck directly at the Republican strategy with the admonition that "the Senate should act within a reasonable time to confirm or reject [judicial nominees]." He pointedly observed that some nominees had been waiting "for a considerable time" for a Senate Judiciary Committee vote or a final floor vote. "Vacancies cannot remain at such high levels indefinitely without eroding the quality of justice," he added. He also urged passage of the bill recommended by the Judicial Conference in 1997 creating fifty-three new judgeships.[41]

Hatch was caught in the middle between the more zealous conservatives and his duty as chairman of the Judiciary Committee to insure the effective operation of the federal courts. Like everyone else, he knew the system was in deep trouble because of the vacancies and the many judicial emergencies. Nevertheless, his first response was to deny that the vacancies created a serious problem, and to accuse the White House of trying to pack the courts with activists, a charge undercut by many studies and general agreement to the contrary. While agreeing that nominees should be voted up or down, Hatch advised Clinton to withdraw nominees who were opposed, threatening a filibuster if the president did not.[42]

Rehnquist's criticism had an immediate effect however, and indeed changed the dynamics for 1998. Within a month, the Senate confirmed three more nominees, including one much-needed appointment to the woefully shorthanded Ninth Circuit. One of the successful District Court nominees, Ann Aiken, had waited almost twenty-six months to be confirmed to the District Court in Oregon even though she was supported by Republican Senator Gordon Smith as well as by Oregon's Democratic senator. Here, as with Judith McConnell, the opposition focused on a single decision she had made as a state judge, this time in a child rape case: She had given a defendant a shorter jail sentence rather than a longer prison term because she thought the former, which involved long-term supervision, would produce a longer period of oversight than a prison sentence, a decision she admitted was probably a mistake. Nevertheless, Hatch praised her a few weeks after the Rehnquist report, and after two years of waiting she was confirmed, though with thirty votes against her.

The vote on Aiken was the beginning of a modest break in the logjam over nominations. Two weeks later, on February 11, 1998, Margaret Morrow was confirmed as a district judge to the Central District of California by a 67-28 vote; she had been nominated almost two years earlier in May 1996. A forty-seven-year-old former president of the California and Los Angeles County bar associations, and a corporate lawyer with a major national law firm, Morrow was supported by many prominent Republican figures. She had, however, been an advocate for equal treatment for women lawyers, having also been president of California Women Lawyers, a respected nonpartisan group, so Ashcroft went after her for that. She had also criticized special interest domination of voter initiatives, and this criticism also became an Ashcroft target. "This reflected a disdain for voters," he charged. Additionally, in a law review article, she had written that "the law is, almost by definition, on the cutting edge of social thought." This particularly incensed the Missouri senator who declared that "her statement reflects a belief that the law can and should be used by those who interpret it to change social norms. . . . Truly, that is a definition of activism, the ability of judges to impose on the culture those things which they prefer rather than have the culture initiate through their elected

representatives those things which the culture prefers. . . .
[T]hat is anti-democratic." [43]

After a hearing in June 1996 and a unanimous committee
vote, her nomination languished. Clinton renominated her in
1997, and when the Senate convened she was called back for a
second hearing in March. There, she was kept waiting for hours
and then subjected to repeated rounds of questioning. After the
hearing, Ashcroft and other Republicans had her reveal her
votes on some 160 California initiatives, and answer many
other questions which were described by an angry Patrick
Leahy, the ranking Democrat on the committee, as "the 'when
did you start beating your husband type.' " Democratic Senator
Dianne Feinstein from California, who sponsored Morrow, was
furious. At Morrow's hearing on May 8, Feinstein exclaimed, "I
see a test applied to Margaret Morrow that has been applied to
no other district court candidate. . . . In the time I have been on
this committee, I have never seen a male district court nominee
asked these questions about initiatives." [44]

Morrow's nomination was again reported favorably a few
weeks after Feinstein's protest, but no vote was taken until February 1998. This time she was openly supported by Hatch, who
said, "While I initially had some concerns that Ms. Morrow
might be an activist, I have concluded—based on all the information before the committee—that a fair case cannot be made
against her." She was easily confirmed in late February 1998. [45]

A few weeks later, on March 11, 1998, Hilda Tagle, a state
court judge in Corpus Christi, Texas, was confirmed as the first
Hispanic woman on the federal District Court in Texas. Clinton
first nominated her in August 1995 to fill the longest-standing
District Court vacancy in the country, but Texas Republican Phil
Gramm continually blocked her, without explanation. Almost
two and a half years later, on March 5, 1998, she finally received
a ten-minute hearing and was confirmed six days later.

Margaret McKeon was another woman who had to wait several years. A Seattle litigator and a former White House fellow, she was the first woman partner at a major law firm, and represented Boeing Aircraft, Citicorp, and other corporate clients. She had also done a good deal of pro bono work. She was first nominated in March 1996 from Washington State to the desperately shorthanded Ninth Circuit. According to Republican staff aides, she was held up because she signed an American Bar Association resolution affirming a woman's right to an abortion. She had also been chairwoman of the ACLU legal committee in the early 1980s, which drew fire from Sessions, who asserted that the ACLU "has a history of taking positions outside the mainstream"; he questioned McKeon closely on school vouchers, drug decriminalization, and moments of silence in public schools. When finally voted on in late March, she sailed through easily with an 80-11 vote.

Judge Sonia Sotomayer's confirmation was also delayed—sixteen months in her case—and it was directly related to her dual status as a member of the Hispanic minority and as a woman. Because of this, she was a likely candidate for a possible Supreme Court vacancy, and she was someone who would be politically difficult to block. By denying her a Court of Appeals seat, the Republicans hoped to decrease the likelihood she would be nominated if a Supreme Court vacancy opened while Clinton was president.

Sotomayer was, however, a much too attractive Circuit Court candidate to block easily. She grew up in the Bronx housing projects, graduated *magna cum laude* from Princeton, was an editor of the *Yale Law Journal*, and then a federal prosecutor. She was also a board member at the Puerto Rican Legal Defense and Education Fund for twelve years, and sat on the board of the State of New York Mortgage Agency, where she helped give mortgage insurance coverage to low-income housing and AIDS hospices. In her leisure time, Sotomayor became a founding member of the New York City Campaign Finance Board, which distributes public money for city campaigns.

In 1992, Bush appointed her a federal judge in the Southern District of New York with a unanimous confirmation vote. She gained national prominence when she ended the 1995 baseball strike. Clinton nominated her to the Second Circuit in January 1997. Republicans tried to stop her first by citing her refusal to dismiss without a hearing a prisoner's claim that he was discriminated against because he was gay. That failed when she pointed out that she had ultimately ruled against him. She was also criticized for commenting, during the sentencing of a first-time drug offender, that the Federal Sentencing guidelines were too harsh in such cases. That too fell flat because Sotomayer had nevertheless correctly applied the guidelines. Congress later revised them to allow judges discretion in first-time drug cases.

In September 1997, eight months after her nomination, she finally obtained a hearing. For six months, nothing further happened. In early March 1998, she was reported out with a 16-2 vote, but she still did not receive a prompt floor vote. Finally, after seven more months, in October 1998 she was confirmed by a 68-28 vote.

One of the more imaginative efforts to block a nomination, nicknamed the "throw momma from the bench" tactic, related to William Fletcher, and it held up his confirmation for three and a half years. Fletcher, a law professor at the University of California at Berkeley, was nominated to the Ninth Circuit in April 1995. His "problem" was his mother—Judge Betty Binns-Fletcher, one of the liberals on a court that Republicans thought was far too liberal already, being about equally divided between liberals and conservatives. Republicans feared that the son might be as liberal as his mother. The Republicans dug up an 1887 antinepotism statute that barred appointment to any federal court position of someone who was a first cousin or closer of a judge. The Clinton administration argued that the law was not intended to apply to presidential appointments, but the language of the statute expressed no such limitation.

Fletcher's opponents had a problem, however—Republicans had consistently ignored the law in the past. In 1992, they voted to confirm George Bush's nomination of Morris Arnold to the Eighth Circuit Court of Appeals on which his brother Richard already sat. Earlier, Judge Augustus Hand was appointed to the Second Circuit, on which his cousin Learned Hand already sat. In 1997, Charles Breyer, the brother of Supreme Court Justice Stephen Breyer, was confirmed to a California district judgeship.

None of this made any difference to the Republicans who, while willing to give Fletcher a hearing and an approving committee vote in 1995, refused to take any further action. After waiting three years, Clinton decided to make a deal with the Republicans whereby Betty Fletcher would take senior status and Clinton would nominate Judge Barbara Durham, a very conservative Washington State judge urged by Senator Slade Gorton. Fletcher was then called for a second hearing in April 1998, and reported out favorably in May. Even then, he was held up another four and a half months until September when he was confirmed 57-41. The Republican tactic failed, however, when Judge Durham, whom Clinton nominated in January 1999, withdrew the following August because of her husband's poor health.

Others were not so lucky. Judge Michael Schattman was nominated by Clinton in December 1995 to the District Court in Dallas, a court badly understaffed and overloaded. Schattman had been a highly respected state judge since 1979. Initially supported by Texas Senators Phil Gramm and Kay Bailey Hutchinson, Schattman expected to be easily confirmed, and did not run for reelection as a state judge. Gramm soon turned against him, however, charging that Schattman could not be impartial because he had campaigned for Democratic candidates and had been a delegate to the 1992 Democratic National Convention. It turned out, however, that Gramm himself had supported GOP activists for a federal judgeship, including one man who contributed to Gramm's campaign while Gramm was promoting his nomination. Gramm then switched to a charge that since Schattman had been a conscious objector to the Vietnam War in the 1960s, he could not be impartial in cases involving the many people in the district who worked for military contractors. David Broiles, a Fort Worth lawyer who had represented Bell Helicopters before Schattman, dismissed Gramm's complaint as "preposterous." In July 1998, Schattman angrily withdrew.[46]

Frederica Massiah-Jackson got further than Schattman but fared no better. Nominated in July 1997 to be the first black federal trial judge in Philadelphia, with the support of both Pennsylvania Republican Senators Arlen Specter and Rick Santorum, she was attacked by the Philadelphia District Attorney and the Pennsylvania District Attorneys Association as too lenient. She was nevertheless backed by the Philadelphia Bar Association, as well as by many prominent lawyers, including former prosecutors, and the press. The *Philadelphia Inquirer* editorialized in her favor, referring to a poll of lawyers who gave her "overwhelmingly high marks for integrity, judicial temperament, and work ethic," and observed that "there's nothing in Judge Massiah-Jackson's record that disqualifies her from the federal bench." Another editorial declared that if Massiah-Jackson failed "to win confirmation despite [her] qualifications, that would be worth protesting."

In the face of the Philadelphia District Attorney's attack, Santorum withdrew his support. After being reported favorably in

November, Massiah-Jackson was called for a second hearing in March 1998 to face a new set of allegations based on material forwarded from the Philadelphia District Attorney to Ohio Republican Senator Michael DeWine the night before the hearing. They concerned cases that Massiah-Jackson had handled at the beginning of her judgeship. This time, she performed badly, responding vaguely to some questions and changing her story about one matter. Specter continued to support her and expressed "outrage" over the lack of notice and late production of information, saying "I think it was wrong for her to be questioned on materials that she had not seen. It is a matter of fundamental due process that one receives notice to prepare a defense." Facing probable rejection, Massiah-Jackson withdrew her nomination five days later.

As 1998 ended, sixty-five judges had been confirmed, but many nominations still languished, including four reported by the Judiciary Committee and on the executive calendar of the Senate: Judge Richard Paez, Missouri Justice Ronnie L. White, Judge William J. Hibbler, and Timothy Dyk; Paez had been waiting since January 1996.

Judicial nominations were also stalled at earlier steps in the process. Marsha Berzon, Annabelle Rodriguez, Clarence Sundram, and Matthew Kennelly were denied votes by the committee after a hearing. Seven others did not even get a committee hearing: James Beaty Jr., Helene N. White, Jorge C. Rangel, Ronald M. Gould, Robert S. Raymer, and Barry P. Goode; White had been waiting since January 1997. Rangel withdrew his name in October 1998, writing Clinton that "Our judicial system depends on men and women of goodwill who agree to serve when asked to do so. But public service asks too much when those of us who answer the call are subjected to a confirmation process dominated by interminable delays."

Numbers tell much of the story. For Bush nominees in

1991–1992, with a Democratic Senate, the average number of days between the time a District Court nomination was received by the committee and a hearing was 92.1. For Clinton in 1997–1998, it jumped to 160.6. The average number of days for a Circuit Court hearing to be held during 1991–1996 ranged between 77.4 and 80.8. In 1997–1998, it jumped to 230.9.[47]

The role of majority leaders Dole and Lott was crucial to the slowdown. Bush and Clinton had their District Court nominees confirmed by a Senate vote during 1991–1992 and 1993–94 within an average of 3.2 and 4.3 days after the committee report, respectively. In 1995–96 and 1997–98, the figure rose to about ten times that for Clinton—35.3 and 38.4. The numbers were similar for Circuit Court nominees: For Bush and Clinton in 1991–94, the figures were 14.4 and 8.7. In 1995–96 and 1997–98, they were 39.5 and 38.4.

Trent Lott was not overly disturbed. Discussing the delays in the confirmation process at the close of the session, Lott commented, "Do I have any apologies? Only one: I probably moved too many already." When asked in 1997 whether the Republicans were deliberately delaying the process, he had "smiled broadly," according to NPR's Nina Totenberg and answered "Sounds like a good idea to me."[48]

1999–2000

During the winter months of 1998–99, the Clinton presidency hit rock bottom. After Clinton denied having sexual relations with Monica Lewinsky in January 1998, Republicans, especially in the House, joined with Independent Counsel Kenneth Starr to hound him relentlessly. This sudden burst of moralism turned out to be bipartisan, however, as two Republican leaders were forced to resign over their own extramarital sexual activities—House speaker Newt Gingrich and his expected successor, Bob Livingston of Louisiana. House elder and Judiciary Committee chairman Henry Hyde, the silver-haired, portly model of rectitude, was also forced to admit to "youthful indiscretions" some years earlier when at 41 he entered upon a seven-year affair with a woman named Cherie Snodgross that ended only after Hyde's wife learned of it.[49]

In August 1998, Clinton backed down and admitted he had engaged in a "relationship with Ms. Lewinsky that was not appropriate. In fact it was wrong." In October Kenneth Starr issued a pornographically detailed report to the House of Representatives describing Clinton's sexual activities with Lewinsky; much of the report was written by one of his top lieutenants Brett Kavanaugh, who would later join the George W. Bush White House and then be nominated to a seat on the D.C. Circuit in 2003.[50]

A month after the Starr report, in November 1998, the House impeached Clinton, and in January 1999, a public trial before the Senate was held. The effort to convict him failed and Clinton remained in office.

In the November 1998 elections, the Democrats did better than expected, though the Senate stayed at 55-45. Perhaps emboldened by the failure of the impeachment and their electoral success, Democrats soon went on the offensive, focusing on the Republican's treatment of minorities and women. It did little but draw indignant outbursts from Hatch and other Republicans.

Nineteen ninety-nine opened with a stalemate on judicial nominations, and ended with the second-lowest number of confirmations in twenty years. Although Clinton sent up sixteen Circuit Court and thirty-one District Court nominations, none got a hearing during the first five and a half months, and only seven hearings were held all year. Orrin Hatch wanted Clinton to nominate Brian Theodore "Ted" Stewart to a district judgeship, but environmental groups protested, charging that Stewart was an extreme anti-environmentalist. While executive director of the Utah Department of Natural Resources, he eliminated wildlife protection programs, advocated limiting the scope of the Endangered Species Act, and called those who sought to protect public lands the "enemy." When Clinton went along with the environmentalists, Hatch shut down the confirmation process until a deal was made: Clinton would nominate Stewart, and in return, Berzon and Ronnie White would get hearings and floor votes, as would Paez, who had already had two hearings. Liberal groups condemned the deal as a "bad bargain," and Hatch immediately seemed to renege, warning that he would not be rushed on nominations (other than Stewart) and that "judicial activists" would be stalled.[51]

When Republicans tried to force a vote on Stewart in September, Democrats insisted on votes for Paez and Berzon first, but the Republicans refused and the Democrats began a filibuster. After two weeks, the Democrats folded, hoping that the Republicans would allow votes for Berzon, Paez, and White. Acting in a way Senator Barbara Boxer later called "real sweet," Democrats also decided to vote for Stewart, allowing him to be confirmed by a 93-5 vote on October 5. In return, they did obtain a vote, but on only one nominee and it was hardly what they expected. On the same day that Stewart was confirmed with almost solid Democratic support, every single Republican (except one absentee) voted to deny Justice Ronnie White, the first African-American judge on the Missouri Supreme Court, a seat on a Missouri District Court. The vote was 54-45. This was the first rejection of a nominee on the floor of the Senate since Robert Bork, and the first of a District Court nominee in more than fifty years.

The refusal to confirm Justice White was orchestrated by John Ashcroft, in what the St. Louis Post Dispatch characterized as Ashcroft's "shameless battle of character assassination. White, a 46-year-old native of St. Louis, was appointed to the Missouri Court of Appeals in 1994 and to the Missouri

Supreme Court in 1995. On the two courts, he had written some 140 opinions. During this period, he had heard fifty-eight capital cases, and upheld the death penalty in forty-one; in ten of the cases overturning the death sentence he was part of a majority. Because of these seventeen votes against the death penalty, out of fifty-eight, Ashcroft attacked him as "procriminal and activist," although that judges whom Ashcroft had put on the Missouri courts when the governor had voted more often than White to overturn the death penalty. Most observers believed that Ashcroft, in a tight race for reelection against the popular Democratic Governor Mel Carnahan, was looking for an issue. Although Ashcroft claimed that Missouri police organizations opposed White—it was actually just one sheriff's organization and was only because of a White vote against a Missouri sheriff—the 4,500 member Missouri State Fraternal Order of Police supported White. In a letter to the sheriffs, the organization's president said,

Justice White on the death penalty has been far more supportive of the rights of victims than of the rights of criminals. While in fact voting 17 times for death penalty reversals, he has voted to do so in far fewer instances than the other justices on the court. . . .

And his letter closed with:

Nothing can undo the needless injury which has been inflicted on the reputation of Justice White, and our nation has been deprived of an individual who surely would have proven to be an asset to the federal judiciary.

. . . .

On behalf of the membership of the Fraternal Order of Police, I would encourage you to exercise greater judgment in

> future battles of this sort. It is a great disservice to the members of your organization, and the nation as a whole, to choose to do otherwise.

The Missouri Police Chiefs Association also backed White, turning down several requests by Ashcroft's office to oppose him, including a telephone call from one of Ashcroft's staff.[52]

African-American organizations were furious, particularly with Ashcroft's Missouri colleague Christopher Bond. The year before in a tight fight for reelection, Bond had assured African-American organizations that he would support White. "Absolutely I am," he had assured African-American groups, and thereby managed to pick up 33 percent of the black vote. In presenting White to the Judiciary Committee, Bond called White "a man of the highest integrity and honor" with the "necessary qualifications and character" to serve as a federal judge, who "understands the role of the federal district judges is to interpret the law, not to make the law." He said he found it a pleasure "to urge that this committee act favorably upon his nomination and send it to the floor for confirmation." On another occasion he told the committee "I believe Judge White has the necessary qualifications and character traits which are required for this most important job," and reaffirmed his support for White in January 1999, the same year as his vote against him.[53]

Bond was not the only Republican to support Judge White initially, and then to abandon him. Three Republicans on the Judiciary Committee—Orrin Hatch, Arlen Specter, and Strom Thurmond—voted for him in committee. Yet when Justice White was voted on by the full Senate on Tuesday, these senators and all the other Senate Republicans voted against him and killed his nomination. Afterward, Vermont Senator Jim Jeffords and some others said that they didn't know White was African-American! Bond later asserted, "first I never told

Judge White nor anyone else how I would vote on his nomination," and secondly, "after careful consideration, I determined that Judge White was not the appropriate candidate to serve in a lifetime capacity as a U.S. district judge for eastern Missouri." He gave no other reasons.[54]

African-Americans had a different view of it. "Senator Bond's words are not his bond," said the Rev. B.T. Rice, president of the St. Louis Clergy Coalition and pastor of New Horizon Seventh Day Church. "He did not mislead us," Rice said. "He literally lied to us."[55]

The Ronnie White vote was a rare deviation from the Republican strategy of avoiding up-or-down votes. As NPR's Nina Totenberg observed later, they would not again make that mistake. Instead Republicans perfected a system of Senate inaction on judicial nominations. People like Hatch and Ashcroft figured out that it was better to stall behind the scenes, often for years, rather than have a confrontation that would embarrass them or that they might lose. "[I]t's just better to kill them in committee," a Republican staff member of the Judiciary Committee told Goldman later.[56]

There was so much criticism of the Republicans for White's rejection, not just among Democrats but from more disinterested observers, that in November, the Senate Republican Policy Committee found it necessary to circulate a memorandum describing White as "notorious among law enforcement officers in his home state of Missouri for his decisions favoring murderers, rapists, drug dealers, and other heinous criminals." Nobody took that seriously.

In March 2000 Paez and Berzon were finally voted on. Paez had waited four years and two months, and Berzon two years and two months.

Richard Paez was the first Latino judge on the Los Angeles

District Court, having been nominated and confirmed in early 1994; before that, he was first a public interest lawyer for ten years and then a municipal court judge for fourteen. In January 1996, Clinton nominated him to the Ninth Circuit. He immediately ran into trouble. Sessions led the assault. While giving a speech to a law school class in 1995, Paez criticized Proposition 209, which barred racial preferences, as an anti–civil rights initiative, and called Proposition 187, which denied benefits to illegal immigrants, divisive. "This was stunning to me," said Sessions explaining his opposition, since as he saw it, Proposition 209 merely reflected the Constitution. Although Paez later said he regretted his comments about Proposition 209, Hatch conceded that the Judicial Code of Conduct allows judges to "give speeches and lectures on the law in effort to improve the law, the legal system, or the administration of justice. This exception may be read to exonerate Judge Paez of potential violations." Sessions also called Paez hostile to law enforcement, and Oklahoma Republican James Inhofe called Paez an extremist. However, a detailed study of Paez's career and seven of his court rulings published earlier that year by the *Los Angeles Daily Journal*, a legal publication, concluded that Paez was a "thoughtful, unbiased and even-tempered judge."[57]

Despite the senatorial opposition, Paez picked up support from prominent Republicans. Among those endorsing Paez were Representative James Rogan of Glendale and Los Angeles attorney Sheldon H. Sloan, an adviser to former California Republican Governor Pete Wilson on judicial nominees. Rogan, a floor manager during the impeachment hearings against President Clinton, called Paez a fine jurist whose "character and integrity have never been questioned."[58]

Newspaper reports on the Paez fight suggested that the primary target was the Ninth Circuit, which, as noted earlier in connection with Fletcher, many conservatives considered too liberal already. "The 9th Circuit is a big enough mess now without another liberal judicial activist, and I'm opposed to [Paez]," majority leader Trent Lott said. Ohio Republican Mike DeWine called the circuit "totally out of control." One wonders whose "control" he had in mind, and what kind.[59]

In October 1999, after the White vote, Lott agreed to hold votes on Paez and Berzon. To assure no further evasion, minority leader Tom Daschle had Lott declare in the *Congressional Record* that votes on the two nominees would be held no later that March 15, 2000, a concession Lott made only after California Senator Boxer put a hold on a nomination that Lott wanted.

Lott stalled as long as he could, and no vote was taken on either Paez or Berzon for many months. When the Republicans took over in 1995, Hatch had reinstated the traditional blue-slip system that Democrats had dropped, whereby a senator from a nominee's home state could veto the nominee by not returning the blue slip. Although Hatch later denied that the absence of a blue slip from a home state senator was fatal, Nina Totenberg reported that in 1998 Hatch added to the form: "Please return this form as soon as possible. No further proceedings on this nominee will be scheduled until both blue slips have been returned by the nominee's home-state senators." As a matter or practice, Hatch subsequently expanded the policy to allow *any* senator to veto a nomination and to do so anonymously. Although Lott and Daschle later agreed to abolish secret holds, Lott did not implement the agreement. As a result, despite Lott's scheduling agreement in October, Paez and Berzon did not get a vote until March 2000. When the *Washington Post* looked into the matter, it discovered that New Hampshire Republican Bob Smith had put the hold on anonymously and Lott was honoring it, even though Smith was not a home state senator.[60]

It was not until March 9, a few days before the March 15 deadline, that Paez finally came up for a vote. Even then, fourteen

Republicans tried to block the vote with a filibuster and other parliamentary maneuvers. Cloture was invoked, but Sessions moved
to "postpone indefinitely," an unprecedented maneuver that was
too much even for Hatch but which drew thirty-one Republican
votes. When the vote was finally taken, Paez was confirmed 59-39.

Marsha Berzon was first nominated to the Ninth Circuit in
January 1998. She was a nationally renowned appellate and
Supreme Court litigator, a former clerk for Justice Brennan,
and a Cornell Law School professor. She had worked on the
National Housing Law Project, the board of directors for the
AFL-CIO Lawyers Coordinating Committee, the Legal Aid
Society of San Francisco, and the ACLU of Northern California. At a Judiciary Committee session, Hatch noted Berzon's
bipartisan support and called Berzon "one of the best lawyers
I've ever seen." She obtained the support of a broad range of
Republicans, Democrats, law enforcement officials, and business leaders, including former conservative Republican Senator James A. McClure of Idaho and California appeals court
justice Paul Haerle, a key aide to Ronald Reagan when he was
governor of California. She also had the support of many corporate lawyers who had opposed her on major labor cases. "I
can think of no other union-side lawyer who would command
so strong and so compelling a consensus from management
lawyers," wrote Fred Alvarez, a former EEOC commissioner
and Assistant Labor Secretary under President Ronald Reagan.

Nevertheless, she was given the same treatment as Margaret
Morrow. She was asked her views on each of 160 California ref-
erendums. Then, after her hearing ended, she was called back
for a second hearing, kept waiting all day, and then taken to a
small room by Sessions containing a small table, and grilled by
him alone, with an occasional visit by Democrats.[61]

Like Paez and Fletcher, her primary problem was the hostility to the Ninth Circuit, although Smith, who also put an

anonymous hold on her, also considered her too liberal. She received the same treatment as Paez when she was finally voted on—a fourteen-senator filibuster led by Imhofe, and then cloture. She was confirmed by a 64-34 vote.

The Ronnie White, Paez, and Berzon episodes intensified the Democratic attack on the Republicans for the racial and gender discrimination that seemed to be taking place. Clinton, speaking before the US Hispanic Leadership Institute a few days after the Ronnie White defeat, attacked the Republicans for rejecting White's nomination and for their failure to vote on four outstanding Hispanic nominees: Paez, Judge Julio Fuentes, nominated to the Third Circuit in Philadelphia; Enrique Moreno to the Fifth Circuit; and Ronald Guzman to a District Court in Illinois.

Clinton's complaints in October 1999 were somewhat late in the day. Long before the Democrats raised the issue, the Republican majority had targeted minorities. Studies by the Citizens for Independent Courts, a nonpartisan organization, and a Georgetown University project reported that during the 1997–98 session there was a much higher rate of failure and much longer delays for minority nominations than for white males: 35 percent of Clinton's minority nominees had been rejected but only 14 percent of his white nominations, and it took an average of 186 days to accept or reject his white nominees but 246 days for minorities.[62]

Minorities and women continued to be the primary victims in 2000. In July, Clinton charged that minority nominees were being held "in a political jail," and added, "I'm worried about the people whom I've tried to put on the court of appeals who are African-American and Hispanic . . . because they can't get a hearing from this Republican Senate." According to an Alliance for Justice summary in its 2000 report:

Although women were confirmed at basically the same rate as

men, they waited significantly longer for confirmation. On average, the Senate took nearly 100 days—over three months—longer to act on the nominations of women and minorities, than it took on the nominations of white males.

The list of those candidates who were not confirmed in 2000 also suggests a bias toward white males. The 42 lapses and two withdrawals include nine African-Americans, two Asians, three Hispanics, and fourteen women, and the statistics show that white males were confirmed at significantly higher rates than women and minorities. Of the year 2000 nominees, fourteen, or 17%, were African-Americans. Of those confirmed, only five were African-Americans, making them less than 13% of the candidates confirmed in 2000. In contrast, 59 of the candidates, or 73%, were white, and of the 39 confirmed, 30 were white—77%. In other words, while white nominees were confirmed at a higher rate than the rate at which they were nominated, African-American nominees were confirmed at a lower rate. Moreover, the 12.8% year 2000 confirmation rate of African-Americans is lower than the overall rate of 16.8% from 1993 through 1999.[63]

The most egregious examples involved the Fourth Circuit and Senator Jesse Helms of North Carolina. The Fourth Circuit, which covers Maryland, Virginia, the Carolinas, and West Virginia, has more African-Americans than any other—25 percent of the population. It is also probably the most conservative Court of Appeals in the nation, and until 2001, it had never had an African-American member.

Clinton tried four times to place an African-American Fourth Circuit appointment, and ultimately succeeded with Roger Gregory, but only after he left office.

Clinton's first nominee was James Beaty. After Beaty served thirteen years as a North Carolina Superior Court judge, Clinton put him on the federal District Court in North Carolina in 1994. He then nominated Beaty in December 1995 to the Fourth Circuit. Hatch immediately attacked Beaty as "soft on crime" because of a habeas corpus decision in a murder case, in which a juror made an unauthorized visit to a crime scene and told the other jurors what he saw. Beaty, sitting temporarily on a panel of the Fourth Circuit, joined the other two judges in ordering a new trial. "Will the president chastise [!] Judge Beaty," thundered Hatch, "or does he agree with his decision to release a convicted double murderer on a technicality?" In fact, the defendant was not going to be released but only given a new trial, as Hatch certainly knew. Before that could happen, however, the full Fourth Circuit overturned the panel's ruling.[64]

More important than Hatch's attack was home state Senator Jesse Helms's refusal to allow the nomination to go forward. Although racism was always possible where Helms was concerned, and many have charged him with that in connection with the Fourth Circuit, the primary reason Clinton's refusal to name federal District Judge Terence Boyle, a Helms protégé to the Fourth Circuit. Helms, incidentally, had supported Beaty for the district judgeship a few years earlier.

Helms claimed that even though the court had four vacancies out of a complement of fifteen, the circuit didn't need more judges. Critics noted that while the circuit disposed of its cases faster than any other, it heard only 27 percent of them orally, the lowest of any court, and dismissed 87 percent of the appeals in brief unsigned opinions. Moreover, it frequently imported judges from other circuits or lower courts to fill out its panels; that was where Beaty had gotten into trouble in the *Sherman* case.[65]

What especially angered liberals and others were the swift confirmations of two white nominees to the Fourth Circuit— Robert B. King and William Traxler—with no objection by either Helms or Wilkinson; both are conservative.

After Beaty waited three years without ever getting a hearing, Clinton dropped the nomination and nominated James Wynn, another African-American, in August 1999. Wynn, a North Carolina Court of Appeals judge, considered a moderate, fared no better, for Helms blocked him too. North Carolina Democratic Senator John Edwards tried to revive Wynn's nomination in 2001 in return for Edwards's support of Terence Boyle, but failed. Democrats still had not learned.

In June 2000, Clinton nominated African-American Roger Gregory, a highly regarded Virginia lawyer. Also considered a moderate, he was supported by Virginia Republicans Senator John Warner and Governor George Allen, and Democratic Senator Charles Robb. Gregory too was left dangling without a hearing for months, and it looked as if he would suffer the same fate as Beaty and Wynn. Clinton then resorted to a recess appointment for Gregory in December 2000, which would integrate the Fourth Circuit for the first time in its history, though only for a year. Allen was elected a senator in 2000, however, and since both home-state senators were Republicans and supported Gregory, Bush renominated him in May. Helms and Wilkinson apparently decided another judge was now needed, and raised no objection; three other judges would soon be added. Gregory was easily confirmed in July 2001.

In July 2000, Clinton again attacked the Republican treatment of minorities in a speech before the annual NAACP convention. Lambasting Jesse Helms for blocking his every effort to integrate the all-white Fourth Circuit, Clinton exploded, "This is outrageous! . . . The Circuit Court with the highest percentage of African-Americans in the country—but not one single black judge on the Court of Appeals." He also condemned presidential candidate Texas Governor George W. Bush for his silence over the Republicans' refusal to confirm Enrique Moreno of Texas to the Fifth Circuit. "Why don't they want to give these people hearings and a vote? Because they don't want them on the court. But they don't want you to know they don't want them on the court." They only "want people who are ideological purists." [66]

Clinton had nominated Moreno in September 1999. Born in Mexico, Moreno grew up in El Paso, went to Harvard Law School, and returned to Texas to practice. Phil Gramm and Kay Barkey Hutchinson, the two Texas senators who had blocked Schattman, claimed that a panel of lawyers they had set up found him unqualified for lack of experience. The ABA, however, gave Moreno its highest rating, and Gramm had never found Texas Republican nominees Edith Jones, Jerry Smith, or Harold DeMoss unfit for appellate judgeships because they lacked judicial experience. In fact, of President Reagan's and George H.W. Bush's twelve appointments to the Fifth Circuit, half had never had prior judicial experience, and only four had been judges for more than three years before their appointment. It appeared too that the lawyers panel set up by Gramm and Hutchinson focused primarily on Moreno's views about the death penalty, abortion, and especially affirmative action for minorities, a particular target for many Republicans. Moreno was never given a hearing. Here too, Republicans apparently decided it was better to "kill them in committee," because an open hearing might have embarrassed them in an election year in which the Hispanic vote was a major target for both parties. Clinton renominated Moreno again in January 2001, but Bush withdrew it—he had Miguel Estrada in the wings, another Hispanic nominee but one on whose adherence to conservative doctrine he could count. [67]

Clinton's explosion did do some good. A few days later, the Republicans confirmed Johnnie B. Rawlinson of Nevada as the first African-American female on the Ninth Circuit.

Another African-American female was not so lucky. The Sixth

Circuit, which covers Michigan, Ohio, Kentucky, and Tennessee, had four vacancies by summer 2000. It was among the slowest federal courts in the country, frequently calling on judges from other parts of the country to fill in. In spring 2000, Chief Judge Gilbert Merritt wrote the president that the court was "hurting badly and will not be able to keep up with its workload due to the fact that the Senate Judiciary Committee has acted on none of the nominations." For two of these slots, Clinton nominated two women: Helene White, a Michigan appeals court judge and cousin of Michigan Democratic Senator Carl Levin, and Kathleen McCree Lewis, a distinguished African-American female lawyer. Lewis was first nominated in September 1999. She was never afforded a hearing. White was first nominated in January 1997 and renominated in January 1999. She too never received a hearing, even though strongly backed by Michigan Democrat Carl Levin. Michigan Republican Senator Spencer Abraham blocked them both, claiming that Clinton failed to consult him in the nominations. Facing a tough reelection fight in 2000—which he lost—Abraham backed down. Nevertheless, neither ever got a hearing from Hatch.

As the Helene White and other examples show, minorities were not the only victims of the Republicans' tactics. Women were also targeted. Elena Kagan was nominated in June 1999 to the D.C. Circuit Court of Appeals to replace Patricia Wald, one of the court's stronger and most effective liberals. Kagan, now dean of the Harvard Law School, was a former clerk to Abner Mikva on the District of Columbia Circuit appeals court and to Supreme Court Justice Thurgood Marshall, and a top deputy to Bruce Reed at the Domestic Policy Council at the time of her nomination. She too never got a hearing. The District of Columbia Circuit was closely divided between Democratic and Republican appointees, and Wald's departure provided an opportunity to affect the balance. For this reason the Republican strategy that started in 1996 with refusing to allow Clinton to shift the balance in the appellate courts doomed the Kagan appointment. The claim that the D.C. Court of Appeals did not need more judges provided a convenient cover for the refusal to act on either Kagan or the widely respected Allen R. Snyder, 53, longtime leader in District of Columbia legal circles, a former Rehnquist clerk, and an aide to White House Deputy Counsel and Clinton confidante Bruce Lindsey. Snyder did get a hearing at which he drew nothing but praise, but that did not get him a floor vote, and the nomination died in committee. Other distinguished Circuit Court nominees left hanging without hearings included Bonnie Campbell, former Attorney General of Iowa and head of the Justice Department's Office of Domestic Violence; Barry Goode, who was a distinguished California lawyer, and many others.

At the end of 2000, eighteen appellate court nominations had not been voted on; only thirteen had been confirmed in Clinton's last two years. In his eight years, Clinton had appointed only sixty-one appellate judges, well below the number Reagan appointed.

Many District Court nominees were also left hanging after long delays. James Klein, nominated for the Washington, District of Columbia Court as chief appellate lawyer of the District of Columbia Public Defender's Office, was a typical example. He was first nominated in January 1998. Despite the absence of any negative comments about his views or his abilities during his three-year wait, he never had a hearing. Dolly Gee, the daughter of Chinese immigrants, was a brilliant graduate of UCLA and an award-winning labor lawyer who represented both management and labor. Nominated in May 1999, according to the *Los Angeles Times* "Gee is not a controversial choice . . . [Her] support is not limited to Democrats. Among others, Republican Congressman James E. Rogan, one of the

House impeachment managers, has written in support of her nomination." The chief judge of the court where she would be serving—already short-staffed, with four vacancies—also has written urging the committee 'to take action.'" Frederic Woocher, a May 1999 nominee, was a distinguished California lawyer who had done a great deal of free public-interest work, and was a former clerk to Supreme Court Justice William Brennan. Woocher had opposed Robert Bork's nomination to the Supreme Court. He received a hearing and strong bipartisan support, but was never voted on. Clarence Sundram, born in Bombay, India, was nominated to a seat on the Northern District of New York in 1995. An advocate for people afflicted with mental illness, he would have been the first person of South Asian heritage on the federal bench. He had a hearing in 1996, but his nomination lapsed. Clinton renominated him, and Sundram had another hearing in 1997 at which Hatch praised him saying: "Frankly, there are very few witnesses who have come before the committee that appear to be as intelligent as you are. . . . I believe you will be a great judge when you get there." However, Thomas Jipping published an op-ed in the *Washington Times* making the unfounded charge that Sundram favored drug legalization—which Sundram denied—because Sundram had written a law review article some twenty-five years earlier, when he was a particularly young law student. Sundram never received a committee vote.[68]*

Sixty-three Clinton appellate and district nominees were denied either a hearing or a committee vote during the six years of Republican control. According to a 2001 study by People for the American Way, during the six years of Republican control, 45.3 percent of Clinton's appellate nominations were returned to the White House without a vote. During the six years of the Reagan-Bush administrations in which Democrats controlled

---

* In the interests of full disclosure, I should note that I was one of Sundram's professors and he was one of my best and favorite students.

the Senate, only 26.3 percent of their appellate selections were returned. During Clinton's last two years, Republicans blocked 56 percent of the Circuit Court nominees, 60 percent more than for Reagan and Bush, each of whom lost only 35 percent of his nominees during 1987–88 and 1991–92, respectively.[69]

Four factors determine whether a president will have an ideological mark on the bench after he leaves office: the president's interest in ideological choices; the number of choices he has, which is in turn determined in part by how many new judgeships are created on his watch; the makeup of the Senate; and the makeup of the already existing judiciary. All four worked against an ideological shift on the bench during the Clinton administration. He was a conservative Democrat; he was not interested in ideology; did not consider judges politically important, and he faced a very hostile Senate that considered the ideological cast of judges very important; his appointees took office in what was already a very conservative judiciary; and despite the Judicial Conference recommendation of fifty-three new judgeships, he was denied the creation of a substantial number of new judges. Between them, Reagan and Bush were given more than 200 new judgeships.

The moderation of Clinton's appellate appointments was highlighted in a 2001 analysis of federal appellate decisions by three political scientists, Susan B. Haire, Martha Anne Humphries, and Donald R. Songer. They attributed that moderation primarily to the hostile environment created by the Senate Judiciary Committee and the Republican-controlled Senate. They ignored Clinton's sluggishness in sending up nominees during his first years while he had a Democratic Senate majority, which was in sharp contrast with George W. Bush and Ronald Reagan, each of whom quickly sent up a swarm of strongly ideological nominees upon taking office with a favorable Senate.[70]

Haire, Humphries, and Songer found that from 1993

through 1999 Clinton's nominees voted somewhat less liberally than Carter's nominees in civil rights, criminal, and labor/economic cases, and quite close to Bush and Reagan nominees in criminal and labor/economic cases. Clinton's nominees were more liberal than those of the two Republicans in cases where the appellate panel was split. In the latter cases, however, Clinton's nominees were still less liberal than Carter's, though much more liberal than judges appointed by Reagan and Bush. This group, however, comprised a small sample, accounting for only 10 percent of the total number of cases, and Haire et al. caution that the overall policy impact of these cases is probably very modest. Moreover, many of these decisions may have come in the Second and Ninth Circuits, where there were a large number of Clinton appointees, in relation to the size of the circuits, thus diluting the effect of the liberal decisions in the overall federal appellate system.

As conservative commentator Bruce Fein said, Clinton's nominees were "as centrist as can be." He went on to say, "I don't think you can detect any change from Reagan's and Bush's judges in the vastly more conservative approach on the judicial bench from criminal justice to affirmative action to church/state issues." Only in a few areas like abortion and affirmative action did Clinton judges support liberal positions and even then, not very much more than their Republican colleagues.[71]

Nevertheless, by the time Clinton left office, he had changed the face of the federal judiciary. In a joint article, Sheldon Goldman and three colleagues concluded that "the Clinton judicial legacy is one of diversity and appointing mainstream high quality judges and lawyers." Despite the Republican hostility toward minority and female nominations, Clinton managed to increase the number of minority and female judges by about 68 percent from what it was on Inauguration Day 1991, and to reduce the federal judiciary from 80 percent white male to about

66 percent. Goldman and his colleagues found that "diversification was more successful during the first term than during the second, although the record for both terms is impressive. For the first term a record-breaking 52.1 percent of all appointees were nontraditional. Never before in American history had an American president recruited a majority of his appointees from women and racial minorities. During the second term that proportion dipped, but even so more than four in ten appointees were nontraditional, a record surpassing that of every other president." Seventeen percent of his District Court appointees were minorities and 28.5 percent were women, one in seven of whom was a minority. On the Courts of Appeals, of his sixty-one appointees sixteen, or more than 28 percent, were minorities, and twenty, or thirty-two percent, were female. Overall, for his entire presidency, minorities and women accounted for almost 51 percent of his appointments.[72]

Clinton's appointees also had higher ABA ratings than Bush, Reagan, or Carter; it was the highest level since the ratings began under Eisenhower. And, like those of his immediate predecessors, Clinton's appointees, particularly in his second term, were very affluent. More than half his appellate court appointees were millionaires, as were 38 percent of his district judges, with an increasing number in his second term. Clinton appointed more judges from large law firms than any of his immediate predecessors, and as political scientist Robert Carp, who studied the comparative liberalism and conservatism of judges appointed by Clinton and prior presidents put it, "You cannot be a radical or too liberal at these big firms." The Alliance for Justice also tracked the public interest activities of his nominees and found that public interest involvement declined as Republican opposition to liberals increased.[73]

Although the number of vacancies and judicial emergencies was still high when Clinton left office—eighty, including twenty-six appellate seats—Trent Lott remained untroubled. In January 2001, George W. Bush was inaugurated as President after one of the most bitterly disputed and problematic elections in American history. He took office pledging to unite the country, raising hopes that he would help cure what had become a troubled and malfunctioning judicial selection process. Those hopes would not be fulfilled.

• • •

1. David M. O'Brien *Judicial Roulette: Report of the 20th Century Fund Task Force on Judicial Selection* (Washington, D.C.: The Century Foundation Press, 1988).
2. Brown and Rodriguez, "A Judicial Legacy Can Now be Written," *The Legal Times,* November 11, 1996, p. 6.; David Maraniss, *First in His Class: A Biography of Bill Clinton* (Touchstone Books, 1996) p. 453.
3. Sheldon Goldman, "Judicial Selection Under Clinton: A Midterm Examination," 78 *Judicature* 276, 278 (1995) (Acheson)
4. Neil A. Lewis "G.O.P. to Challenge Judicial Nominees Who Oppose Death Penalty," *The New York Times,* October 15, 1993, p. A26.
5. Letter in author's file.
6. Linda Greenhouse "The Supreme Court: A Sense of Judicial Limits," *The New York Times,* July 22, 1993, p. A1.
7. Neil A. Lewis "High Court Nominee Defends Judges' Use of Broad Powers," *The New York Times,* July 7, 1993 p. A12.
8. Friends of the Earth, Inc. v. Laidlaw Environmental Services, Inc., 528 U.S. 167 (2000).
9. Karen O'Connor and Barbara Palmer, "The Clinton Clones: Ginsburg, Greyer, and the Clinton Legacy," 84 *Judicature* 262 (March-April 2001).
10. Neil A. Lewis, "For This Court Choice, Policy Is Passion," *The New York Times,* July 11, 1994, p. A13; William H. Freivogel., "Breyer Nomination Stirs Outrage, Delight: Liberal on Civil Rights, Conservative on Business," *St. Louis Post Dispatch,* May 15, 1994, p. 1A.; Sheldon Goldman, et. al., "Reactions to the Breyer Appointment," *Legal Times,* May 16, 1994. p. 21.
11. Eva M. Rodriguez, "Clinton's Justices: Not a Matched Set," *Legal Times,* November 14, 1994, p. 6.
12. Sheldon Goldman, "Judicial Selection Under Clinton: Mid-Term Examination," 78 *Judicature* 276, 285 (May-June 1995).
13. *Alliance for Justice,* 9th Annual Report on the State of the Judiciary 1994, p.10, p. 2. (hereafter AFJ).
14. Eva M. Rodriguez, "Judge-Pickers' Last Waltz," *Legal Times,* November 14, 1994, p. 6.
15. Naftali Bendavid, "Avoiding the Big Fight; Seeking Diversity, Not Confrontation; Missed Opportunity To Reshape Bench?," *Legal Times,* September 11, 1995, p. 1; Ibid.
16. Ibid.
17. Henry Weinstein, "Boxer Backs LA Judge, Attorney for Federal Bench; Courts Richard Paez and Samuel Paz are Recommended. They would be the First Mexican-

American to Serve on the Local District Court," *L.A. Times,* August 13, 1993, p. B1.;"Judiciary Watch; Two Pluses," *L.A. Times,* August 16, 1993, p. B6.

18. Weinstein and Hall, "L.A. Brutality Case Lawyer's Road to Judgeship Blocked; Courts: A Senate Panel Approved Samuel Paz. But Vehement Opposition From Police Groups has Stranded Him," *L.A. Times,* December 17, 1994, p. A1.

19. Joan Biskupic, "Facing Fights on Court Nominees, Clinton Yields," *The Washington Post,* February 13, 1995, p. A1.

20. George F. Will, "Edelman's Cloaked Agenda," *The Washington Post,* December 18, 1994, p. C7.

21. Anthony Lewis, "Abroad at Home; A Political Mugging," *The New York Times,* December 26, 1994, p. 39.

22. Carrie Johnson, "Why Clinton Shares Blame for Rejection of Missouri Bench Nominee," *Legal Times,* October 11, 1999, p. 1.

23. Joan Biskupic

24. AFJ 1995, p. 13.

25. J. Harvie Wilkinson III, "We Don't Need More Federal Judges," *The Wall Street Journal,* February, 1998, p. A19.

26. United States v. Bayless, 913 F. Supp. 232 (S.D.N.Y. 1996).; United States v. Bayless, 921 F. Supp. 211 (S.D.N.Y. 1996).

27. The study was by Ronald Stidham, Robert A. Carp, and Donald R. Songer, "The Voting Behavior of President Clinton's Judicial Appointees," 80 *Judicature* 16, 19 (July-August 1996).

28. Joan Biskupic, "Hill Republicans Target 'Judicial Activism'; Conservatives Block Nominees, Threaten Impeachment and Term Limits," *The Washington Post,* September 14, 1997, p. A1.

29. Cass R. Sunstein, "In Court v. Congress, Justices Concede One," *The Washington Post,* Outlook Section, December 21, 2003, p. B3.

30. Bush v. Gore, 531 U.S. 98 (Dec. 2000).

31. Jonothan Groner, "As Judge-Picker, Dole Is No Ronald Reagan; Likely GOP Presidential Nominee Favors Mainstreamers - to Dismay of Some Conservatives," *Legal Times,* April 1, 1996, p. 1.

32. Al Kamen, "Benched," *The Washington Post,* June 5, 1996, p. A21.

33. The criteria for a "judicial emergency" have since been changed to take a court's workload into effect.

34. Neil A. Lewis, "Move to Limit Clinton's Judicial Choices Fails," *The New York Times,* April 30, 1997, p. D22.

35. Joan Biskupic, "Hill Republicans Target 'Judicial Activism'. . ." *The Washington Post,* Sept. 14, 1997.

36. H. Lee Sarokin, "Sarokin's Letter Of Resignation," *New Jersey Law Journal,* June 10, 1996, p. 27.

37. *Alliance for Justice,* 12th Annual Report on the State of the Judiciary 1997. When where not specifically noted, the statistics in this and later chapters are drawn largely from the annual reports of the Alliance for Justice and from Sheldon Goldman's biennial reports in *Judicature,* both available online.

38. Sheldon Goldman, "Clinton's First Term Judiciary: Many Bridges to Cross," 80 *Judicature* 254, 271 (June 1997).; Neil A. Lewis, "Republicans Begin Clearing Backlog of Nominees," *The New York Times,* October 25, 1997, p. A9.

39. Saundra Torry, "Reno Blames Senate for Judicial Vacancies," *The Washington Post,* August 6, 1997, p. A1.

40. Orrin Hatch, "There's No Vacancy Crisis in the Federal Courts," *The Wall Street Journal,* August 13, 1997, A15.

41. Robert Schmidt, "Volunteering for Trouble," *The Legal Times,* November 10, 1997, p. 1.

42. "Judiciary Report: Congress Is Prodded," *The New York Times,* January 1, 1998, p. A14.
43. Neil A. Lewis, "Hatch Defends Senate Action On Judgeships," *The New York Times,* January 2, 1998, p. A1.
44. Comments from Senator Ashcroft on the "Proper Role of Judges," *The New York Times,* December 24, 2000, p. 16.
45. Cong. Rec. S 4418 May 14, 1999; Biskupic and Dewar, "More Scuffling Over Judgeships; Senate Confirms One Long-Pending Nominee, Keeps Another Waiting," *The Washington Post,* February 2, 1998, p. A21.
46. Neil A. Lewis, "Republicans Begin Clearing Backlog of Nominees" *The New York Times* 10/25/97 [ck]; Schmidt, Robert, "Senate Easing Judge Jam-Up," *The Legal Times,* February 9, 1998, p. 6.
47. Terry M. Neal and Lena Sun, "Gramm Taking Partisan Shot at Judicial Nominee," *The Washington Post,* August 19, 1997, p. A06; Neil A. Lewis, "Jilted Texas Judge Takes On His Foes in Partisan Congress," *The New York Times,* November 16, 1997, p. 1
48. Sheldon Goldman "Clinton's Second Term Judiciary: Picking Judges Under Fire," 82 *Judicature* 265, 271 (May-June 1999).
49. Quoted in AFJ 98:4; Nina Totenberg, National Public Radio, April 24, 2001
50. See www.cnn.com September 19, 1998.
51. Neil A. Lewis, "President Moves Quickly on Judges," *The New York Times,* March 11, 2001, p. 34.
52. *Alliance for Justice,* 13th Annual Report on the State of the Judiciary 19 99, p. 20.
53. Editorial Page, "Ashcroft's Ugly Victory," *St. Louis Post Dispatch,* October 6, 1999, p. B6. Donna Britt, "Judging Nominee by the Color of his Skin?," *The Washington Post,* October 9, 1999, p. A23. Deirdre Shesgreen and Jo Mannies, "Law Enforcement's Opposition to White was Courted by Ashcroft; Police Group's President Says it Rejected Senator's Request to Oppose Judge," *St. Louis Post Dispatch,* October 8, 1999 p. A6.
54. Ben White, "Deepening Rift Over Judge Vote; Minorities confirmed At a Lower Rate," *The Washington Post,* October 7, 1999, p. A03.; Thomas Oliphant, "Four senators play partisan politics and help derail a judge's nomination," *The Boston Globe,* October 11, 1999, p. A17; Ben White, "Deepening Rift Over Judge Vote; Minorities Confirmed At a Lower Rate"; Colbert I. King, "The Ghost of Ronnie White". WP, 10/9/99; Editorial "The Ronnie White Vote," *The Washington Post,* October 8, 1999, p. A28.
55. Christopher A. Bond, "My Judge White Decision," *The Washington Post,* November 1, 1999, p. A26
56. Deirdre Schesgreen and Bell, "Clinton May Renominate White for Bench, Official Says," *St. Louis Post Dispatch,* October 9, 1999, p. 4.
57. Nina Totenberg, *National Public Radio* 4/24/01; Goldman et al. "Clinton's Judges: Summing Up the Legacy," 240.
58. Henry Weinstein, " GOP Stonewall Creates Judicial Limbo; 9th Circuit: Lengthy Impasse Blocks Senate Vote on Two Nominees, Angering Latino and Women's Rights Activists," *The L.A. Times,* October 3, 1999, p. B1; Pianin and Babington "Long in Limbo, Judge Finally Will Get a Ruling," *The Washington Post,* March 6, 2000, p. A01; Joan Biskupic, "Politics snares court hopes of minorities and women Federal judges are more diverse, but minority nominees still twice as likely to be rejected," *USA Today,* August 22, 2000 p. 1A.
59. Henry Weinstein, n. 58
60. Eric Pianin and Charles Babington, "Long in Limbo, Judge Finally Will Get a

Ruling"; Johnson, Carrie, "Amicus Effort Pays Dividends for Chamber of Commerce," *The Legal Times,* June 28, 1999, p. 1.

61. Nina Totenberg, *National Public Radio* 4/24/01; Helen Dewar and Thomas B. Edsall, "Democrats Block Justice Picks; Senators Protest GOP Change in Judicial Vetting," *The Washington Post,* May 4, 2001, p. A01.; Editorial "A Shameful Performance," *The Washington Post,* October 6, 1999, p. A32.

62. Interview with former Democratic staffers, Sept. 23, 2003.

63. Herman Schwartz, "The Courts; The GOP's Judicial Delays and the Cost to Minorities," *The L.A. Times,* February 15, 1998, p. M1.; Joan Biskupic, n. 58

64. 2000 AFJ p.9

65. Sherman v. Smith, 70 F.3d 1263 (4th Cir. 1995) (Unpublished)

66. Edwin Chen, "Clinton Fumes about Judgeships; Politics: Talking to the NAACP, the President Unleashes an Emotional Attack Over GOP Obstacles to Minority Nominees to the Federal Appeals Court," *The Los Angeles Times,* July 14, 2000, p. 12.; Ibid.

67. Joan Biskupic

68. Nancy L. Choy, "Judicial Confirmation Logjam must be broken; Federal Courts: A Chinese American Woman Nominated to a State [sic] Judgeship Has Been Waiting for More than a Year for a Hearing," *The L.A. Times,* July 19, 2000, p. B9;

69. People For the American Way Foundation, President Bush, The Senate and the Federal Judiciary; Unprecedented Situation Calls for Unprecedented Solution"; October 17, 2001, p.6]

70. Goldman, et al. n. 70 at p. 84.

71. David Byrd, "Clinton's Untilting Federal Bench" p. 556; Ibid., p. 112

72. Sheldon Goldman, Elliot Slotnick, Gerard Gryski, and Gary Zuk, "Clinton's Judges: Summing Up the Legacy" 2001 p. 84 *Judicature* (2001).

73. David Byrd, "Clinton's Untilting Federal Bench," *The National Journal,* February 19, 2000, p. 555.

Chapter 5

George W. Bush's Judges

2001–2002

George W. Bush took the oath of office as a minority president. He had received a half-million votes less than Vice President Al Gore and was clearly the choice of only about 48 percent of the electorate, since most of the 2.6 million Nader votes were almost certainly hostile to him; he had eked out a five-vote Electoral College victory, because of a Florida election that was a textbook case of how things can go wrong, both deliberately and unwittingly. In the eyes of many, he was president only because of a politically motivated Supreme Court decision by five Republican justices that immediately became one of the most bitterly disputed and widely criticized Supreme Court rulings in American history. In addition, the Republicans had a thin House majority and the Senate was evenly split at 50-50; only the vice president's tiebreaking vote enabled the Republicans to organize and control the Senate. Even that was shaky because the Republicans included the frail 98-year-old Strom Thurmond and an unhealthy Jesse Helms.

In similar circumstances in 1824, John Quincy Adams, also a president's son, had said, "less possessed of your confidence, in advance, than any of my predecessors, I am deeply conscious of the prospect that I shall stand more and oftener in need of your indulgence." Bush had no such inhibitions, once again reaffirming the political maxim that no matter how slim the victory or how it was won, the victor will use the office to its utmost. Acting as if he had been given a mandate, Bush immediately embarked on a hard-right conservative course, later using the nation's shock and fear as a result of the September 11, 2001 tragedy to promote his domestic policies as well as his foreign policy. Although he had talked during the campaign about uniting the country and had presented a moderate face with the slogan "compassionate conservatism," he chose not to govern that way. Immediately after his inauguration, corporate lobbyists were handed the bill-writing for major economic legislation over such matters as energy, the environment, and worker safety; severe tax cuts favoring the top brackets were proposed and soon passed; pollution control and other environmental measures were rolled back by executive orders; worker safety and health regulations that had been worked on for years were canceled. Social conservatives also got what they wanted: These included an anti-abortion measures at home and abroad; lowering of the wall of church/state separation with "faith-based" social programs; prosecutions and other penalties for the medical use of marijuana and for assisting terminally ill patients to commit suicide; and cutbacks on family planning programs abroad. Hard-core Federalist Society members were placed in key positions throughout the administration. Two months after Bush was sworn in, the *Washington Post* wrote, "President Bush is quietly building the most conservative administration in modern times, surpassing even Ronald Reagan in the ideological commitment of his appointments, White House officials and prominent conservatives say. . . . [There is] an absence of moderate dissent." Conservative

Michael Horowitz concurred, saying, "In many respects, this is better than the Reagan administration." [1]

Some speculated that Bush's rightward tilt resulted from his fear of losing his conservative base, which had contributed to his father's loss in 1992. Now, however, there is little doubt that his heart was with the far right from the start, and conservatives quickly recognized this. His choice of Dick Cheney as his vice president over many moderates was an early signal. While a congressman, Cheney had voted against the Safe Water Drinking Act, fair-housing legislation, federal support for AIDS testing and counseling, funding for school lunches for poor children, and even against a resolution urging freedom for Nelson Mandela. Cheney was very close to the elder Bush. He had been the latter's secretary of defense, and was obviously going to be a key policy-maker in the new administration and a mentor to the inexperienced son.

Unlike Clinton, Bush took the ideology of his judicial nominees very seriously. According to Alberto Gonzales, Bush's White House counsel, for Bush, "filling these judgeships is a priority." Gonzalez himself described judicial selection "as perhaps the most important thing a president does." What Bush was looking for was clear during the presidential campaign when he named Supreme Court Justices Scalia and Thomas as the judges he most admired. [2]

As soon as Bush took office, the administration moved on judges. Bush appointed John Ashcroft, who had lost his bid for reelection to his opponent's widow, as his attorney general over strong opposition; forty-two senators voted against him. Within two months after inauguration, Ashcroft and Gonzalez organized a Judicial Selection Committee of young conservative lawyers from the White House and the Justice Department. Most were Federalist Society members and had clerked for conservative judges like Scalia, Thomas, Luttig, Silberman, and others. Some, like Associate White House Counsel Brett Kavanaugh, had worked for Kenneth Starr in the Whitewater and Monica Lewinsky cases; Kavanaugh wrote part of the Starr report on the Lewinsky affair. Others had worked on the Florida election proceedings. Viet Dinh, a Georgetown law professor, O'Connor clerk, and a John Ashcroft protégé, was appointed assistant attorney general in the Office of Legal Policy, and was in charge of the confirmation process. Their mantra was "no more Souters." Many were still furious about the Bork nomination, one of their heroes and a cochair of the Federalist Society board of governors. "For some of these people, these conservative lawyers, the issue of who gets to be a federal judge is the only thing that matters," Professor Michael Gerhardt, who has closely studied the confirmation process, told the *New York Times*. In keeping with the administration's penchant for secrecy, the administration refused to reveal the names of the team except for Kavanaugh and Dinh; preceding administrations had not been so secretive. Clint Bolick was very pleased with the group. "Gonzalez has put together a top notch team of young lawyers who are very committed to conservative ideals."[3]

Federalist Society members were not only involved in judicial selection but were strategically placed throughout the administration. Lee Liberman, now Lee Liberman Otis, became general counsel to the Department of Energy, and Spencer Abraham, another of the Federalist Society founders, was named secretary of energy. (Abraham had lost his senatorial seat.) Ashcroft and his chief subordinates were also Federalist Society members, as were Solicitor General Theodore Olson, five of the eleven lawyers in the White House Counsel's office, and Interior Secretary Gale Norton (who had once said in 1996 that when the South lost the Civil War, states' rights suffered a grievous blow). Grover Norquist, among the nation's most influential right-wing political strategists, said happily, "If

Hillary Clinton had wanted to put some meat on her charge of a 'vast right-wing conspiracy,' she should have had a list of Federalist Society members and she could have spun a more convincing story."[4]

The team had much to work with. By March, there were 100 judicial vacancies including thirty-one appellate slots, and there would soon be thirteen retirements. The committee worked fast. By April, they had screened some seventy candidates. According to the New York Times, seventeen of the first twenty candidates were recommended by the Federalist Society.[5]

In March, the right finally got its revenge against the American Bar Association for the ABA's failure to support Bork in 1987. On March 22, the White House announced that the ABA would no longer be given the names of potential nominees as part of the screening process but only after their nomination, ending a fifty-year policy adhered to by nine presidents. This made it unlikely that lawyers would speak openly to the ABA committee, for if the nominee was confirmed and it was revealed that a lawyer had spoken against the nominee, the lawyer was in trouble. Nan Aron of the Alliance of Justice attributed the ABA's removal also to the administration's insistence on "total and complete secrecy" in all of its doings. The Democrats protested, but to no avail.

Removal of the ABA greatly upset the organization, and it appears that it decided to placate the administration. The ABA works through circuit representatives and the District of Columbia Circuit representative was Fred Fielding, a former Reagan administration lawyer involved in that administration's judicial selection process. After reviewing two of Bush's nominees to the District of Columbia Circuit and voting favorably on them, he left the ABA committee in order to cofound the Committee for Justice. C. Boyden Gray and Bush Sr. to promote the president's nominees. Cheryl Dinkins, another Republican Party activist, was appointed chairman of the ABA's judicial review committee in August 2002.

Democrats were more incensed over Hatch's announcement that the blue-slip system would no longer be honored so long as the White House "consulted" with both home-state senators. Hatch claimed to be following past practice, but his claim was belied by the language he himself added to the blue-slip form in 1998 that "no further proceedings will be scheduled until both blue slips have been returned by the nominee's home-state senators."[6]

A word about the blue-slip system. Although its origins are not entirely clear, it appears that it developed in the 1950s as what one student of the process calls "the institutionalization of 'senatorial courtesy.' " When a judicial nomination is made, the chair of the Senate Judiciary Committee sends "blue slips" (so called because of the color of the paper) to the senators of the nominee's home state. The practice has been that if even one senator declines to return the slip, then the nomination is dead, or at least that further action is unlikely, depending on what the chair decides to do. The blue-slip procedure is employed only by the Judiciary Committee and only for federal judges. Other nominees to any post, however, including judges, can be stopped by senators who put a "hold" on a nominee, or by chairs of committees who refuse to hold confirmation hearings. The Senate majority leader can also halt a nomination by refusing to schedule an up-or-down vote.[7]

Although the blue-slip system applied only to judicial nominees, the other blocking devices can be used against a nominee for any office that requires senatorial consent. All of these methods were used frequently by the Republicans to block Clinton nominees, with anonymity usually cloaking the senator who either withheld a blue slip or placed a hold on a nominee.

There is some research indicating that until recently, a refusal to return a blue slip was actually quite rare. The system is designed to give senators, even those of the other party, the ability to force the president to negotiate on the vacancy. In the past it was therefore used primarily to delay, but in recent years it has come to be used by senators from each party to kill a nomination. In 2001, when the Democrats took control of the Senate after Vermont Republican Jim Jeffords's change of party, the Republicans for the first time agreed to disclose who was using the blue slip, a reform Senator Kennedy had sought many years earlier. An effort to force disclosure of all floor "holds" has never succeeded, however, despite an agreement by Daschle and Lott in 1999 and further attempts in 2003.

The Democrats' concern about Hatch's modification of the blue-slip system was not lessened by what the White House considered "consultation." According to Gonzalez, he had met with the Judiciary Committee periodically since early February "to solicit their input, to get their advice, to ask for their help in getting the president's nominations," but even Hatch admitted that these meetings were little more than a "listening session," as New York Democrat Charles Schumer put it. Democratic Senator Dianne Feinstein commented that "consult" really amounted to "insult." Maryland Senators Paul Sarbanes and Barbara Mikulski received this treatment when discussing a possible Fourth Circuit nominee from Maryland, Peter D. Keisler, a leading member of the Federalist Society and a former law clerk to Robert Bork. During their half-hour meeting with Gonzalez, he never asked for their opinion but simply praised Keisler.[8]

By May, the Democrats were ready to fight, particularly over what were now five Fourth Circuit vacancies out of fifteen. Little was heard any more from Helms about too many judges. When Wilkinson was asked about his prior comments on the virtues of small courts, he said merely that "my position remains the same as it has been for the past decade." During the following years Bush made five nominations to Wilkinson's court, but nothing more was heard from him about the damage to "collegiality" that filling the vacancies would produce.[9]

Before leaving office in January 2001, Clinton had renominated nine appellate judges, including Roger Gregory, who was already sitting on the Fourth Circuit by virtue of a recess appointment, as well as female and minority candidates Helen White, Bonnie Campbell, Kathleen McCree Lewis, Enrique Moreno, and James Wynn. Taking Bush at his word about "setting a new tone in Washington," the *Washington Post* urged him to look closely at the nine Clinton nominees and to renominate Ronnie White. Bush promptly made it clear that he would not even consider renominating White and withdrew all nine in March.

By the end of April, Bush was ready with his first group of nominees. White House officials told the *Wall Street Journal* they hoped to send up fifty nominations. At the urging of Virginia Republicans John Warner and George Allen, Bush included Roger Gregory. Overall, the federal appellate bench was almost evenly split and about 15 percent vacant, largely because of the Republican tactics during Clinton's administration. If Bush filled all the appellate vacancies "with one fell swoop" Republicans would be able to "dominate the courts of appeals," observed Sheldon Goldman. Aware of this, Democrats threatened to block all nominations unless the blue-slip system were kept just as it had been under the Republicans. Though uncomfortable with ideological battles, according to Nina Totenberg most Democrats felt they had no choice in the face of a determined effort to tilt the federal courts even further to the right for many decades to come. "We are not going to be rolled over," warned Schumer.[10]

Republicans professed to find Schumer's remarks "stunning," as Sessions put it. "We don't need to have litmus tests on judges. The qualifications of judges is discipline, and will they enforce the laws passed by Congress." As the *Washington Post* pointed out, however, Sessions "was among the most tenacious of senators in . . . being that single senator who could frustrate the president's will. He, along with Senator Bob Smith, is believed to have been responsible for stalling the nominations to the Ninth Circuit Court of Appeals of the well-qualified Richard Paez and Marsha Berzon. Now that President Bush is scheduled to send up his first nominations today, Sen. Sessions is waxing eloquent about respect for presidential appointment powers, and doing so without blushing." [11]

On the eve of Bush's announcement of the nominations, the *Wall Street Journal*'s Paul Gigot complained that the "Democrats have decided to turn judicial selection into political blood-sport." Gigot had apparently slept through the preceding six years.

Bush had originally planned to send up fifteen names. In a gesture aimed at easing the way for his nominees, he held back a few of the most controversial choices, and named two Democratic African-Americans, Roger Gregory to the Fourth Circuit, and Judge Barrington Parker Jr. to the Second, 39-year-old Hispanic lawyer Miguel Estrada to the District of Columbia Circuit, and three women. The controversial choices he postponed included Caroline Kuhl, a California state judge who had been one of the most extreme members of Reagan's Justice Department, and Christopher Cox, an equally conservative member of Congress, against whom both California senators protested.

Bush lost little by delaying the Kuhl and Cox nominations. The Ninth Circuit had so many Clinton appointees that the two would have made relatively little difference except on occasional panels. The Parker and Gregory nominations also changed little, for the Second Circuit to which Parker was nominated was already Democratic, and the Fourth was not only solidly conservative but Bush sent up two more conservatives with Gregory.

It was not immediately apparent, but all the nominations besides Gregory and Parker were very conservative. Many of them like Miguel Estrada, Jeffrey Sutton, Priscilla Owen, Edith Clement, and Michael McConnell were members of the Federalist Society. The choice of Gregory for the Fourth Circuit, who might be expected to line up with the few liberals on that court, was more than balanced by the nomination of Judge Dennis Shedd, a former aide to Strom Thurmond, and Judge Terence Boyle, Jesse Helms's protégé. North Carolina Democrat John Edwards, who had seen his nomination of James Wynn blocked by Helms, threatened to fight Boyle's nomination unless Gregory and Wynn were put on the circuit. To the Sixth Circuit, which was balanced between seven Democratic and seven Republican appointees, Bush nominated Sutton, the chief advocate for the conservative attack on federal authority in the name of federalism, and Ohio Supreme Court Justice Deborah Cook, an equally conservative nominee. Bush's other picks were McConnell, a law professor who frequently argued in the Supreme Court and in the law journals against church/state separation, abortion rights, and for other right-wing causes, and Texas Supreme Court Justice Priscilla Owen, who frequently voted against plaintiffs in abortion rights; in some cases she was the lone dissenter on a conservative court. McConnell was proposed for the Tenth Circuit, which covers Oklahoma, Kansas, New Mexico, Colorado, Utah, and Wyoming, and Owen to the Fifth, which is Texas, Mississippi, and Louisiana. The only May 9 nominee who drew no opposition was District Judge Edith Clement.

A week later, Bush nominated two district judges. A week

after that, on May 22 and 23, Bush nominated Hatch aide Sharon Prost to the Federal Circuit, which handles patents, customs matters, and suits against the United States for the lost value of property resulting from environmental regulation. He also nominated Levinski Smith, an antiabortion advocate and a conservative African-American, and William Riley to the Eighth Circuit.

Although fights loomed, it seemed likely that Bush would obtain most and perhaps all his choices despite the narrow Republican majority. Republican discipline is very strong, as the Ronnie White vote showed, and although some Democrats seemed ready to fight, their holding together on judicial nominations was dubious, especially since the party included very conservative Democrats like Zell Miller of Georgia and Ben Nelson of Nebraska, who usually voted with the Republicans, and John Breaux of Louisiana who often did.

Less than two weeks later, on May 21, Hatch scheduled hearings to be held May 23 for John Roberts, Sutton, and Cook. Democrats protested the speed with which the hearings were called, denying them time to investigate the nominees and to prepare. They also complained about the scheduling of three circuit nominees at one hearing, together with two Justice Department nominees. Hatch had not moved so swiftly during the Clinton years; indeed, he had continually asked for extensions when Democrats controlled the Senate. The Senate was working into the night on the tax bill, however, and Hatch agreed to postpone the hearing. But it was a sign of things to come.

And then the world—or at least the United States Senate—turned upside down.

On May 24, Vermont Republican Senator Jim Jeffords announced he was leaving the Republican Party to become an independent and would vote with the Democrats on organization. The Republican Party had moved too far to the right for him and the administration and Senate leadership had treated him with near-contempt. The Judiciary Committee and judicial nominations would now be under the control of Democrats. Within days, Cox withdrew.

The Senate Republicans were appalled by the switch. Those who had been on the bottom were now on top. Judiciary Committee and other Republicans feared payback time—what they had done to Clinton might now be done to Bush and to them by the Democrats.

The judicial nomination process was just one of the Republicans' many worries, but it was a big one. Lott threatened to shut down the Senate reorganization with a filibuster unless Republicans were guaranteed that all their nominations would be speedily moved to the Senate floor for a vote, even when they were rejected by the committee. Although he soon backed off the filibuster threat, the Democrats nevertheless assured him that they would handle the Bush nominees fairly and expeditiously.[12]

Undeterred by Jeffords's defection, Bush continued to send up controversial nominations. On May 25, he nominated Timothy Tymkovich to the Tenth Circuit, and Mississippi District Judge Charles Pickering to the Fifth. Tymkovich had vigorously opposed gay rights, and Pickering had a controversial civil rights and abortion record. On June 6, the Senate formally changed hands. The Democrats would not engage in "payback," said the new majority leader Tom Daschle of South Dakota. In June, Bush nominated Harris Hartz, a former New Mexico appeals court judge and Federalist Society member, to the Tenth Circuit.

One result of the switch was a final agreement on California nominations that would give each party the ability to veto unacceptable district judges for the state's four districts.

Schumer also scheduled hearings on judicial selection criteria, opening on June 26 with hearings on the proper role of ideology in the process.

Reorganization moved slowly, primarily because the Republicans insisted on an assurance that if any home-state senator wanted to veto a judicial nominee, it should be public. That is a "good government, sunshine provision," said Gramm solemnly. He was obviously right, regardless of the blatant hypocrisy, and the Democrats soon acquiesced. Conveniently forgetting the preceding six years, Republican Mitch McConnell of Kentucky insisted at a Senate hearing that "a president is entitled to tilt the judiciary any way he wants." Committee for Justice founder C. Boyden Gray condemned "ideological inquiries" as "perilous because of the message they send to the public at large." There was no more talk from Hatch, Sessions, and others about the need to block "judicial activists." Hatch had one of his now frequent memory losses, declaring that Republicans had not blocked Clinton appointees because Clinton got almost as many nominees confirmed as Reagan. The sixty-three Clinton nominees who never even got a floor vote apparently did not count.[13]

The Judiciary Committee was finally organized, and on July 11, it held its first hearing. To start on a positive note, it heard only Roger Gregory and two Montana district judges, who were easily confirmed on July 20. There would be no such smooth sailing for other Circuit Court nominees.

The Democrats seemed totally uninterested in district judges. Throughout the seventeen months that the Democrats controlled the Senate, they confirmed almost all of the District Court nominations Bush sent up in 2001–02, a total of eighty-three out of ninety-eight nominations. Of the fifteen who did not get hearings, thirteen lacked either an ABA rating or a positive blue slip from a home-state senator. Several of these could have been expected to face opposition. For example David Bunning, the son of Kentucky Senator Jim Bunning, was rated "not qualified" by a majority of the ABA because his legal career and experience was "very limited and shallow," and he was otherwise undistinguished. Paul Cassell was a Utah law professor who had devoted his career to expanding use of the death penalty and to opposing rights for defendants in criminal cases. His particular target was *Miranda v. Arizona*, which he unsuccessfully urged the Supreme Court to overturn.

Perhaps more noteworthy was the Democrats' refusal to challenge Terry Wooten. Wooten was Thurmond's counsel during the Clarence Thomas hearing, and he was accused by David Brock of having improperly given Brock papers from a raw FBI file on Angela Wright, who had been ready to corroborate Anita Hill's story about Thomas's behavior. According to Brock, Wooten was assisting Brock with a book that smeared Anita Hill in order to vindicate Thomas after the latter took his seat on the Court. When Wooten allegedly leaked the file to Brock, the Senate was investigating leaks of other FBI files during the Thomas hearings. Brock recanted the scurrilous comments he had made in the book about Hill and Wright, and when Wooten was nominated by Bush for a South Carolina district judgeship, Brock filed a sworn statement with the Judiciary Committee describing what he now claimed Wooten had done. Wooten denied this, of course, though he admitted talking to Brock and having had the file. Brock's charges met with skepticism by Leahy who said "I can't believe he [Wooten] would lie before the committee." The FBI investigated and found that Brock had indeed obtained the file, but made no finding about how he got it. The committee approved Wooten and the Senate confirmed him 98-0.

That Ron Clark was guilty of improper behavior was not in dispute. Clark was a Texas state legislator and a close friend of

George W. Bush. He was running for reelection in an election in which the speakership of the Texas House of Representatives was also at stake, with the vote for the latter expected to be close. Eight days after his Senate confirmation, it was revealed that he had asked Bush to postpone signing his commission as a judge until after the Texas election, so he could be reelected and vote for his choice as Speaker. Even though Clark's seat was classified as a "judicial emergency" and Bush's spokesman Ari Fleischer was complaining that the Senate was not filling vacancies fast enough, Bush acceded to Clark's request.

Clark's postconfirmation campaigning violated Canon 7 of the Code of Conduct for United States Judges, which bars judges from participating in partisan elections; Canon 1 of the code expressly applies the canons to "judges and nominees for judicial office." This obviously applied to Clark, for as legal-ethics expert NYU Professor Steven Gillers observed, "this man is, for all intents and purposes, a judge." When the press reported Clark's request, and Bush's willingness to go along, it drew wide criticism, and Bush quickly signed the commission. Clark agreed to give up active campaigning but "said he still hopes to win," which he did.[14]

In making his District Court nominations, Bush virtually ignored the Democrats, and refused to consult with home-state senators, apart from the agreement on California and a somewhat similar arrangement in Washington. Both states were in the Ninth Circuit, where the appellate court was dominated by Clinton appointees, so it was not that important to the White House who the district judges were.

By early August, Leahy had held numerous hearings on executive branch nominees, two hearings on judicial nominees, and was preparing to hold two more hearings in August during the recess, an unusual move. Hearings had not yet been held on Estrada, Roberts, Sutton, or McConnell, and Leahy came under heavy fire from the Republicans for not moving faster on these and Bush's forty-four other nominations. Leahy pointed out that no hearings were held in May or June while Republicans still controlled the committee. He also noted that the takeover did not take place until June 5, but the Republicans had jockeyed for power until early July, and he had scheduled two hearings during the August recess, which was virtually unprecedented. By Labor Day, four nominees had been confirmed and three more had hearings.

Then, September 11 happened and after that the anthrax scare, which forced evacuation of Senate office buildings. The administration quickly introduced what was to become the USA-PATRIOT ACT, and the Senate Judiciary Committee promptly turned its attention to the administration bill.

In the USA-PATRIOT ACT, Ashcroft, Viet Dinh, and the FBI dumped in everything that Justice Department prosecutors and the FBI had been trying to get for years but without success. Obviously, this was the time. The bill contained so many potential civil liberties violations that even conservative Republicans objected. Nevertheless, the law that emerged six weeks later, 342 pages long, was filled with provisions that few of those who voted for it had even read, and it became subject to increasing criticism as people began to realize what was in it.

All this was still in the future, as Judiciary Committee members tried to decipher the massive bill. The bill and the evacuation of Senate offices because of the anthrax letters which were sent to Daschle and Leahy, necessarily delayed the committee's consideration of judicial nominees and provided the Republicans with further ammunition for their attacks on Leahy and the Democrats. Following a suggestion of a *Wall Street Journal* editorial shortly after September 11, the Republicans linked judicial nominations to the war on terrorism. "Anyone who is interested in helping the president in the war on terrorism should support the president's judicial nominees," Hatch told reporters. There weren't enough judges to issue wiretap and other warrants and subpoenas, he argued. When reporters pressed him for evidence of a slowdown in these matters, he admitted there was none.

Nevertheless, on November 7, the *Washington Post* reported that:

> Chris Myers, senior communications adviser for the Senate Republican Conference, is working to put something together that will use the war on terrorism to force Democrats to confirm more GOP judges.
>
> Myers, in an e-mail Thursday to White House and other GOP aides, said that Sen. Rick Santorum (Republican-Pa.) has been talking with Senate Republican Leader Trent Lott (Miss.) about "a press event to speed the pace of confirmations," with "a more specific linking of the new terrorism bill to the need for judges. Our message would be: You can't get wire taps, search warrants, etc. without judges; confirm the president's slate so that efforts to capture terrorists won't be delayed
>
> . . . .
>
> In his e-mail, Myers wanted some specific help: "Also, we'd love to have evidence of a slowed investigation because of the lack of judges. Who could help us with this? Judiciary Committee? Dept. Of Justice?"[15]

Unhappily for Myers, as for Hatch earlier, there still was no such evidence. Nor could there be, for warrants, subpoenas, and initial hearings for people who are arrested are usually handled by magistrates. These are not appointed by the president, are not subject to Senate confirmation, and there was no evidence of any shortage. Moreover, the Republican complaints were primarily about appellate nominees, who have virtually nothing to do with warrants, subpoenas, and arrestees. Even the Republicans did not charge delay in confirming district judges, who would handle these matters if no magistrates were available—by November 7, the committee had held hearings on eighteen of the twenty-two District Court nominees sent up before Labor Day, despite the crises and the evacuation of Senate offices.

All this, however, did not affect the Republican strategy of claiming that the Democrats' delay was impeding the war on terrorism. The Republican senators held a press conference on November 8, and billed the meeting as a "push for quick confirmation of federal judges in the war on terrorism." At the meeting, Santorum declared, "At a time when we're facing unprecedented, not just terrorism, but other kinds of actions here in this country, it's vitally important that our federal judiciary is as robust as possible and able to deal with the issues at hand." [16]

Right-wing groups chimed in. The Center for Reclaiming America wailed that "the holdup of these nominees threatens the war on terrorism, because these judicial vacancies need to be filled as soon as possible to act on law-enforcement requests." Concerned Women for America complained that "Senate Democrats are deliberately limiting the ability of federal courts to bring criminals to justice." Radio talk-show host Hugh Hewitt claimed that the effect of the Senate Democrats' actions was literally to "endanger the national security" as "American soldiers, sailors, airmen, and marines are in harm's way and the nation's civilians are under attack."

By the session's end, the Senate had confirmed twenty-seven judges, the same as the first full year of the Clinton administration, when Democrats were in control. These included twenty-one of thirty-six District Court nominees and six of twenty-eight appellate nominees. The committee had held more hearings and at a faster pace than during any of the last two terms of the Clinton administration when the Republicans controlled the process, especially with respect to appellate court nominees. Moreover, as Hatch well knew, the Democrats did not have seven full months but closer to five, and even that was interrupted by the summer recess, (during which Leahy held hearings) and the September 11 attack and its legislative aftermath. Even during the anthrax scare, Leahy held a hearing on Charles Pickering, concluding it minutes before the Capitol police evacuated the entire Capitol complex.[17]

At the end of the year, the *Washington Post*, which had urged Leahy to hold hearings on Estrada, Roberts, McConnell, and other circuit nominees, nevertheless commented, "We have been critical of Mr. Leahy for not moving more swiftly to confirm some of Mr. Bush's judges. But he did not create the current mess—a situation made all the more galling by the pious carping of those who presided over the system's collapse."[18]

Opening the second session of the 107th Congress, Leahy noted that in July Gonzalez had said he did not expect the Senate to confirm more than five judges in 2001, but as of January 25, 2002, the committee had reported thirty-two, confirmed twenty-eight, and was about to confirm two more. He compared this progress with prior Congresses and asserted that "for the first time, the Judiciary Committee is making public the blue slips." He also pointed out that senators still wanted ABA "peer review" and that removing the ABA from the prenomination screening process was partly responsible for many delays. Instead of having that ABA peer review done simultaneously with the FBI background check and having the ABA report come to the Senate about the same time as the FBI report and the nomination, the Senate now had to wait six or eight weeks after the administration sent up the nominee to get the ABA's views. He therefore urged the administration to reinstate the ABA in the prescreening process. He also promised another hearing on Pickering in two weeks, and hearings later for Owen, McConnell, and Estrada, all of whom had been nominated the previous May. Leahy went on to criticize what he called "the White House's unilaterism," and called on the president to work with and consult home-state senators, in order to find "consensus nominees" as Clinton had done.

To no one's surprise, his report was not well received by the Republicans and their allies. The same week, Bush sent up twenty-four more nominees. In his January 25, 2002, report, Leahy had praised Hatch and said he looked forward to working with him. In its year-end editorial, the *Washington Post* had described Hatch as "one of the good guys." No longer.

The first pitched battle was over Mississippi District Judge Charles Pickering, a Bush Sr. appointee who was nominated to the Fifth Circuit. Pickering was not a typical Bush appellate court nominee, for he was 64 when nominated and was not the high-powered intellect that so many of the right-wing nominees since Reagan had been. He was the father of a Mississippi congressman and a good friend of Trent Lott, however, and was nominated on May 25, two weeks after the first group. As noted above, he received a hearing on October 18, 2001, during the height of the anthrax scare.

The Democrats initially expected the nomination to be non-controversial. It soon appeared, however, that Pickering was very hostile to civil rights laws. He had published only ninety-nine written opinions in his eleven years on the bench, and some 1,100 unpublished opinions. In the latter, he displayed a special hostility to the Voting Rights Act and to the one-person-one-vote principle, calling the principle "obtrusive." He had also dismissed a very high proportion of employment discrimination cases because, he told the committee, the Equal Employment Opportunity Commission usually resolves the meritorious claims. This was ludicrous, because everyone knew that the EEOC had a backlog of 35,000 cases and litigated only 3.5 percent of the cases in which it found reason to believe there was discrimination.

His most troubling actions occurred in a 1994 case in which defendant Daniel Swan was convicted of burning a cross on the lawn of an interracial couple, and received the mandatory five-year sentence. After the conviction, Pickering aggressively and successfully sought to have the charges reduced after describing the cross-burning as a "drunken prank." First, Pickering pressured the government prosecutors in Mississippi. When they refused, he privately called Frank Hunger, a high-level official in the Justice Department from Mississippi and Vice President Gore's brother-in-law. This was a violation of the Judicial Code of Conduct. Hunger said he did not recall contacting the Civil Rights Division after Pickering called him, but the division ultimately dropped the cross-burning charge and Pickering reduced the sentence to two years. He claimed that he worked to have Swan's sentence reduced because Swan's two codefendants had received lower sentences. However, the other two defendants were a juvenile and a young adult with a borderline IQ, each had pled guilty to a lesser offense, and each testified against Swan. Furthermore, Swan had been the instigator of the cross-burning, had built the cross, and provided the gasoline and transportation to the interracial couple's lawn.

Problems with Pickering's candor before the committee also developed. When he was nominated for the District Court in 1990, he denied having had anything to do with Mississippi State Sovereignty Commission, a segregationist group infamous for harassing civil rights workers. It was now revealed that when Pickering was a state senator in the 1970s, he had asked the commission to "be advised of developments" in their investigations of unions in his hometown, and he approved appropriations for them. As a law student in 1959, Pickering had written an article to suggest ways in which the state could amend its Constitution to make interracial marriage unconstitutional. At his hearing, he said he was merely showing *how* the state could do it, not that it *should*, and said that he did not oppose such marriages.

Additionally, he was very hostile to *Roe v. Wade*. He was the primary mover behind the 1976 Republican platform plank calling for a Human Life Amendment to ban abortions, and he supported a plank in the platform opposing the Equal Rights Amendment for women. According to Leahy, religious groups initiated a phone campaign to Democratic senators' offices to urge them to vote for Pickering.[19]

As a trial judge, Pickering had a high reversal rate in his eleven years on the court—twenty-six—and all but one were by unanimous reversals. Particularly troubling was that fifteen of the reversals were of unpublished rulings, which under court rules are supposed to be issued only in cases involving well-settled principles of law. By contrast, Judge Edith Brown Clement, whose appointment to the appellate court the Democrats easily approved despite her known conservatism, had published fourteen times the number of opinions that Pickering had in her ten years on the district court. She had been reversed only seventeen times, and only once in an unpublished ruling.

Particularly troubling to many who were not partisan was Pickering's solicitation of letters supporting his nomination from lawyers who appeared before him and his demand that these letters be sent to him to forward to the Justice Department.

On the other hand, some of this, like the 1959 law review article, was in the distant past. Also, in 1967 he had testified against a Ku Klux Klan grand wizard accused of fire-bombing a civil rights activist. According to the *Washington Times* this testimony cost Pickering his reelection as a state prosecutor. It appeared, however, that this was not quite as noble as it seemed—Pickering challenged the Klan only after it bombed a local segregationist newspaper, frightening business leaders in Pickering's hometown of Laurel, Mississippi. He was a member of an interracial reconciliation commission and was supported by African-Americans from Mississippi who knew him, including Charles Evers, brother of murdered civil rights worker Medgar Evers. Some in the black community in his hometown admired him. He seemed to be someone who had accepted the need for racial harmony, but not the laws necessary to bring it about.[20]

On March 14, in three straight 10-9 party-line votes, the committee rejected Pickering, and the Republicans exploded. Hatch called it a "lynching" and a "smear job," and accused "the groups" of trying to change the ground rules; he did not specify what rules he had in mind. Lott threatened to retaliate and when majority leader Daschle refused in accordance with well-settled rules to send the nomination to the floor despite the rejection, Lott put a hold on a Daschle nominee to the Federal Communications Commission. Lott also tried to cut off Judiciary Committee funds for post–September 11 oversight.

Among the angry reactions was a *Wall Street Journal* op-ed by Virginia Thomas, the wife of Clarence Thomas and director of executive branch relations at the Heritage Foundation. Ms. Thomas, who was vetting résumés for the Republicans while *Bush v. Gore* was being decided, accused the Democrats of not considering Pickering "as human right now . . . Facts matter little" to Senate Democrats, she said, for they are "impervious to the truth." And, she added, their opposition to Pickering "doesn't hurt their fund-raising efforts." [21]

Bush went on the attack, characterizing the Democrats' refusal to send the nomination to the floor as "unconstitutional," and

praised Pickering as a fighter for racial justice. Bush also used
the issue in a major fund-raising drive in the states where senatorial contests were to take place during the fall, hoping to
develop a major campaign issue in the South. Other Republicans suddenly discovered a serious concern about judicial
vacancies.

Much more was involved, however, than another presidential fund-raising effort to shape the Senate according to his
liking. The Republican eruption was hardly spontaneous, nor
was it solely the result of the Pickering vote. Events soon
showed that it had been planned for some time. According to
John Nichols of *The Nation*, the very evening of the vote, Karl
Rove, Bush's chief political adviser, had a closed-door meeting
with 300 members of the Family Research Foundation, an
ultraconservative Christian group, at which he assailed the
Democrats for a "judicial lynching" of "a good man." The fundamental fight, Rove told the antiabortion group, was about
the courts, and the crucial fight was for the Supreme Court.[22]

Rove's goal was to mobilize the religious right. According
to his calculations, 4 million people who identified themselves
as Christian fundamentalists didn't vote in 2000. He wanted
their votes in 2004. Christian right activists like Gary Bauer
and James Dobson had told him that overruling *Roe v. Wade*
was the key to turning them out, and Rove decided to focus
on the courts.

Nichols also reported that in July Rove began to attend
meetings of the White House Judicial Selection group and to
hold strategy sessions with key senators and even House members to urge them to attack the Democrats for "politicizing"
confirmations. As usual Republican discipline was tight, and
even moderate Republican senators like Susan Collins of Maine
wore a "Remember Pickering" sticker. In July, Boyden Gray
reentered the scene, joining with Bush's father to raise money

for a public relations campaign against Senate Democrats up for reelection.

Rove's pet project was getting a seat on the Fifth Circuit, the same court to which Pickering had been nominated, for Priscilla Owen, a Texas Supreme Court judge and arch antiabortion judge. Rove and Owen had a long-standing relationship. Owen was a lawyer for oil and gas firms in 1994 when she hired Rove and paid him $250,000 to help her become a justice of the Texas Supreme Court in Texas's partisan elections for that bench. She was among Bush's first group of Appeals Court nominations in May 2001, and as Rove and Bush surely expected, her nomination set off another bitter fight, this time centering on abortion, as well as her close relationship with Texas business interests.

Owen's hearing was scheduled for July 23, 2002. But before that there was D. Brooks Smith. A 50-year-old federal District Court judge in Pennsylvania, Smith was nominated to the Third Circuit, which covers New Jersey, Pennsylvania, and Delaware. The court was fairly evenly split with six Democratic appointees and five Republican judges; there were three vacancies. During his fourteen years on the District Court, Smith, a Reagan appointee, was reversed some fifty times, most notably in cases involving rulings against workers and injured plaintiffs. In an age discrimination case, he dismissed a factory worker's suit because it was filed 300 days after the worker was fired, and not within 300 days after the man had received a performance evaluation. The appellate court reversed. In another case, the Court of Appeals ruled that Smith wrongly upheld a school rule allowing only women, not men, to take a year's unpaid leave when a child is born. In still another reversal, the court held that Smith should not have dismissed a suit by parents of a 15-month-old child who choked to death on a toy alleged to be dangerous.

Smith also took a narrow view of the Commerce Clause, telling a Federalist Society meeting in 1993 that Congress was passing laws that went far beyond its authority under the Commerce Clause. That clause, he argued, should be used only against "trade barriers." Under Smith's interpretation, African-Americans, women, and other groups would lose rights established under the current interpretation of the Commerce Clause. As Neil Lewis of the *New York Times* wrote, Smith's "talk before the conservative Federalist Society was the kind of thing that gets one noticed in influential administration circles." [23]

On the other hand, Smith had an expansive reading of the Fifth Amendment's Takings Clause, which is being used to challenge health, safety, and environmental regulations. In a case under the Coal Industry Retiree Health Benefit Act, Smith ruled that forcing a company to pay benefits to retired miners would constitute an illegal taking of the company's property even though the miners had earned the benefits, an interpretation other courts had rejected. [24]

At his hearing, Smith adopted what became the standard tactic used by right-wing nominees like Thomas, Ashcroft, Pickering, William Pryor, and others: a repudiation of what they had done, said, and written, and a promise that from now on, they would just follow the law. But as Lewis also observed, "it was those very arguments before the Supreme Court or their public statements or their active membership in the Federalist Society that won them the consideration to be nominated." [25]

The *Washington Post* editorial page was not usually sympathetic to the Democrats who opposed Bush's judicial nominees. As the judgeship wars intensified during the Bush administration, the *Post* became more and more angry with the Democrats. It recognized that they faced a dilemma created by Republican obstructionist tactics during the Clinton administration on the one hand, and Bush's nomination of very conservative judges on the other. The paper nevertheless insisted that Democrats let bygones be bygones, play by the previous rules, and consider only intellect, integrity, and judicial temperament. Only the most extreme reactionaries or those with ethical shortcomings were to be rejected.

What persuaded even the *Post* to oppose Smith was the combination of a failure to quit a club that discriminated against women, a conflict of interest, and attendance at junkets funded by conservative groups, often to elegant resorts that involved not only golf, but attendance at conservatively oriented seminars on antitrust, environmental law, reform, and similar issues. The *Post* summarized the ethical case against Smith as follows:

> For years, Judge Smith was a member of a fishing club whose bylaws exclude women. Before the Judiciary Committee in 1988, when nominated for the district bench, he acknowledged that norms of judicial ethics forbid membership in such an organization, and he committed himself to quitting the group if unable to persuade it to change its rules. On becoming a judge, he did urge change. He did not, however, resign. Not, that is, for 11 years—until the judgeship for which he has been nominated became vacant.
>
> Judge Smith also failed to recuse himself in a timely fashion from a case involving a bank for which his wife worked and in whose parent company he and his wife owned substantial amounts of stock. [Smith's wife, Karen Smith, was the vice president of Mid-State Bank at the time. Smith held $100,000 to $250,000 in Mid-State Bank stock and his wife had the same amount invested in a 401(k) with the bank.] The bank was not a party to the litigation. But it quickly became clear that the bank had potentially enormous liability. Yet Judge Smith remained on the case and issued a significant ruling before

finally recusing himself. [He admitted he should have withdrawn earlier, after ethics experts criticized his conduct.]

Finally, Judge Smith has offered an unacceptable defense of
his attendance at privately funded judicial junkets. Among the
many seminars Judge Smith attended was one sponsored by
the Law and Economics Center at George Mason Law School,
a very conservative group. Among the center's numerous con-
tributors was a company that had pending litigation before
Judge Smith and in whose favor he later ruled.

. . . .

Cumulatively, such infractions paint a picture of a judge
who has pushed ethical lines and then sought to rewrite the
rules retroactively to justify his behavior. It isn't a pattern this
Senate ought to reward.[26]

Pennsylvania senior Senator Arlen Specter nevertheless supported Smith vigorously. At the time, the Third Circuit had
three vacancies out of its fourteen-judge complement, and the
highly respected Judge Edward Becker spoke to Biden on
Smith's behalf. At first, Biden seemed dubious, but after Specter
worked on him, Biden came around to supporting Smith.
Edwards and Wisconsin's Herbert Kohl then followed suit, and
Smith received a 12-7 vote from the committee. Confirmation
followed on July 31, 2002, with a 64-35 vote.

A digression on the seminars attended by Smith may be
useful here. The Smith nomination was not the first time the
issue of attendance by judges at all-expenses-paid seminars at
elegant resorts funded by right-wing organizations had arisen.
In the late '70s and in 1980, news of such attendance first
appeared in the press. The Alliance for Justice challenged the
practice, many critical comments were made, but the Judicial
Conference did nothing. In 1993, the Alliance for Justice published *Justice for Sale*, one chapter of which studied judges'

judicial disclosure forms for 1989–90, and found that two of the most popular seminars were the "law and economics" program and "civil justice reform," the latter of which was intended to reduce plaintiff recoveries in product liability and other personal injury cases; the "civil justice reform" seminars were funded by Aetna Life and Casualty Foundation.

Then, in 1998 the Community Rights Council issued a report revealing that the Foundation for Research on Economics and the Environment, which described itself as promoting "free-market environmentalism," was holding seminars at elegant Montana ranches. (The 1996 seminar on Environmental Economics and Policy Analyses was held in September at Elkhorn Ranch, Big Sky, Montana.) In July 2000, the CRC issued a 122-page report that studied the financial disclosure forms of every judge from 1992 to 1998. It reported that during those years, 1,030 federal judges had gone to 5,800 of the privately funded seminars; more than 10 percent of the judges who attended did not report their attendance. The CRC found that

> the judicial education is overwhelmingly dominated by pro-market, anti-regulatory seminars offering a single and unchallenged line of reasoning in areas of law with many competing views. Indeed, the three organizations hosting the most trips—the Law and Economics Center (LEC), the Foundation for Research on Economics and the Environment (FREE) and Liberty Fund (collectively the "Big Three")—share a remarkably similar, and in some respects extreme, conservative/libertarian ideology.[27]

The report focused on the seminars' approach to agency regulations, expanding the Fifth Amendment Takings Clause, environmental protection efforts, the Commerce Clause, and access to the courts in environmental cases. In each area, reported the CRC, the author of every leading conservative decision attended at least one Big Three seminar. Most of the judges attended many times, sometimes while a pertinent case was before their court, and sometimes ruling in favor of a litigant backed by the same special interests that sponsored the judge's trip. The 1993 Alliance for Justice report quoted one judge as saying, "As a result of better understanding the concept of marginal costs . . . he said, 'I have recently set aside a $15 million antitrust verdict.'" The CRC report also noted that the most frequent attendees included District of Columbia Circuit Judge Douglas Ginsburg, District Judges Kenneth Ryskamp, and D. Brooks Smith.

Introducing the 2000 CRC report, former District of Columbia chief judge, White House counsel and congressman and now law professor Abner Mikva wrote:

> It may be a coincidence that none of these seminars and study sessions take place in Chicago in January, or Atlanta in July. It may be a coincidence that the judges who attend these meetings usually come down on the same side of important policy questions as the founders who finance these meetings. It may even be a coincidence that environmentalists seldom are invited to address the judges in the bucolic surroundings where the seminars are held. But I doubt it. More importantly, any citizen who reads about judges attending such fancy meetings under such questionable sponsorship will doubt it even more.[28]

The Federal Judicial Center also provided seminars. These however, were in such places as South Bend, Indiana, which did not feature golf or fishing, and were considered to "work the judges too hard."

Again, nothing happened, except that the ultraconservative

Leonidas Ralph Mecham, picked by Chief Justice Warren Burger to head the Administrative Office of the United States Courts, attacked the report.

Some senators were nevertheless disturbed. In 2000 Democrats John Kerry of Massachusetts and Russ Feingold of Minnesota introduced a bill to restrict judges to Federal Judicial Center seminars, but at this point Rehnquist weighed in, charging that the bill was "antithetical to our American system and its tradition of zealously protecting freedom of speech," and that the seminars "are a valuable and necessary source of education for judges." That ended that.[29]

The Texas Supreme Court is only one of ten state supreme courts whose members are chosen by partisan elections. Thanks to a major effort by Texas business groups to elect probusiness judges, it became one of the nation's most conservative state courts where business is concerned, noted for what Molly Ivins has called a "canine fidelity to corporate special interests." According to Ivins, Karl Rove has been involved in electing all nine justices. Priscilla Owen found even that court insufficiently conservative for her on corporate, abortion, and other matters, and she frequently dissented. As of July 2003, she had dissented eighty-seven times from such decisions.[30]

In its July 2002 report, the Alliance for Justice listed scores of cases in which Owen voted for the corporate litigant in worker, consumer, taxpayer, and environmental cases, often in dissent. In one case, the Texas Supreme Court struck down as unconstitutional a state law written to let a particular developer get around the City of Austin's water-quality rules. Owen wrote a scathing dissent, criticizing the majority for curtailing the development company's property rights. The majority, including Justice Alberto Gonzales (currently White House counsel), stated that "[m]ost of Justice Owen's dissent is nothing more than inflammatory rhetoric, and thus merits no response." She had received a total of $2,500 from the chairman of the company for her campaign as well as $44,958 from the developer's legal counsel.[31]

In another case, the court ruled that the Texas law on age discrimination, which is modeled on Title VII of the Civil Rights Act, required only that age be "*a* factor" in the discrimination, not *the* decisive factor; she dissented. She also broke with the majority in a case upholding a lower court ruling granting damages to the family of a teenager who was paralyzed when he was ejected through the car's sunroof in an accident.

The most disturbing of these cases is the Searcy case. Willie Searcy was an African-American teenager paralyzed in a head-on collision when a Mercury Cougar ploughed into the Ford pickup that Searcy's stepfather was driving, leaving Willie a ventilator-dependent quadriplegic. It would cost between $22 and $26 million to keep him alive.

Major donors to the Texas justices' political campaigns do particularly well. A study by Texans for Public Justice found that from 1994 to 1998, major donors won in twenty of twenty-six cases before the court. In Owen's case, she came out favoring her top donors in twenty-two of twenty-six.

One example of that was Willie Searcy's suit against Ford. The jury decided that Ford's seat belt had failed and awarded Willie's mother $30 million plus $10 million in punitive damages. Ford raised the usual delaying tactics that defendants use, but an appellate court upheld the $30 million while setting aside the punitive $10 million.

On appeal to the Texas Supreme Court, Ford was represented by Baker, Botts, which had given $20,450 to Owen's election campaign.

Willie needed care desperately and quickly, and his lawyer asked the Supreme Court to expedite the appeal. Willie's condition apparently made no impression on Owen, to whom the opinion was assigned. After sixteen months, she handed down a decision for a majority, but didn't rule on the award. Instead, she granted Ford's motion to retry the case in Dallas, a place that Ford considered friendlier, and his mother appealed. The court acknowledged that it should have granted a request by Willie's lawyer to speed up the case.[32]

In Dallas, the result was as Ford wished. Willie lost. On June 29, 2001, an appeals court ruled for Willie in a way that guaranteed he would win. It was too late. The patchwork system of family and volunteers that his mother had put together to care for Willie failed. On July 3, 2001, the night nurse left at 4 AM, no one was there, the ventilator wasn't working, and by 5 AM Willie was dead.

During the Judiciary Committee's hearing, Feinstein asked Owen why she took so long when the boy's life was at risk. "He did not pass away while the case was pending in my court," Owen replied.[33]

There are many more instances of her probusiness bias and hostility to environmentalism. They are set out in detail in the Alliance for Justice report on Priscilla Owen. By themselves, probusiness rulings would not be enough to doom a nomination, for many Democrats are as dependent on the business community as Republicans, although with less to show for it. It was the abortion issue that produced the number of Democratic votes necessary to kill the nomination, at least temporarily.

Owen's record in abortion cases was about as extreme as possible, leaving even fellow conservatives behind. Owen was a very committed evangelical Christian and showed it in her rulings. In a series of cases dealing with the rights of minor girls to an abortion, she came down again and again on the antiabortion side. The cases usually involved teenagers asking for court permission to have an abortion without getting permission from their parents, known as the "judicial bypass." In nine of twelve cases, she ruled against the teenager. In the most widely publicized of these cases, known as Jane Doe No. 1, involving a pregnant seventeen-year-old, she interpreted a newly enacted statute to require a minor who wanted permission from the court to have an abortion to "indicate to the court that she is aware of and has considered that there are philosophic, social, moral, and religious arguments that can be brought to bear when considering abortion." She claimed to be relying on the Supreme Court decision in the 1992 *Casey* case and a case from Akron, Ohio, but neither involved judicial permission for minors or required consideration of "religious arguments." A majority of the court sharply disagreed with her. Justice and now White House Counsel Alberto Gonzalez described Owen's interpretation of the statute as "an unconscionable act of judicial activism." As White House Counsel, Gonzalez, of course, supported her nomination.[34]

There were also ethical questions. In 1994, Enron's political action committee and executives gave Owen $8,600. In 1996, she wrote the majority opinion in a unanimous decision that reversed a lower court order and reduced by about $15 million the amount of school taxes paid by Enron. In another case, Owen voted to dismiss a malpractice suit against a law firm whose partner had made a substantial contribution to her election campaign. But this may be just the way Texas justice works.

Owen was also a notoriously slow judge whose backlog routinely held up the court. Several clerks recall times when Owen was so far behind that other justices ordered opinions to be taken from her chambers. One clerk cited as many as 200 pending cases in her chamber in a recent year.[35]

Owen went through the usual ritual of promising to abide by
the law, but few were fooled. Owen's fate at the 10-9 committee
turned on California Democrat Dianne Feinstein. At first, Feinstein seemed sympathetic to Owen, but then changed her mind
after talking to consumer advocates from Texas. On September
5, 2002, a 10-9 vote turned down the nomination making Owen
the second of the two negative votes handed down by the
Democratic-controlled committee.

That was not the end of the story, however. When the Senate
returned to Republican hands in the 2002 elections, Bush
renominated her over Democratic protests.

The most bitterly fought nomination was not over Owen but
over Miguel Estrada, a Washington, District of Columbia,
lawyer who had migrated to this country from Honduras. He
did well at Columbia and Harvard Law School, clerked for
Supreme Court Justice Anthony Kennedy, and then served as
an Assistant United States Attorney and as a junior lawyer in
the solicitor general's office, first under Bush and for four years
under Clinton. When nominated for the District of Columbia
Circuit with John Roberts, he was a 38-year-old partner in a
Washington law firm and a member of the Federalist Society.
Though a Honduran immigrant, he was hardly the typical Central American immigrant. The son of a well-to-do lawyer and
banker, he arrived in the United States as a 17-year-old,
having attended elite private schools in Honduras where he
learned English.

Estrada's nomination was unusual for the District of
Columbia Circuit because while he was certainly bright, he had
not held high public office and was not a well-known law
teacher or even a particularly distinguished lawyer. All the
members of that circuit, both the current judges and those of
recent memory, Republican and Democrat, have either held
high executive branch positions, usually at the presidential

appointment level, like Thomas, Scalia, Garland, Starr, Warren Burger, and Patricia Wald; were judges like Sentelle, Judith Rogers, and Skelly Wright, scholarly law professors like Stephen Williams and Harry Edwards, or distinguished middle-aged lawyers with extensive careers like David Tatel and, soon, John Roberts. Estrada was none of these, for he was not too different from many other bright lawyers under forty who had held junior government posts.

But he was Hispanic and known to be reliably, indeed extremely conservative. He was immediately seen on all sides as a possible Supreme Court candidate. However, he had not said or published anything that indicated what he thought, and at his hearing, he continually avoided answering any questions about his views, questions that had been asked and answered by many other nominees, from Supreme Court justices like Souter and Ginsburg to trial court judges. Estrada gave the impression that he could not recall discussing any Supreme Court rulings— including the most controversial—while working in the office of the solicitor general. When senators tried to pin him down on whether he agreed with key rulings, he gave highly evasive answers, asserting that he would have to read all the briefs and the oral argument to comment on such decision as *Roe v. Wade*! He was promptly labeled the "stealth" nominee. As one observer suggested: "If we are to accept his testimony on its face, he demonstrated an inordinate lack of intellectual curiosity within his professional field. At best, his responses were disingenuous. At worst, he may have lied to the committee." Scalia had also refused to answer any questions, perhaps because he might have to expose his views. But they were already well-known from his opinions on the Court of Appeals and his articles. In any event, attention was focused on Rehnquist, and Scalia received a free ride.[36]

It was also rumored that the Bush White House was advising

nominees to say as little as possible, but this was never sub-
stantiated. What is undisputed is that such advice was indeed
given by a high-level Republican—District of Columbia Circuit
Judge Laurence Silberman. At a Federalist Society luncheon in
April 2002, Silberman told his audience of 150 that in 1986,
when his colleague Antonin Scalia was nominated to the
Supreme Court, Silberman (who had been appointed to the
bench the year before), served as an advisor to Scalia. Said Silberman, "I was his counsel, and I counseled him to say nothing
[at his confirmation hearings] concerning any matter that
could be thought to bear on any cases coming before the
Court." Silberman claimed this kept Scalia out of trouble. He
added that Scalia should not even answer questions about *Marbury v. Madison*, the nearly 200-year-old case that established
the principle of judicial review. "I told him that as a matter of
principle, he shouldn't answer that question either," Silberman
said. He explained that once a prospective judge discusses any
case at all, the floodgates open and he would be forced to discuss other cases. Such a decision is, of course, not at all unethical so long as nominees do not commit themselves to voting
a particular way. And, as noted earlier, the White House had
instructed Clarence Thomas not to reveal his opposition to
Roe v. Wade.[37]

There was no justification for Estrada's refusal to respond to
the committee. As Professor Michael Gerhart, an expert on
judicial nominations wrote, "It is hard to see how the questions
Estrada has declined to answer would jeopardize his independence. He would not identify a single Supreme Court case
with which he disagreed and initially wouldn't even name
judges he admires (though he cited three in writing later).
Other Bush judicial nominees have answered such questions.
Reagan and Bush White House officials asked them of people
under consideration for nomination. Republican senators have

quizzed numerous Democratic nominees about the Supreme Court precedents with which they disagree. Democratic senators are now asking judicial nominees the same questions.[38]

There was, however, evidence of Estrada's views from one of his former superiors—dean emeritus of the Arizona State Law School Paul Bender. Bender had served as principal deputy solicitor general during three of Estrada's years in the solicitor general's office. When he heard of the nomination, Bender told the *Philadelphia Inquirer*, "Miguel is too much of an ideologue to be an appellate judge. . . . You could not count on him to be fair or neutral. He is a terrific oral advocate, but I could not rely on his written work as a neutral statement of the law." [39]

The response to Bender's statement was sulfuric. Hatch let loose one of his special brands of personal vilification which he had refined in his assault on Anita Hill, accusing Bender of being an "extremist" defender of pornography for thirty years. Leahy and Kennedy defended Bender but the attack had an effect, for though Bender was willing to talk publicly, he refused to expose himself to the Hatch treatment, which would almost certainly be matched by Sessions, Kyl, and others.

Bender has an impeccable reputation for integrity and great intellectual power—he was a law clerk to both Judge Learned Hand and Justice Felix Frankfurter, and is a prominent scholar and writer. In an interview with the author in October 2002, he said that his strong language about Estrada was based on his experience working with Estrada and on personal conversations with him. Bender cited a labor case in which a Virginia court had imposed a $52 million fine on a union without a jury trial. Estrada filed an *amicus curiae* brief for the United States in which he grossly misstated the law in order to support the Virginia courts in denying the union a jury. Bender raised the matter with him and learned that Estrada had also failed to check with the National Labor Relations Board before filing the brief, contrary to standard practice. Estrada's argument was so inconsistent with the governing law that it was dismissed by a unanimous Supreme Court, as Bender expected. There were other such instances, according to Bender, who ultimately concluded that Estrada was more conservative than even Scalia.[40]

Hatch had argued that Bender had rated Estrada highly from 1994 to 1996. In the October interview Bender explained that he did not normally do evaluations; Solicitor General Drew Days did. One year, however, when the evaluation forms came in, Days was going out of town. He therefore gave them to Bender, his principal deputy. Both considered the ratings a matter of form. Bender said that he asked Days, "What do I do with these?" and Days had responded, "Say they are all fine." This was the only evaluation Bender said he did.

In addition, the *Washington Post* reported that privately, many of those who have known Estrada over the years described him as an acerbic ideologue who likes to pick fights at the office over political issues and did not suffer fools gladly. "He has a very intellectual kind of snideness of the kind you see on the *Wall Street Journal* editorial page," a former colleague said.[41]

Nevertheless, he received support from well-known Democrats like Ron Klain, former Chief of Staff to Gore. Klain had worked with Estrada, and said, "I think Miguel Estrada takes the law very seriously. He's a very independent thinker and confident enough to come to his own conclusions, and won't just follow along with the Republican herd."[42]

The purpose of the committee's hearings, and the necessary condition for the Senate to exercise its advise and consent authority is to learn a nominee's views on basic constitutional and legal principles. Most Court of Appeals nominees have a public record on these matters and all the committee need do is explore and develop that, as the hearings of Bork, Ginsburg, and others described in this book show. But with someone like Estrada, who had no public record and about whom serious questions had been raised, it was necessary to look further. The committee therefore asked the Justice Department to release to the committee Estrada's memoranda recommending what position the United States should take in the Supreme Court, either as a party or as an *amicus curiae.* Such recommendations indicate how someone wants the law to be in areas which are usually uncertain, and where there is much room for judicial discretion. The memos are thus the best indications of that person's ideas about basic legal issues and how he would exercise his discretion as a judge.

The Justice Department refused, even though there is no legal or other justification for such a position, as Hatch, Assistant Attorney General Viet Dinh, and many others pointed out during the Clinton administration. Despite the department's claim that it has a "longstanding policy" against such disclosure, in 1941, United States Attorney General Robert Jackson wrote that "committees called upon to pass on the confirmation of persons recommended for appointment by the attorney general would be afforded confidential access to any information that we have—because no candidate's name is submitted without his knowledge and the department does not intend to submit the name of any person whose entire history will not stand light." [43]

Accordingly, the department has often turned over to the Senate Judiciary Committee in-house memos by government attorneys in connection with judicial and other nominations. These include the nominations of Rehnquist, Ninth Circuit Judge Stephen Trott, the Supreme Court nomination of Robert Bork, and Justice Department nominees Benjamin Civiletti and William Bradford Reynolds. As recently as summer 2001, the administration turned over memos by a nominee for an Environmental Protection Agency position when he worked in the Office of the White House Counsel during the first Bush administration, directly advising the president.

In order to bolster the case for the department's refusal, eight previous solicitors general, Democrats as well as Republicans, filed a letter in June 2002 with the Judiciary Committee threatening dire consequences to the Republic if the memos were provided the committee. They apparently were unable to cite any legal or historical authority for their position, for there was none in their letter. They argued only that "attorneys inevitably will hesitate before giving their honest, independent analysis if their opinions are not safeguarded from further disclosure." Apart from this being inherently implausible, there is no evidence that turning over the memos of other nominees for judicial or other offices has deterred government lawyers from "giving their honest, independent analysis." If an attorney does shape his or her advice in hopes of some future nomination, that attorney has no business being either a government lawyer or a nominee for public office.

There was also a question about Estrada's candor before the committee. Estrada served on a screening committee to select clerkships for Justice Kennedy. One lawyer he interviewed reported that "Miguel told me his job was to prevent liberal clerks from being hired"; a second lawyer had a similar experience. Both concluded they were being "subjected to an ideological litmus test." The two lawyers refused to identify themselves, a not-uncommon fear among lawyers when speaking publicly about someone before whom they may appear. Hatch's vitriolic attack on Bender also served to discourage witnesses from testifying.[44]

When asked about these interviews, Estrada first denied saying what the lawyers had charged. At lunch, however, he apparently decided a flat denial would not do. When the hearing resumed, he asked to explain further and he gave a lengthy but very murky response. Schumer tried repeatedly to get Estrada to answer yes or no to the question of whether he had said what the two lawyers reported. Schumer had no luck. Estrada repeatedly responded with lengthy evasive answers. Finally, Hatch broke in to rescue him with an outburst about Schumer's questions, and Schumer gave up.

The administration continued to refuse to turn over the memos, even though Estrada said he was willing, and the Democrats refused to move. The Republicans charged that the Democrats were hostile to Hispanics. "If we deny Mr. Estrada the position on the District of Columbia Circuit, it would be to shut the door on the American dream of Hispanic Americans everywhere," said Iowa Republican Senator Charles Grassley. The racism charge was ludicrous given the Republican treatment of Clinton's many Hispanic nominees, and it was not taken seriously by the Hispanic community, many of whom, including the Congressional Hispanic Caucus, opposed Estrada. But it was a harbinger of the tactics that the Republicans would often use. Estrada would later withdraw his nomination in September 2003.

Three other Circuit Court nominees, all of whom might have been expected to be controversial, were easily confirmed, though the latter two—Michael McConnell and Dennis Shedd—were confirmed after Democrats lost the midterm election.

Levinski Smith, an African-American Arkansas Public Service Commission member, was nominated by Bush to the Eighth Circuit, which covers Minnesota, Iowa, Missouri, Kansas, Nebraska, and the Dakotas. This was a surprising nominee to be approved without controversy. Smith was executive director of the Arkansas branch of the Rutherford Institute, the Christian-right group that paid for Paula Jones's

lawsuit against Clinton; he was also affiliated with funda-
mentalist John Brown University in Arkansas. He was a lawyer
for the plaintiff in a case called *Unborn Child Amendment Committee v. Dr. Harry Ward*, a largely unsuccessful suit to prevent
abortions from being performed in public hospitals, even with
private funds. In a failed run for the Arkansas Court of
Appeals, Smith received donations from a political action
committee whose sole purpose was to promote opposition to
abortion.

Nor was Smith a distinguished lawyer. He had had a brief
stint as an appointed Justice of the Arkansas Supreme Court to
fill out a vacancy before his failed effort to be elected to the
lower-level Court of Appeals. He had not published anything,
and at his hearing on May 25, 2002, he was criticized for failing
to cite a well-known precedent that contravened the argument
he made in his *Unborn Child Amendment Committee* case even
though the American Bar Association ethics code requires
lawyers to cite relevant legal authority. He had little experience
as a litigator, and few lawyers who worked with him even
remembered him. Nevertheless, he was confirmed a few
months after his hearing with only three senators reported in
opposition.

Michael McConnell and Dennis Shedd were much more
prominent and controversial. McConnell was among Bush's
May 9, 2001, nominations. The Alliance for Justice provides a
concise summary of his record:

> He was well-known as a strong opponent of *Roe v. Wade* and
> statutes that protect abortion clinics from violent protests, an
> outspoken opponent of the Supreme Court's separation of
> church and state doctrine, and a strong believer in "origi-
> nalism" as the correct method of Constitutional interpreta-
> tion, opposing any Constitutional rights that he did not believe

the framers of the Constitution had in mind when the document was written.

.... He signed a document saying "Abortion kills 1.5 million innocent human beings in America every year. There is no longer any serious scientific dispute that the unborn child is a human creature who dies violently in the act of abortion" ... [He opposed a law that protected clinics and women seeking abortions from violence. When the Freedom of Access to Clinic Entrances (FACE) Act passed despite his opposition, he praised a judge who refused to enforce the law.]

[On the basis of his "original intent" views], McConnell opposes several important Constitutional rights, claiming that they are not protected by the Constitution because the framers did not believe that these rights existed. As a result, he opposes the one-person-one-vote principle, ... the rule that the federal government cannot discriminate on the basis of race or sex protected in the desegregation case of *Bolling v. Sharpe*; and other basic rights. Because of his views on freedom of religion, he also believes that Bob Jones University should have been allowed to retain its tax-exempt status in spite of its policy of racial discrimination. He called the Supreme Court decision upholding the IRS's revocation of Bob Jones University's tax-exempt status "notorious." [45]

McConnell had strong support, however. Not only was he from Hatch's home state, but he was also endorsed for the judgeship by many academic friends, including some well-known liberals like Laurence Tribe of Harvard, Cass Sunstein of Chicago, and Akhil Amar of Yale. Although it was originally thought that he would not be voted on in the 2001–02 session, after the election the Democrats decided to let the matter go. The nomination was voted out of committee on November 14, and confirmed by unanimous consent on November 15; Leahy warned that McConnell would not have such an easy time if he were nominated to the Supreme Court.

South Carolina District Judge Dennis Shedd, nominated to the Fourth Circuit, had been an aide to Thurmond. When nominated to the District Court in 1990, Shedd had practiced law for less than three years and had very little experience as a litigator. The committee questionnaire asks for a nominee's ten most significant cases litigated to verdict; Shedd could list only four. Both plaintiffs' and defendants' lawyers who appeared before Shedd considered him defendant- and employer-oriented, with some describing him as "a right-winger" and "about as conservative as you can get."

Shedd's sole claim to fame as a judge was his decision in *Condon v. Reno*, striking down the Driver's Privacy Protection Act. He ruled that the federal government lacked the power to prohibit states from disclosing or selling personal information obtained from driver's licenses or car-registration applications. Although the Fourth Circuit affirmed his decision, the Supreme Court unanimously disagreed in a Rehnquist opinion.[46]

The *New York Times* reported that in eleven years as a federal district judge in South Carolina, Shedd sat on 5,000–6,000 cases, but published opinions in only about sixty of these. He submitted about 1,500 unpublished opinions to the committee, which apparently constituted substantially all of his written opinions on the bench.

Shedd had also shown himself to be hostile to employees and to civil rights plaintiffs in race and gender cases. A group of law professors came out against him, but Thurmond made a rare and angry floor appearance in his behalf when it looked as if the nomination might fail. South Carolina Democrat Ernest Hollings came out in Shedd's favor, reportedly because South Carolina trial lawyers wanted Shedd off the District Court. On

November 14, the committee voted him out, even though each member of the Democratic majority present asked to be recorded against him. He was confirmed the next day by a 55-44 vote.

At the end of the session, Leahy summed up what the Judiciary and the Senate Committee had accomplished under his chairmanship since July 2001. It had held hearings on 103 nominations in twenty-six hearings, voting on 102 of them, had confirmed 100 nominees, and rejected two in committee. "This compares most favorably to the thirty-eight judicial nominations averaged per year during the six and a half years when the Republican majority was in control of the Senate," said Leahy. He noted that during 1996, the Republicans had confirmed only seventeen district judges and no circuit judges; in contrast, prior to the 2002 election, the Senate had confirmed fourteen appellate judges and another three in the week after the election. Vacancies had been reduced from 110 in July to fifty-eight, which included forty-seven vacancies that opened up after the Democrats took over; Hatch had earlier said he considered sixty-seven vacancies the equivalent of "full employment."

Overall, the Democrats averaged six confirmations per month during 2001–02, in contrast with the Republicans' 3.2 in 1995–96, 4.25 in 1997–98, and 3.04 in 1999–2000. Twenty Circuit Court nominees were given hearings and seventeen were confirmed. Eleven were left hanging, including many of the most controversial. According to Leahy, many of those nominees who did not have hearings lacked either home-state senatorial consent or ABA review.

Leahy went on to complain about the Republican attacks on him and other Democrats and summarized some of the Republican tactics. "We never tried to override the chairman's prerogative to set the agenda for consideration of judicial nominees by trying to manipulate the committee's cloture rule to force a nomination to a vote in defiance of the chairman. We never tried to use the committee rule to hold off consideration of an agenda item for at least a week to force either legislation or nominations to be voted on in a week's time. We never invoked Senate Rule XIX to make an end-run around our colleague, chairman Hatch, to try to force an executive committee business meeting." [47]

Leahy soon would have more to complain about, for in the November 2002 elections the Republicans narrowly regained the Senate, 51-49.

2003

As the 108th Congress began, eight circuits had solid Republican majorities of active judges, often quite top-heavy like the Fourth (8-4), Fifth (10-4), Seventh (8-3), Eighth (8-3), and the Federal Circuit; two had Democratic majorities, both also top-heavy, the Second (8-4) and the Ninth (17-7); three were tied—District of Columbia (4-4), the Third (6-6), and the Sixth (5-5). Things would soon change.

At the end of November, after Congress adjourned, the *Washington Post*, responding to a Bush proposal that nominees obtain a floor vote within 180 days of nomination, urged him to make gestures of reconciliation on this subject—including showing some flexibility on nominations to key courts—by way of demonstrating his commitment to a new start. An earlier editorial had specified what those gestures should be: to "consult on judges," "to seek Democratic input," to "accommodate," and not to continue to "rub salt in Democratic wounds." [48]

Bush had other ideas. In January he not only renominated all those left unresolved at the close of the prior session, but he also recommended Pickering and Owen despite the committee's rejection, a move that Democrats termed unprecedented. The January nominees included three predictably controversial nominees from Michigan to the Sixth Circuit whom he had earlier sent up, and a fourth Michigan nominee. These nominations were certain to draw fire from Michigan's two Democratic senators, Carl Levin and Deborah Stabenow, who were still fuming over the Republican refusal even to grant hearings to Clinton nominees Kathleen McCree Lewis and Judge Helene White, the latter a cousin of Levin's by marriage; White went four years without ever getting a hearing. Bush also nominated fifteen district judges, and a few weeks later three more appellate judges.

Taking his cue from Bush, Hatch was in no mood to compromise. He was now an angry man in a hurry. Inconvenient committee rules and precedents were brushed aside, in what a *New York Times* editorial soon called "steamrolling judicial nominees" in order to achieve "an era of conveyor belt nominations . . . giv[ing] short shift to [the Senate's] constitutional role of advice and consent." [49]

In January Hatch announced that he was dropping the blue-slip policy he had insisted upon when Clinton was president. "I'll give great weight to negative blue slips, but you can't have one senator holding up, for months, a circuit court nominee." Every nominee was entitled to an up-or-down vote. Hatch and his allies insisted. Forgotten was Helms's continual refusal to allow any African-American nominee to be confirmed for the Fourth Circuit until Bush renominated Roger Gregory, or Michigan Senator Spencer Abraham's blocking Helene White and Kathleen McCree Lewis, to say nothing of Hatch's own holdup of sixty-three Clinton nominees. Leahy pointed out that "during the Clinton administration, [Hatch] would not allow a nomination to move forward unless he had both blue slips, [and that] to do differently during the Bush administration would be inconsistent." That was doomed to fall on deaf ears.

Other rules were also ignored. In 1995, Biden and Thurmond had agreed to follow a hearing schedule on which Hatch had insisted: (1) No hearing could be held less than three weeks after the paperwork is done; (2) no hearing would be held on more than one controversial nominee at a time; and (3) there would be adequate time for post-hearing questions and answers before a committee vote was scheduled. Nevertheless, on January 29, Hatch scheduled Jeffrey Sutton, Deborah Cook, and John Roberts, all controversial nominees, for one hearing on January 29. Also, according to Democratic staff, nominees have been scheduled for a vote even before minority committee members have had a chance to submit written questions or to obtain and study answers; in some cases, the responses arrived the day before the vote. These usually provided little or no information, for they were cleared by Justice Department lawyers.

As Democrats saw it, since Bush refused to consult them on nominees, and since Hatch was breaking the rules that protected the minority, they had nothing left with which to fight extremist nominees except the filibuster. They saw nothing unfair about this. The Republicans' refusal during the eight Clinton years to grant hearings, committee votes, and floor votes was the equivalent of a silent filibuster. Also, Republicans had tried to block Paez and Berzon with filibusters necessitating cloture votes; Democrats also pointed out that Republicans had filibustered six judicial nominees when they had been in the minority.

Later in the year, Hatch decided on more shortcuts in the committee process. When the Republicans were in the minority during the first two Clinton years, Hatch had insisted on the committee rule whereby a committee member's objection to a

vote on a nominee would require a majority vote of the committee to override it, including at least one minority party
member. Democrats tried to block a vote by staying away en
masse twice. The first time it was to protest Hatch's scheduling
votes on Cook and Roberts within a few weeks after the 108th
Congress convened, an act Daschle called an exercise of "raw
power." Hatch agreed to put off the votes in order to persuade
the Democrats to allow votes on Cook and Roberts. He again
violated the rule, however, in July by scheduling a vote on
Alabama Attorney General William Pryor even while an ethics
investigation of Pryor was under way. He now said that the rule
allowed the committee majority to vote on a nominee even if no
minority party senators were included in that majority. Leahy
objected that Hatch had argued the other way just a few years
earlier, to which Hatch blithely responded "And I apparently
was wrong back then when I made that argument." [50]

Other troubles began on January 30, when a 10-9 vote of the
committee voted out Miguel Estrada. When the Democratic
request for Estrada's memos was again rejected, the Democrats
announced that they would delay the nomination until they
received the memos—a filibuster—setting off eruptions of outrage among Republicans. Forgotten was Hatch's insistence
during Clinton's presidency on "more diligent and extensive
questioning of nominees." [51]

On February 14, the Senate recessed for the Presidents Day hol-
idays, with Republicans, led by Bush, charging that the Democrats
were anti-Hispanic. Republican strategists saw the Estrada fight as
helping to persuade Hispanic voters to vote Republican, even
though eight of the ten Hispanic judges on the Courts of
Appeal were Clinton appointees, Paez had been filibustered
by the Republicans, and Hispanic nominees Jorge Rangel,
Enrique Moreno, and Christine Arguello were never voted out
of committee.

"Our current state of affairs is neither fair nor representative of the bipartisan majority of this body," Texas Republican John Cornyn said. "For democracy to work, and for the constitutional principle of majority rule to prevail, this obstructionism must end, and we must bring matters to a vote." Cornyn, a newly elected senator, was apparently unfamiliar with the Senate's history. Not only had the Republicans filibustered Paez and Marsha Berzon but also Abe Fortas in 1968, when Lyndon Johnson nominated him to be chief justice. Moreover, the Senate is not a majoritarian institution. With its holds and its continual reliance on unanimous consent for its operation, one or a few senators can often block the Senate from doing anything.[52]

It has always been like that. The Framers knew about filibusters, and deliberately wrote into the Constitution that "each House may determine the rules of its proceedings." The current rule requiring sixty senators to close off debate is a reform to curtail the power of a minority. For our first 130 years, there was no way to end debate. In 1917 Rule XXII was adopted allowing a cutoff by two-thirds of the senators present and voting. In 1961, majority leader Mike Mansfield put issues subject to a filibuster on a separate track from other matters. This encouraged the use of filibusters since now, other Senate business would not be brought to a halt by a filibuster—other matters could be taken up. In 1975, Rule XXII was again amended to lower the cloture requirement to three-fifths of the Senate, or sixty, regardless of the number present, and that is the current rule. As a result, filibusters are now routine by members of both parties who are in the minority on an issue.

Some six more unsuccessful cloture votes to move the Estrada nomination were tried by the Republicans until, on September 4, 2003, Estrada withdrew. Additional expressions of outrage erupted, but the confirmation fights had now moved elsewhere.

The day before Estrada was reported out, on January 29, forty-six-year-old John Roberts was given a hearing on his nomination to the District of Columbia Court of Appeals for one of the two seats left vacant by the Republican refusal to move on Snyder and Kagan. Unlike Estrada, Roberts was widely considered to be one of the most distinguished appellate advocates in Washington, having also served in key governmental posts. Initially nominated by George H.W. Bush in 1992 when Roberts was thirty-six, his nomination lapsed at the end of the year.

Roberts was also a staunch conservative. While serving in the Reagan-Bush administrations, including a stint as principal deputy solicitor general in 1989–92, Roberts had argued *Rust v. Sullivan*, in which he urged the Court to override *Roe v. Wade* even though that was unnecessary to decide the case; *Rust* dealt only with whether recipients of federal family-planning funds could be barred from mentioning abortion. (The Court held that they could be.) He had intervened as an *amicus curiae* to argue that religious prayers should be allowed at formal graduation ceremonies, a position the Supreme Court rejected. He filed an *amicus curiae* brief in a case involving violence by Operation Rescue at abortion clinics, in which he successfully urged the Court not to use the civil rights laws to protect women against violence when they seek an abortion. He argued against citizens' rights to challenge threats to the environment. In his capacity as deputy solicitor general and in other branches of the Justice Department, and as associate White House counsel, he often displayed a hostility to civil rights enforcement. He had, however, done a significant amount of pro bono work for indigent criminal defendants, and had successfully argued an important case for environmentalists.[53]

In response to the Democrats' anger at the joint hearing for

Roberts, Sutton, and Cook, a second hearing for Roberts was held on April 30. Roberts went through the usual motions of saying he would just follow the law in accordance with the Supreme Court's rulings and insisted that "my practice has not been ideological in any sense. I've argued in favor of antitrust enforcement and in favor of affirmative action, but I have also argued cases against affirmative action and against antitrust enforcement." [54]

Roberts nevertheless refused to answer several written questions about which Supreme Court decisions he disagreed with. When Schumer tried to press him, Hatch broke in with one of his now frequent outbursts, saying "Senator Schumer usually asks good questions. But I know dumbass questions when I see dumbass questions." When a startled Schumer asked Hatch whether he wanted to correct the record, Hatch refused, repeating his comment. After the second hearing, the committee Democrats decided not to oppose the nomination. Roberts was confirmed by unanimous consent. [55]

Two other flash points also failed to ignite: Jeffrey Sutton and Deborah Cook, both nominated to the closely divided Sixth Circuit. Each was quickly reported out after their hearing on January 29; Sutton was reported out two weeks later with an 11-8 vote as California Democrat Dianne Feinstein broke ranks; and Cook two weeks later on February 27, with a 13-2 vote, with four Democratic abstentions. Each represented a major victory for the Republicans.

Jeffrey Sutton was another able, young (40) conservative lawyer. A director of the Federalist Society, he was the chief advocate for the assault on federal and Congressional authority in the name of federalism. His targets included disabled people, the elderly, medical care for poor children, civil rights plaintiffs, and environmental protection. As usual, he told the committee he was "simply representing a client" and had "no idea" whether he personally agreed with the position he advocated. No one took that seriously, except perhaps Feinstein. An officer of the Federalist Society's federalism and separation of powers practice group, he was more than just an advocate for a client. At one point he had said, "I really believe in this federalism stuff"; at another time, moderating a panel discussion, he concluded with "[w]e ought to find a way to continue to push [federalism] in the direction that it is going." [56]

By the time Sutton was nominated to the Sixth Circuit, he had written Supreme Court briefs arguing that Congress could not require a state university to comply with age discrimination laws in its tenure system, could not require a state university running a hospital to comply with disabilities laws, or empower a woman to sue her attackers for domestic violence in federal court. He also challenged the right of private citizens to challenge federally funded state programs that had the effect of discriminating on the basis of race, gender, or national origin. He argued that the Clean Water Act did not apply to small lakes and was unconstitutional if it did; that, even though certain federal statutes authorized a successful party to obtain those fees, plaintiffs could not recover attorneys' fees if, in response to the lawsuit, the state voluntarily changed its programs to comply with federal law. He also unsuccessfully argued that antiloitering statutes that are often used to harass racial minorities are constitutional; he lost that one. [57]

Sutton's record drew opposition from disability and civil rights organizations and the environmental community. Nevertheless, Feinstein found him acceptable, and since the Democrats could not present a united front, they decided not to filibuster Sutton. He was confirmed on April 30, 52-41.

Deborah Cook, a 49-year-old State Supreme Court justice from Ohio, was also nominated to the Sixth Circuit. On the Ohio Supreme Court, she consistently voted in favor of business and insurance companies against disabled workers, older workers, victims of discrimination, and consumers. She was often a minority of one. In one case, she dissented from all the other justices when they allowed the widow of a Wal-Mart forklift operator crushed to death to add a claim of deception when she learned that Wal-Mart employees might have lied and destroyed evidence. In another case, where she dissented, she voted to uphold a law that shielded insurance companies and businesses; trial lawyers called it the Drunk Drivers Protection Act. In another case, she dissented from a decision protecting whistleblowers. She also dissented from an Ohio decision that found unconstitutional the vast disparity in funding for public schools. Even Hatch found her large number of dissents surprising.[58]

There was little organized opposition to her outside Ohio, however, and as the Brooks Smith nomination showed, many Democrats have not been especially solicitous of worker or consumer interests. She received a 13-2 vote in committee. Democrats put a hold on the nomination, but when a cloture petition was filed, they gave up. On May 5, Owen was easily confirmed 66-25, a week after Sutton.

One other controversial nomination was confirmed in the early spring: Timothy Tymkovich, named to the Tenth Circuit. He was a member of the Federalist Society, and as Colorado Solicitor General (1991–96) and in private practice, he took very conservative positions. As solicitor general, he argued that Colorado could deny Medicaid funding to poor women for abortions to terminate pregnancies that resulted from rape or incest; when he lost by a unanimous vote, he pressed the case all the way to the Supreme Court, where his petition for review was summarily rejected. Tymkovich asserted that local ordinances that prohibited discrimination on the basis of sexual orientation conferred "special rights" on homosexuals,

a position rejected by the Supreme Court in *Romer v. Evans.*
He opposed Denver's efforts to restrict assault weapons. He
told Congress that federal clean air and clean water regulations, as well as "motor voter" provisions designed to make it
easier for citizens to register to vote, unconstitutionally inter-
fered with state governments' constitutional autonomy.
Throughout his career, Tymkovich allied himself with legal
organizations that support states' rights and oppose gun control. He also told Congress that the federal government was
"overreaching" and intruding on the states in environmental
protection laws and Medicaid requirements that states provide funds for abortions for poor women who become pregnant because of rape or incest. According to Tymkovich, these
and other federal laws, all of which have withstood constitutional attack, violate the Framers' constitutional plan in
which the states were "the cornerstone of the Nation." [59]

Nevertheless, he was voted out of committee a few weeks
after his hearing by a 10-6 vote and three weeks later was confirmed by a 58-41 vote. The relative ease and dispatch with
which these controversial nominees were confirmed did not
soothe Hatch and his colleagues. Nor did the fact that 100 district judges and twenty-three appellate nominees, many quite
controversial because of their extreme conservatism, were also
approved. The Democrats would not budge on Estrada and
would try to stop Owen and Pickering. Also, John Edwards and
the Michigan senators were continuing to "blue slip" Terence
Boyle and four Michigan Sixth Circuit nominees. Despite his
threats, Hatch was still honoring the "blue slip" tradition at
this time.

To ease the situation, in early May Feinstein wrote to Bush
suggesting that he emulate nationwide the California bipartisan arrangement for district judges noted earlier. Schumer
also worked out an arrangement with New York Republican

Governor George Pataki to divide ten district judgeships on a 7-3 basis. Bush ignored Feinstein's letter and simply continued to inveigh against the Democrats' "obstructionist tactics," charging that there were serious vacancies on the federal bench. Few observers were impressed. The number of vacancies was the lowest since 1990, with just twenty-six vacancies out of 665 District Court judgeships, and only twenty-one out of 179 appellate seats. As a Pittsburgh columnist pointed out,

> of [Clinton's appointments in this region], during the years of the Santorum filibuster that court of 10 judges had as many as five vacancies. Today, the Senate has confirmed four Bush appointees . . . and the fifth nomination has just been sent to the Senate . . . That hardly sounds like obstructionism.[60]

Nevertheless, the Republicans continued to charge that despite the many confirmations, the Republic was in jeopardy because of the Democrats' refusal to move forward on three nominations though they had already confirmed 126. Because of the 1961 Mansfield rule change, Senate business continued without a halt. No attempt was made to break the filibuster the old-fashioned way by stopping everything and holding the Senate in session night and day until the filibustering senators ran out of steam. That strategy is more of a burden on the majority than on the minority because the minority need only keep one speaker on the floor who can rest when yielding for questions by an ally, whereas the majority party must always have a majority of senators available if a quorum call or a roll call vote is suddenly called by those engaged in the filibuster.

There was one possibility, referred to as the "nuclear option," by which the Republican majority could force a nomination or any other matter subject to a filibuster to an ordinary majority vote. It involved a complicated parliamentary maneuver in which the vice president, as presiding officer, would rule that nominations were nondebatable and the Senate parliamentarian would rule against the vice president, in accordance with the established rules. The parliamentarian's rule would then be appealed to the Senate where a simple Republican majority would be enough to support the vice president. If Republican discipline held, the parliamentarian would be overruled and judicial nominations would no longer be subject to filibuster. This would not require a formal rules change, which requires a two-thirds vote. (Lott, demoted to chairman in the Senate Rules Committee for expressing sympathy for Strom Thurmond's 1948 Dixiecrat segregationist presidential campaign, had nevertheless pushed a rule change through the committee but no floor vote was scheduled.) This could of course be applied to all issues, and would make the Senate like the House, where a disciplined majority can always rule over the minority, no matter how slim the former's margin.

Like the real nuclear weapon, this one is just too dangerous to use, for it could destroy its user as well as its target. As political scientist Norman Ornstein observed, if it were attempted, "all hell would break loose, probably affecting all issues for the remainder of the Congress. . . . If Republicans unilaterally void a rule they themselves have employed in the past, they will break the back of the comity in the Senate. Democrats could block Republican legislative efforts at every turn. For a short-term victory now, Republicans would reap the whirlwind." Nevertheless, throughout the rest of the session, the new majority leader Bill Frist of Tennessee, Hatch, and others continued to threaten its use.[61]

The assault on the judiciary continued on other fronts with amendments to the Sentencing Guidelines legislation. The guidelines generally imposed harsh sentences and drastically limited judicial discretion. They did, however, allow judges to vary the sentences a bit to account for individual circumstances. Hard-line members of Congress felt that judges were making too many downward adjustments. The amendments curtailed that discretion even further by requiring reports to Congress of all adjustments and close review by appellate courts. The amendments were adopted, much to the dismay of many judges.

The House Judiciary Committee also started investigations into the activities of "liberal" judges. The first was actually directed at the "political bias" reflected in the sentencing practices of a conservative Reagan-appointed Minnesota District Judge, Chief Judge James Rosenbaum, who had indicated that he thought the sentencing guidelines for low-level drug offenders were too harsh. Chairman of the House Judiciary Committee James Sensenbrenner, whose chief counsel is Kenneth Starr deputy Jay Apperson, indicated he was prepared to subpoena the judge's records to see if he had given any "unlawfully lenient sentences"; in summer 2003, Sensenbrenner sent a magistrate to check Rosenbaum's records when the General Accounting office refused to. The media and even Rehnquist have supported Rosenbaum.[62]

The second investigation was into the actions of the Sixth Circuit Court of Appeals in the *Grutter* affirmative action case, in which that court had decided in favor of the University of Michigan Law School by a 5-4 vote in 2001, and which was affirmed by the Supreme Court. Dissenting Judge Danny Boggs, a Reagan appointee and one of the most conservative judges on that court, charged that Chief Judge Boyce Martin Jr. had rigged the schedule to ensure a favorable majority; Martin denied this. In mid-October 2003, the House committee sent a staffer on an unannounced visit to interrogate the judges and to look into court files for an "impeachment investigation"; the Democrats were not informed of this and only read of it in the press.[63]

Also in August, Attorney General Ashcroft ordered federal

prosecutors to collect information on judges who were sentencing below the guidelines. Even Rehnquist objected to what "could amount to an unwarranted and ill-considered effort to intimidate federal judges."[64]

Throughout the summer tempers flared. Committee hearings grew more and more acrimonious. At one point, a furious Edward Kennedy, normally a good friend of Hatch despite their political differences, exploded at Hatch with "you may bully some, but you are not going to bully me," to which Hatch responded, "you're not going to bully me either." In July, Hatch declared he would follow through on his decision to scrap the blue-slip policy and announced that there would be hearings on all four Michigan nominees even in the face of negative blue slips from the two Michigan senators. Despite his announcement, he held hearings on only one—Henry Saad—but as of November 25, no committee votes on Saad were taken; no hearings were held on the others. The blue-slip system was apparently too important to all senators on both sides of the aisle for the Republicans to risk abandoning it completely.[65]

The bottom was hit in the fight over Alabama Attorney General William Pryor. Of all the Bush nominees, Pryor was one of the most extreme. He was against almost every progressive reform of the past half-century. Fellow Republican Attorney General Grant Woods of Arizona described him "as probably the most doctrinaire and the most partisan of any attorney general I dealt with in eight years." The *Atlanta Journal-Constitution* described him as "the perfect Christian Right extremist." Pryor's record confirmed those judgments on almost every issue.[66]

- He had filed an *amicus curiae* brief in the Supreme Court's landmark 2003 gay rights case, *Lawrence v. Texas*, supporting the Texas statute criminalizing male homosexual conduct, arguing that striking down the statute would "most logically extend to activities like prostitution, adultery, necrophilia, bestiality, possession of child pornography and even incest and pedophilia." Scalia, Rehnquist, and Thomas picked up Pryor's argument, throwing in masturbation and fornication. Santorum also echoed Pryor's brief saying before the decision, "If the Supreme Court says that you have the right to consensual sex within your home, then you have the right to bigamy, you have the right to polygamy, you have the right to incest, you have the right to adultery. You have the right to anything." [67]

- He was the only state attorney general who argued for striking down the Violence Against Women Act (with Sutton as his attorney).
- He filed an *amicus curiae* brief supporting Nevada in its unsuccessful effort to block remedies for violations of the Family and Medical Leave Act.
- When the Supreme Court delayed an Alabama execution in 2000, Pryor called the justices "nine octogenarian lawyers."
- Pryor also said he thought the electric chair was a humane method of execution and that innocent people were not executed in Alabama.
- In a prison case, guards twice handcuffed a prisoner to an outdoor "hitching post" with his arms raised above his shoulders for many hours. The second time the guards also forced him to remove his shirt and kept him in that position under the scorching sun all day. Pryor argued that this was not unconstitutional conduct even though case law in the Supreme Court and in his own circuit made it clear that it was. This was so

obvious, according to the Supreme Court, that it should have been clear even to a nonlawyer.[68]

- In the 2000 Florida presidential election case, he castigated the Florida Supreme Court for "undermining public confidence in the presidency and the Republic itself," and added: "I'm probably the only one who wanted it [*Bush v. Gore*] 5-4. I wanted Governor Bush to have a full appreciation of the judiciary and judicial selection so we can have no more appointments like Justice Souter."[69]

- He testified in Congress against the Voting Rights Act and urged it to repeal the provision requiring Justice Department preapproval for changes in voting procedures or jurisdictions because it was "an affront to federalism and an expensive burden that has far outlived its usefulness."

- He supported displays of the Ten Commandments on public property, standing on the steps of the Alabama Capitol at a rally in support of state Supreme Court Justice Roy Moore's display of the Ten Commandments in his courtroom. While Pryor's nomination was pending, the Eleventh Circuit ordered Alabama Supreme Court Justice Roy Moore to remove the stone tablets from the Alabama Supreme Court, and Pryor advised him to do so.

- He has argued against federal enforcement of civil rights and worker protection laws.

- He has supported the tobacco and gun industries against lawsuits by state attorneys general. "You are in the center of a battle for the heart and soul of our legal system," he told the American Shooting Sports Council, a gun-rights group, in 1999. "As a survivor of the tobacco wars, I hope and pray that your industry will prove to be tougher opponents of the trial lawyers and their political allies than Big Tobacco proved to be." [70]

- Pryor was alone among the fifty state attorneys general in challenging significant portions of the Clean Water and the Endangered Species acts. He also asserted that land use and wildlife protection are "traditional areas of state environmental primacy" which the federal government cannot regulate. In *Solid Waste Agency of Northern Cook County (SWANCC) v. US Army Corps of Engineers*, Pryor urged the Supreme Court to strike down federal efforts to protect waters and wetlands that provide critical habitat for migratory birds. Eight states filed a brief supporting federal power. Pryor was the only state attorney general to file an *amicus curiae* brief arguing that the Constitution's Commerce Clause does not give Congress the authority to protect these species, again with Sulton as his lawyer. As the *New York Times* concluded, "As Alabama Attorney General, he has turned his office into a taxpayer-financed right-wing law firm." [71]

There is also a possible conflict of interest that could be very serious. Pryor is a cofounder and former chair of a Washington-based organization of at least six Republican attorneys general who have solicited hundreds of thousands of dollars in political contributions from corporations and trade groups subject to lawsuits or regulation in their states. The companies include some of the nation's largest tobacco, pharmaceutical, computer, energy, banking, liquor, insurance, and media concerns, many of which had faced product liability or other lawsuits in the attorney generals' states. Pryor said earlier that he knew of no funds raised in his name from companies

that did business with his office, but it came out that he had
made many calls to major American corporations, including
Alabama banks and tobacco companies. A confidential bipartisan investigation was started, but Republicans leaked it to a
conservative Mobile, Alabama, columnist, killing the investigation. When Democrats protested and asked for more time,
Hatch and Sessions, Pryor's sponsor, refused. In violation of the
rule requiring a minority senator to agree to a vote, as noted
earlier, Hatch quickly called a committee vote for July 23 and
Pryor was voted out 10-9. This was the first time a nominee
was voted on and reported out without the consent of at least
one minority member.[72]

But it was not Pryor's record, activities, or even his views
that provoked the firestorm: It was religion. Pryor had characterized *Roe v. Wade* as "the worst abomination of Constitutional
law in our history," that "ripped the Constitution and ripped
out the life of millions of unborn children." In his hearing in
June, he vigorously reaffirmed those views. He then went
through the usual motions of pledging that he would "follow
the law" regardless of his personal views on abortion this and
all other issues.

All this was not unusual. Other nominees were known to be
strongly against abortion. But at that point Hatch asked Pryor:
"OK, now just for the record, what is your religious affilia-
tion?" "I'm a Roman Catholic," Pryor promptly responded.
Hatch then asked, "Are you active in your church?" "I am,"
Pryor said, leading Hatch to "commend you for that."

Leahy was outraged, as were the other Democrats; even
Specter objected. "Questions about a nominee's religion had
never before been asked," Leahy told Hatch. It is "irrelevant to
our considerations. . . . [and] should never be asked." Leahy,
Kennedy, Biden, and Durbin were themselves Catholics. That
of course made no difference. As Feinstein said, "each time we

have opposed a nominee, there has been bias used as a rationale for those who do not agree with us."

The Republicans responded by complaining that they had been pushed "to the limit" by the Democratic obstructionism and had to "fight fire with fire." At this point, the Democrats had approved over 140 nominations, and were blocking just two: Estrada and Owen.[73]

Hatch's introducing the religion issue into Pryor's June hearing was the signal for the Rove strategy of stirring up conservative religious groups to swing into high gear. Within days, ads began to run in Maine and Rhode Island, two states with large Catholic populations and moderate Republican senators: Lincoln Chafee of Rhode Island and Susan Collins and Olympia Snowe of Maine. The ads featured a picture showing a locked courthouse with a sign, "Catholics Need Not Apply," and a text that said, "Some in the U.S. Senate are attacking Bill Pryor for having 'deeply held' Catholic beliefs to prevent him from becoming a federal judge. Don't they know the Constitution expressly prohibits religious tests for public office?" They were targeted at religiously conservative Catholics, and produced by the Committee for Justice, the organization founded by C. Boyden Gray and supported by Bush's father, working together with Ave Maria, a right-wing Catholic organization funded by Thomas Monaghan, the founder of Domino's Pizza. The committee probably didn't need Monaghan's money—it had been raising huge amounts of money to support right-wing judges for many months. One fund-raiser in March on behalf of Estrada at George H. W. Bush's home brought in $250,000; in February Gray had hosted a $10,000-per-donor dinner at his Georgetown home featuring Frist, Hatch, and George W. Bush's former top aide Karen Hughes; some fifty people attended.

Of course it made no difference that, as the Democrats pointed out, they had confirmed numerous Catholics. As *Wall*

Street Journal columnist Al Hunt observed, "based on their own biographies, it's clear that at least twenty-three Bush-confirmed judges are Catholic, and maybe many more; two Catholics have been opposed. It's a little harder to identify Baptists, but over five dozen Bush appointees have been confirmed from Southern and border states, and it's a sure bet more than a handful are Baptists. Orrin Hatch charged this week, 'it all comes down to abortion.' Yet most, if not all, of the 168 confirmed Bush judges are antiabortion; some like Circuit Court nominees Michael McConnell and John Roberts—two of the most distinguished Bush appointees—have been outspoken advocates of reversing the *Roe v. Wade* abortion rights decision."[75]

This was not the first time Hatch had injected religion into the judgeships issue. The previous fall, he had told the Christian Coalition of America that Democrats refused to confirm Bush nominees "based on their religious views."

Leahy opened the committee business meeting a month later with a demand: "One aspect of the recent debate on which I hope we can get closure today is the unfounded charge leveled most recently by special interest groups that Democratic senators are anti-Catholic. The charge is despicable. . . . I trust that our Republican colleagues, who are so quick to castigate policy groups that dare to oppose any nomination, and who are so prone to categorically condemn every critical statement concerning any Republican nominee as a partisan smear, will today, finally condemn the ad campaign." "This smear is a lie," Leahy concluded, "and it depends on the silence of others to survive." The Republicans ignored the request. Tempers flared as Sessions, a Methodist, lectured the Catholic Durbin on Catholic doctrine.

The Democrats continued to respond angrily, charging a "smear campaign" which only brought more media attention;

the director of Gray's Committee for Justice said he didn't use TV ads because the Democrats were providing all the publicity that was needed. Editorials, ministers of all faiths, and others throughout the country condemned the Republican's tactics as "despicable." Many editorials and columnists also noted the difference in treatment that Bush nominees had received at the hands of Democrats in contrast with the Republican treatment of Clinton nominees.

Nevertheless, Hatch, Sessions, Santorum, and others continued to play the anti-Catholic card. "Are we not saying, then, that good Catholics need not apply?" asked Sessions. Santorum said the issue was whether "anybody who believes in church and faith" will be disqualified from public life. "What we are seeing, de facto, from members of the other side is a religious test." The head of the New York State Conservative Party, a close ally of Governor George Pataki, called Schumer "anti-Catholic"; Pataki was silent.[77]

According to some reports, the Rove strategy of rousing the anger of religious groups committed to abortion, hostile to gay rights, and resentful of other social changes was effective. Rove had been particularly concerned about the Catholic vote ever since Bush spoke at the anti-Catholic Bob Jones University in the 2000 campaign. The ads played well in Catholic blue-collar areas where the former Reagan Democrats lived, and although Gray appeared embarrassed when asked about them, similar ads were scheduled for September to run in three major national Catholic newspapers.[78]

It was a win-win situation for the Republicans. If the Democrats filibustered—as they decided to do after Pryor was reported out in July with Arlen Specter making a 10-9 vote—it played into Rove's strategy; if they allowed a floor vote, Pryor might win, for, as the Ronnie White vote showed, Republican discipline was tight. Arlen Specter was a good indicator. Facing a primary fight for reelection in 2004 with a Republican who was more conservative than he, Specter voted for Pryor in committee, explaining that he just wanted to move the nomination to the floor where he might vote differently. It was a lame excuse, because everyone knew that if Pryor got out of committee and Frist tried to schedule a floor vote, the Democrats would filibuster. By the time the sessions ended, there had been several unsuccessful efforts to force a vote on Pryor.

The Pryor battle was not the only bitter fight on the horizon. Bush had nominated two female judges from California, each of whom was also headed for a filibuster—Los Angeles County Superior Court Judge Caroline Kuhl and California Supreme Court Justice Janice Rogers Brown. Both were among the most conservative of Bush's very conservative nominees, especially Brown. Kuhl was nominated to the Ninth Circuit and Brown to the District of Columbia Circuit.

Caroline Kuhl is a California state trial court judge, whom both California senators oppose, though Feinstein agreed to a hearing on April 1 whereas Barbara Boxer did not. As Leahy pointed out, it was the first time a hearing was held for a nominee who did not have both blue slips from the home-state senators. When the committee vote was taken, both Feinstein and Boxer opposed her. The Democrats reminded Hatch of statements he made to NPR's Nina Totenberg that even if only one senator withholds a blue slip, the nomination would be held. On May 8, she was voted out with the usual 10-9 vote.[79]

Kuhl was particularly notorious for two matters: her ruling in a privacy case and her role in the 1983 *Bob Jones University* case when she was a high level aide in the Reagan Justice Department.[80]

The privacy case grew out of a visit to an oncologist by a woman who had just completed chemotherapy. The doctor asked her to remove her blouse and bra for a breast examination in the presence of an unidentified man who appeared to be a professional, and was introduced as someone "looking at [the oncologist's] work." Upon leaving, however, the woman learned from the receptionist that the man was a drug salesman, and burst out crying in shame and anger. She sued the oncologist and the drug company for an invasion of her privacy, but Kuhl dismissed the claim on the ground that the woman's participation in the exam was "voluntary." A unanimous appellate court reversed Kuhl in a sharply worded opinion.

The other case involved a tax exemption for the segregationist Bob Jones University. Throughout the 1970s Bob Jones University had been denied a tax exemption, a position initially defended by the Reagan administration in 1981. When Kuhl arrived, she apparently decided to reverse the policy. With but one other Justice Department official, she persuaded Attorney General William French Smith to support Bob Jones. She was strenuously opposed by the solicitor general, the Treasury Department general counsel and more than 200 other lawyers, including Theodore Olsen, George W. Bush's Florida lawyer and now his solicitor general. The Supreme Court rejected her position 8-1, with only Rehnquist supporting Kuhl's position. At her hearing she said she had changed her mind about overturning the exemption denial, writing the committee that she now believed her position "had been insensitive to minorities" and that the initial IRS ruling against Bob Jones was "legally defensible."

Kuhl also tried to persuade the Supreme Court to overturn *Roe v. Wade* and failing that, to limit abortion rights. In briefs to the Supreme Court as deputy solicitor general and as a private lawyer, Kuhl called on the Court to overrule *Roe*, even when it was unnecessary to the decision of the specific case. She also coauthored a government *amicus curiae* brief calling for a very narrow construction of Title VII's ban on sexual harassment in a case involving a male supervisor's pressure on a female employee to have sex with him, which, for fear of losing her job, the woman did. Kuhl argued this was "voluntary" and fell outside the law. The Supreme Court unanimously rejected her position. Kuhl also worked vigorously both in and out of government to cut off the ability of environmental groups like the Sierra Club and unions to go to court on behalf of their members; she lost all of these cases. She opposed access to the courts for veterans' claims, and as a judge she tried to deny attorney's fees to a whistleblower, on which she was again reversed unanimously. She was also unanimously reversed in a personal injury suit by a railroad employee against the railroad in which she denied the employee the right to use a crucial piece of evidence.

All of this produced an outpouring of opposition from numerous women lawyers and from environmental and civil rights groups. Kuhl also received support from some California lawyers who described her as a fair and impartial trial judge. Because of her overall record, however, Democrats blocked a floor vote.

The 54-year-old Judge Janice Rogers Brown, an African-American, was even further to the right. She was obviously nominated to the District of Columbia Circuit despite being a Californian to set her up for a Supreme Court appointment, for that Circuit is seen as a stepping stone to the High Court. The *Washington Post* described her as "the most unapologetically ideological nominee of either party in many years." Since Bush knew she would be opposed with a filibuster if she were voted out of committee—and she has been—she was clearly nominated only to embarrass the Democrats. Her background is similar to that of Clarence Thomas—she is the daughter of Alabama sharecroppers, and that was obviously a factor. On the merits, however she was an unlikely nominee. The California Bar Association had rated her "unqualified" for the California Supreme Court. Unlike Thomas, she was opposed by every African-American organization to take a position including the NAACP, the National Bar Association, the California Association of Black Lawyers, and the Congressional Black Caucus. The ABA, described by the *New York Times* as "all but a rubber stamp for the administration's nominees," gave her only a split "qualified/not qualified" rating.[81]

Considered the most conservative justice on the California court, which has six Republicans and but one Democrat, Brown was a frequent dissenter in opinions and often lashed out at her colleagues. Her positions in her opinions and in speeches were so extreme that they were far to the right of the conservative majority of the United States Supreme Court. For example, she praised *Lochner v. New York* and its progeny, in which the Supreme Court asserted the right to decide what governmental economic regulation was permissible, and in the process struck down numerous health and safety laws as infringing on the rights of business. No Supreme Court justice today approves of these cases, nor have they for almost seventy years.[82]

A thirty-nine-page report by People for the American Way and the NAACP summarized her many extreme positions so thoroughly that it is worth quoting at length:

> Brown has written many disturbing dissenting opinions, often joined by not a single additional state supreme court justice, that would have erected significant barriers making it much harder for victims of discrimination based on race, age, disability, and other grounds to obtain relief, if they had been adopted by a majority of the court. In one case, she asserted that a bank employee should not even have been able to file a

lawsuit for race and age bias under California's fair employment law because a 135-year-old federal bank law purportedly pre-empted the claim, an argument specifically rejected by the majority of the court. In another case, her dissent claimed, contrary to established precedent, that racially discriminatory speech in the workplace that creates a hostile working environment is protected by the First Amendment and cannot be limited, even suggesting that Title VII of the 1964 Civil Rights Act could be partly invalid under her reasoning.

California's chief justice severely criticized Brown's opinion in a controversial case concerning affirmative action, writing that her opinion incorrectly claimed that past Supreme Court decisions approving affirmative action were "wrongly decided" and that her analysis "represents a serious distortion of history." She was criticized for a dissenting opinion in an important case concerning reproductive choice, in which she argued, contrary to past precedent, that the California constitution does not provide greater privacy protections than the federal constitution.

Brown has also argued for overturning established precedent in cases concerning corporate power, the rights of workers, and government authority to enact economic and environmental regulations. Her dissent in one case argued for abandoning Supreme Court precedent and giving greater protection to even allegedly misleading commercial speech by corporations. Her dissent in another case ... advocated a "return to an earlier view" of employee rights that even Brown acknowledged has not been the law for many years. . . . Brown has also claimed that a basic Supreme Court principle of constitutional review, that strict scrutiny applies to violations of fundamental rights while general social and economic legislation is upheld if it has a rational basis, is "highly suspect, incoherent, and constitutionally invalid." In a speech to the Federalist Society, she has stated that what she has called the "Revolution of 1937," when the Supreme Court began to consistently sustain New Deal legislation against legal attack, was a "disaster" that marked "the triumph of our socialist revolution." In another speech to the same group, she said "Where government moves in, community retreats, civil society disintegrates and our ability to control our own destiny atrophies. The result is: families under siege; war in the streets; unapologetic expropriation of property; the precipitous decline of the rule of law; the rapid rise of corruption; the loss of civility and the triumph of deceit. The result is a debased, debauched culture which finds moral depravity entertaining and virtue contemptible."[83]

Questions have also been raised about her judicial temperament. She has been openly contemptuous of other justices, some of whom have privately complained of her "poison pen." She has also said that seniors benefitting from government programs, such as Medicare and Social Security, are "blithely cannibaliz[ing] their grandchildren."

At her hearing, Brown said her speech to the Federalist Society, which was delivered to about forty law students, was meant to "stir the pot" intellectually. Since she was preaching to the choir, it is difficult to see what she was "stirring." Idaho Republican Senator Larry Craig declared that Brown's speeches "were ringing statements of what our founding fathers believed were the rights of individuals in dealing with government."

She did write some decisions favoring individual rights. In one case, she denied police the right to stop and search a car just because it had crossed a yellow divider line. She also issued a favorable environmental decision. And she did have some supporters, including fourteen California law professors as well as a local NAACP official, though more than 270 law professors opposed her, including thirty from California.

At her hearing in October, Brown did nothing to dispel the concerns. Her promise that she would follow the law and that she knew "the difference between speeches and decisions" was belied by her many opinions. All this led even the *Washington Post*, which has found fault with very few Bush nominees, to complain that

> Mr. Bush cannot reasonably expect Democratic senators to support such a nominee. Given their propensity to rail against judicial activism, in fact, the wonder is that so many Republicans seem willing to back a candidate who—at least until her hearing—made no secret of her yearning for a judiciary "audacious enough to invoke higher law." . . . As long as the president so nakedly plays to his own base, he courts exactly the obstruction of which he complains.[84]

The *Post* did not offer any advice as to how the minority Democrats should prevent her confirmation other than by "obstruction."

On November 6, a 10-9 vote, including Specter, voted her out. That same day a second cloture vote on Pryor failed, with only Zell Miller and Ben Nelson breaking ranks.

The Brown nomination, together with that of Kenneth Starr aide Brett Kavanaugh, rubbed salt into Democratic wounds. The two nominees were to take the eleventh and twelfth seats on the District of Columbia Circuit, despite the repeated insistence of Republican senators like Grassley and Sessions that the court needed no more than nine or ten members.

Other battles were also on the horizon. Not only Kavanaugh, but Fourth Circuit nominee Claude Allen, who, while campaigning for Helms, said Helms's Democrat opponent had links "with the queers" and called abortion activists "Nazis." And there were the four Sixth Circuit nominees. There were others and the Bush-Rove strategy called for many more.

Many of these nominees were likely to go nowhere because their extremism ensured that Democrats would block them. The Republicans would then assail the Democrats as anti-Catholic, anti-Hispanic, anti-black, anti-Baptist, or anti–anything else they could think of. This would more than satisfy Karl Rove, for it would promote the strategy of ensuring that social conservatives, whether Reagan Democrats or the evangelical right, would vote and vote right in November 2004. Getting these votes became ever more important as Bush's numbers dropped because of Iraq and joblessness.

On October 30, a cloture vote on Pickering failed. The vote was apparently timed to help Haley Barbour, former Republican National Committee chairman and premier lobbyist, in his successful effort to win the Mississippi gubernatorial election on November 4.

On November 12–14, the Republicans engaged in a forty-hour "marathon" on judges, apparently suggested by Rupert Murdoch's conservative *Weekly Standard* and coordinated by his Fox News. In a move obviously designed for television, they brought cots and food into the Senate chamber to dramatize their effort though almost no one used the cots. "Our goal is very simple: an up-or-down vote on the nominations," said Frist. "People can vote up or they can vote down. Just give us a vote." Frist had apparently forgotten that he had voted against cloture on the Paez nomination, which had then been pending for four years. "It is a solemn responsibility of the Senate to act on the president's nominees," solemnly intoned Jon Kyl of Arizona. Democrats countered with reminders of the Republicans' treatment of the many Clinton nominees denied a hearing or a committee vote. Few people paid attention—the session was broadcast solely on C-SPAN—but conservative talk-show listeners were the real target. As Santorum acknowledged, many conservatives "don't think we're fighting hard enough." Stephen

Moore, president of the conservative Club for Growth, said a recent mailing to raise money for candidates yielded empty envelopes from two dozen former givers who said they would not contribute again until Republicans were harder on Democrats over the judges issue. "They want to see that at least Republicans are able to exact a pound of flesh, and that hasn't happened," Moore said. There were also unsuccessful additional cloture votes on Owen, Kuhl, and Brown.[85]

Republicans were not eager to vote on all the Bush nominees. J. Leon Holmes, a former law partner of Arkansas Democrat Mark Pryor, was nominated to a district judgeship in Arkansas in January 2003. It soon appeared that while supporting a constitutional amendment banning abortion, Holmes had rejected a rape and incest exception as unnecessary, saying "the concern for rape victims is a red herring because conceptions from rape occur with the same frequency as snow in Miami." Holmes had also written that "the wife is to subordinate herself to the husband . . . and [that] the woman is to place herself under the authority of the man." In an unusual move, on May 1, Holmes was voted out of committee 10-9, without a recommendation and without a vote being taken on whether to report out the nomination favorably, a very unusual procedure. Specter was one of the ten, with his usual disclaimer that he had done so only to enable the full Senate to vote on the nominee.

Six months later, by early November, majority leader Frist still had not scheduled Holmes's nomination for a vote. After the Republican "marathon" Senator Pryor, who supported his former law partner, moved for unanimous consent to consider the nomination. Obviously pursuant to instructions from the Republican judgeship strategy group—whose meetings Specter attends—Republican John Ensign of Nevada, the lone Republican in the chamber, quickly objected, and Specter and the other Republicans were spared having to vote on so embarrassing a nominee as Holmes. Nothing was heard from Hatch, Kyl, Frist, Santorum, Sessions, or Boyden Gray about "the solemn responsibility of the Senate to act on the president's nominees." Frist did not return phone calls on the matter. [86]

Republicans also had trouble with their antifilibuster plans. Not only were they unable to muster a two-thirds majority for a formal rules change, but they were apparently unable to minister fifty-one votes for the nuclear option.[87]

By the time the first session of the 108th Congress ended on December 9, the Democrats had approved 169 out of 179 nominations to reach the floor, including thirty appellate judges, 138 district judges, and one judge to the International Court of Trade. One nominee, Miguel Estrada, had withdrawn under fire. Ninety-seven percent of the Bush nominees were confirmed. The vacancy rate in the federal judiciary was down to 4.7 percent.

Shortly before the session ended, a bizarre episode occurred.

On November 14 and 15, first the *Wall Street Journal* and then the *Washington Times* published fourteen 2001 and 2002 memos to Durbin and Kennedy taken from the computer files of Senate Judiciary Democrats. The memos outlined strategies and arguments, including suggestions from liberal organizations on blocking or delaying judicial nominations. Democrats cried "foul" and called for an investigation.

Hatch's initial reaction was a denial that Republicans had anything to do with the matter.

> That's typical. Whenever they get their hands caught in the cookie jar, then they start to attack the process. . . . We have no evidence that anybody hacked into their computers, and I don't think they have any evidence of that. It very well

could have been a staffer who was conscience stricken and decided that this type of inappropriate conduct must end.

He and the other Republicans then used the memos to charge that, as Hatch put it,

If what is reported in the media is true about the memoranda . . . then it proves everything I've been saying. That is that Democratic senators are completely under the thumb of those inside the beltway vicious groups that have been labeling and slandering our judicial nominees.[88]

The Senate sergeant-at-arms started an investigation on November 21. On November 25, Hatch declared that his own investigation had turned up no evidence of Republican culpability. It soon appeared, however, that someone on Hatch's staff was probably responsible for the theft. Later the same day Hatch reversed himself and announced that his investigation had now discovered that at least one Republican Judiciary Committee staff member had, in Hatch's words, "improperly accessed at least some of these documents," and that a former staff member might also be involved. Echoing Captain Renaud in *Casablanca*, Hatch professed himself "shocked." The Republican staffer was suspended, and a full investigation was launched with Hatch's agreement, but to the fury of other Republicans, who continued to pound away at the Democrats as tools of "vicious Beltway groups." As of December 9, a full investigation was underway, with arguments about its scope.[89]

The year 2004 would be a presidential election year, and the combination of a sputtering and bloody war in Iraq, a smoldering conflict in Afghanistan, and severe joblessness at home meant the election and everything else political in 2004 would be hard-fought and rough, with the judgeship wars among the roughest of those fights.

The Republicans were prepared. They had already begun to pressure businesses to contribute heavily to the judicial wars on both the federal and state levels. Santorum told the press that "every time I talk to any kind of K Street group, I talk about judges and the importance of getting them involved in the judge issue; I think it's one of the most fundamental issues we have."

The business interests had already contributed heavily to Gray's Committee for Justice. According to *The Hill* weekly, the Chamber of Commerce had also involved itself deeply in state judicial races and had plans to get into many more. It was considering joining the Business Industry Political Action Committee to get into the federal judgeship fights. "Business leaders looking down the road calculate that they will likely have to do more to increase their influence on the nomination and approval of federal judges, especially if Congress passes the Class Action Fairness Act or other tort reform that would move class action suits out of state court and into federal courts. 'Then we would have to create a whole new set of points of influence,' said a consultant to a business trade association." [90]

Orrin Hatch was making his own preparations. To ensure that his rhetoric would be sufficiently vigorous and colorful, he hired Thomas Jipping to write his speeches.

• • •

1. The Adams statement is quoted in Arthur Schlesinger, Jr., "Eyeless in Iraq," *New York Review of Books* (October 23, 2003) pp. 24-25; The other statements are in Dana Milbank & Ellen Nakashima, "Bush Team has 'Right' Credentials; Conservative Picks Seen Eclipsing Even Reagan's," *The Washington Post,* (March 25, 2001) p. A01.
2. Gonzales' statements about judgeships being a priority were in interviews with Nina Totenberg, broadcast on *National Public Radio,* April 24, 2001, and with the *St. Louis Post-Dispatch,* March 24, 2001. His description of judicial selection was reported in Deirdre

Shesgreen, "White House Begins Work on Filling Judgeships; Appointments could Transcend Tax Cuts as Bush's Legacy," *The St. Louis Post Dispatch* (March 4, 2001) p. A5.
3. Gerhardt and Bolick are quoted in Neil Lewis, "President Moves Quickly on Judgeships," *The New York Times* (March 11, 2001) p. 34. The differences between the Bush and Clinton Administrations are noted in Sheldon Goldman et. al. "W. Bush Remaking The Judiciary: Like Father Like Son?" 86 *Judicature* 282, 285 (2003).
4. Federalist Society membership is discussed in Terry Carter, "The in Crowd," 87 *American Bar Association Journal* 46 (2001). Norton is quoted in Douglas Jehl, "Norton Record Often at Odds with Laws She Would Enforce," *The New York Times,* (January 13, 2001) p. A9; Norquist is quoted in Thomas Edsall, "Federalist Society Becomes a Force in Washington; Conservative Group's Members Take Key Roles in Bush White House and Help Shape Policy and Judicial Appointments" *The Washington Post,* (April 18, 2001) p. A04.
5. Terry Carter, n. 4.
6. Hatch is quoted in Helen Dewar & Thomas Edsall, "Democrats Block Justice Picks; Senators Protest GOP Change in Judicial Vetting," *The Washington Post,* (May 4, 2001) p. A01.
7. A full discussion of the "blue slip" procedure can be found in Brannon P. Denning, "The Judicial Confirmation Process and the Blue Slip," 85 *Judicature* 218 (2002).
8. Gonzalez's comment was made to Nina Totenberg, National Public Radio (April 25, 2001).
9. Wilkinson's comment is reported in Brooke Masters, "Battle Brewing over 4th Circuit Nominees," *The Washington Post,* (May 5, 2001) p. A06. The "collegiality" remark is from David Savage "Clinton Losing Fight for Black Judge" *The Los Angeles Times* (July 7, 2000), p. A1.
10. Nina Totenberg, n. 8.
11. Editorial, "More Converts in the Senate," *The Washington Post,* (May 9, 2001) p. A30.
12. Helen Dewar, "Democrats Take Reins of Senate; Both Parties Urge Bipartisanship," *The Washington Post,* (June 6, 2001), p. A01.
13. Gramm is quoted in Alison Mitchell, 'G.O.P Reports an 'Impasse' Over Senate Reorganization," *The New York Times* (June 15, 2001) p. A31; McConnell is quoted in Neil A. Lewis, "Ask, or Ask Not, What They Would Do to Their Country," *The New York Times* (June 27, 2001) p. A15; Gray's comment appears in "Panel Debates Senate Role on Court Choices; Clash on Ideology's Role Reflects Battles to Come," *The Washington Post,* (June 27, 2001) p. A23.
14. Gillers' observation can be found in Neil Lewis, "Bush Acting to Forestall Issue in Texas," *The New York Times* (October 10, 2002) p. A36. A discussion of Clark is contained in Alliance for Justice, Judicial Selection in the First Two Years of the George W. Bush Administration (*Alliance for Justice Judicial Selection Project Biennial Report 2003*), p. 37-38. (hereafter "AFJ 2002")
15. Al Kamen, "Pressing the Issue of Judicial Confirmation," *The Washington Post,* (November 5, 2001) p. A21.
16. Quoted in *AFJ* 2002, n. 15 at p. 2.
17. Both administrations' nominations and confirmations are noted in Rengel, "Lawmakers Find Time to Bicker Over Judges" *Legal Times* (October 22, 2001) at p. 13.
18. "Mr. Hatch's Revisionism," *The Washington Post,* (December 30, 2001) p. B06.
19. Audrey Hudsen, "Hatch says Pickering Victim of 'Lynching' on Civil Rights," *The Washington Post,* (March 7, 2002) p. A08.
20. Bill Sammon, "Bush Marshals Backers for Pickering," *The Washington Times* (March 7, 2002) p. A03.

21. Virginia Thomas, "To Judge Pickering: They Can't Take Away Your Honor," *The Wall Street Journal* (March 14, 2002).

22. John Nichols, "Karl Rove's Legal Tricks: Packing the Judiciary With Right Wingers" *The Nation* (July 22, 2002) p. 11; Rove's comments were quoted in Alan Cooperman & Amy Goldstein "Rove to Group: Bush to Press for a Conservative Judiciary," *The Washington Post,* (March 20, 2002) p. A09.

23. Neil A. Lewis, "These Are My Words, Not My Bond," *The New York Times* (September 22, 2002) p. 14.

24. Editorial "Reject Judge Brooks Smith" *The New York Times* (May 22, 2002) p. A26.

25. Id.

26. Editorial, "A Question of Ethics," *The Washington Post,* (May 23, 2002) p. A32.

27. Nothing for Free: How Private Judicial Seminars are Undermining Environmental Protections and Breaking the Public's Trust (Washington, D.C.) July 2000, p. 2.

28. Id., p v.

29. Edward Walsh, "Rehnquist Assails Curbs on Seminars for Judges; Business-Paid Events called 'Valuable'," *The Washington Post,* (May 15, 2001) p. A15.

30. Molly Ivins, "Is Texas America?" *The Nation* (November 17, 2003) p. 26.

31. AFJ 2002, p. 16

32. Dubose, "Slow and Fatal Justice," *L.A. Weekly* (June 13, 2002) p. 19.

33. Id.

34. Owen's decision in the abortion case is discussed in Jonathan Groner, "Activism' Is Question for Priscilla Owen," *Legal Times* (July 19, 2002). Gonzalez is quoted in Jonathan Groner, "War Over Bush Judges to Resume," *Legal Times* (July 8, 2002) p. 01.

35. See AFJ 2002, n. 15, p. 28.

36. The observer is Jillian Jonas, "Democrats Right on Estrada" *The Modesto Bee* (April 15, 2003).

37. Jonathan Groner, "Judge Nominees Told To Speak Softly," *Legal Times,* April 22, 2002, p. 08.

38. Michael Gerhart, "Here's What Less Experience Gets You," *The Washington Post,* (March 2, 2003) p. B1.

39. Davies, "Battle Looming Over Nominee," Miguel Estrada Has a Chance to be The First Hispanic on the Top Court," *The Philadelphia Enquirer* (January 7, 2002), p. A04.

40. United Mine Workers v. Bagwell, 512 U.S. 821 (1994).

41. Charles Lane, "Nominee for Court Faces Two Battles; Senate Panel to Focus on Ideology, Immigrant Past" *The Washington Post* (September 24, 2002), p. A01.

42. Id.

43. The Jackson memo is in the Opinions of the Attorney General (1941). I am indebted to Lisa Graves for bringing this Opinion to my attention.

44. The lawyers' quotes appear in Jack Newfield, "The Right's Judicial Juggernaut," *The Nation* (October 7, 2002) p. 11.

45. See *AFJ* 2002, n. 15 at p. 30-31.

46. Condon v. Reno, 528 U.S. 141(2000).

47. 148 Cong. Rec. S10344, (October 10, 2002).

48. Editorial, "War Over Judges," *The Washington Post,* (November 24, 2002) p. B06. The previous editorial is at Editorial, "Consult on Judges,' THE WASHINGTON POST (October 24, 2002) p. A34.

49. Editorial, "Steamrolling Judicial Nominees" *The New York Times,* (February 6, 2003) p. A38.

50. Hatch is quoted in "Hatch Reverses His Stand," *The New Republic,* (August 11, 2003) p. 8.

51. Hatch's statement appears in Michael Kinsley, "Estrada's Omerta," *The Washington Post,* (February 14, 2003) p. A31.

52. Senator John Cornyn, "Balance of Power" (May 6, 2003).

53. Rust v. Sullivan, 500 U..S. 173 (1991). For a full summary of Roberts' record, See Report of Alliance for Justice: Opposition to the Confirmation of John Roberts to the U.S. Court of Appeals for the D.C. Circuit (February 2003).

54. Jonathan Groner, "Survival Guide," *Legal Times,* (May 5, 2001) p.1.

55. Hatch's comments are reported in Jonathan Groner, n. 54, and Kirk Victor, "Point of Contention" *The National Journal* (July 5, 2003).

56. See Coons, "Courts: Sutton Overcomes Enviros' Objections to Join U.S. Appeals Court," *Greenwire* (April 30, 2003) [client]; Tony Mauro, "An Unlikely High Court Specialist," *Legal Times* (November 2, 1998) p. 8 [federalism]; Report of Alliance for Justice in Opposition to the Confirmation of Jeffrey Sutton to the U.S. Court of Appeals for the Sixth Circuit (January 2003) p. 3.

57. These cases are collected in pp. 3-4, n. 52.

58. Cases in which Cook dissented from worker and other protections are described in Adam Cohen, "Deborah Cook Is The Typical Bush Nominee—So Watch Out," *The New York Times* (February 25, 2003) p. A28.

59. Alliance for Justice Report in Opposition to the Nomination of Timothy Tymkovich to the United States Court of Appeals for the Tenth Circuit. (2003) p. 7.

60. Delano, "Government Busters: Despite Bush's Protests, Court Vacancies are Down," *The Pittsburgh Business Times* (May 16, 2003).

61. Norman Ornstein, "The Debate to End All Debate," *The New York Times* (May 14, 2003) p. A25.

62. David Rubinstein, "Rosenbaum Inquisition, " *The Nation,* (December 25, 2003), p.6.

63. Charles Lane, "Republicans Investigate Judge in Michigan Case; Wrong Doing in School Quota Case Alleged," *The Washington Post,* (November 1, 2003), p. A05.

64. Editorial, "Blacklisting Judges," *The New York Times* (August 10, 2003), p. 10.

65. Kennedy is quoted in Kirk Victor, "Point of Contention," *The National Journal* (July 5, 2003).

66. Woods is quoted in Editorial "Injudicious," *The Washington Post* (June 13, 2003) p. A28. The other description of Pryor appears in Editorial, "Religious Hard-Liner Unfit to Judge" *The Atlanta Journal and Constitution* (May 6, 2003) p. 10A.

67. Alan Cooperman, 'Santorum Angers Gay Rights Groups," *The Washington Post,* (April 22, 2003) p. A04; Ellen Goodman, *The Washington Post,,* May 4, 2003.

68. Hope v. Pelzer, 536 U.S. 730 (2002).

69. Editorial, "Injudicious," *The Washington Post,* (June 13, 2003) p. A28.

70. Gibson, "Judicial Nominee Ardent About Religion, States' Rights," *The Sun-Sentinel* (July 8, 2003) p. 1A.

71. Editorial, "Beyond the Pale," *The New York Times* (June 23, 2003) at A20.

72. See R. Jeffrey Smith & Tania Branigan "GOP Attorneys General Asked for Corporate Contributions" *The Washington Post,* (July 17, 2003) p. A01

73. Brian York, "Catholics Need Not Apply?" *The National Review Online* (July 30, 2003).

74. A discussion at the Catholic organization's efforts is in Periscope, "Political Ads— More Harm than Good?" *Newsweek* (August 11, 2003) p. 8.

75. Albert R. Hunt, "Politics & People: Showtime in the Senate," *The Wall Street Journal,* Nov. 13, 2003, p. A19.

76. Reilly, Religion News Service (August 8, 2003).

77. Sessions' comment is reported in O'Brien, "Charges of Anti-Catholicism Leveled In Debate Over Judicial Nominee" *The Catholic News Service* (July 24, 2003).

78. Editorial, "Despicable," *Roll Call* (August 18, 2003).
79. Henry Weinstein, "Hatch to Seek Vote on Judge," *The Los Angeles Times* (June 21, 2003), p. A12.
80. Bob Jones University v. United States, 461 U.S. 574 (1983).
81. Editorial, "Out of the Mainstream, Again," *The New York Times* (October 25, 2003) p. A18.
82. Lochner v. New York, 198 U.S. 145 (1905).
83. People for the American Way, "Loose Cannon: Report in Opposition to the Confirmation of Janice Rogers Brown to the U.S. Court of Appeals for the D.C. Circuit" (2003) pp. 2-3.
84. Editorial, "Fueling the Fight," *The Washington Post* (October 30, 2003), p. A22.
85. The reference to Fox News is from Klaus Marrel, *The Hill*, (November 3, 2003). The Kyl quote is from Nick Anderson, "The Senators Pull An All-Nighter Over Judicial Confirmations," *The Los Angeles Times*, (November, 13, 2003); the Moore quote is from Mike Allen, "GOP Plans Marathon on Judges; Debate to Spotlight Blocked Nominees," *The Washington Post,*(November 8, 2001), p. A1.
86. Geoff Earle, "In Twist, GOP Blocks Bush Nominee," *The Hill*, (November 19, 2003), p. 12.
87. Paul Kane, "GOP still Lacks Votes on Rules," *Roll Call* (November 17, 2003).
88. Lee Davidson, "Do Demos Take Orders From Left? Hatch Cites Proof; Allegations Over Leaked Memo Could Spur Fight," *Deseret Morning News,* (November 21, 2003).
89. See Neil A. Lewis, "Democrats Suggest Inquiry Points to Wider Spying by G.O.P.," *The New York Times,* February 10, 2004, p. A23. In early February Sergeant-at-Arms William Pickle told the Associated Press that what the Republican staffers had done was "certainly unproper." James Rosen and Julie Asher, "Memo Fireworks Consume Judiciary Panel Hearing," FoxNews.com, (February 12, 2004). Hatch and some other committee Republicans agreed, and Democrats called for a criminal investigation.
90. Alexander Bolton, "K Street Enters Fray Over Bench," *The Hill* (October 8, 2003), p. 1.

Chapter 6
The Impact of The Right Wing Counterrevolution

The right-wing tilt of the Reagan and Bush majority on the Supreme Court is so pronounced in the contentious areas that it is often difficult to pinpoint the specific contribution of the lower courts to this change, for in our hierarchical legal structure, the High Court sets the law that the lower courts apply. Nevertheless, it is not true that lower court judges simply "follow the law" given them by Congress and the Supreme Court, as judicial nominees ritually promise. As noted earlier, the many unresolved constitutional and statutory gaps, uncertainties, and unanticipated situations, even in cases where the High Court has spoken, leave the lower courts a great deal of unreviewed discretion. It is thus possible to analyze how the varying ideological policies of recent presidents have affected what the lower federal courts have done.

The District Courts

When it comes to shaping the law that governs our lives, the trial courts are only a way station, for litigants generally have a right to appeal trial court decisions, with certain exceptions (if they can afford to). Trial judges can, however, have a strong influence on the outcome of a case by the way they shape the record and by their fact-findings, both of which usually go unreviewed. Their rulings as to what evidence is admissible determine what is legally relevant. Their findings as to subjective matters like credibility and intent are particularly immune to review and will frequently determine the outcome of criminal justice and discrimination cases.

A study in 2001 by political scientists Robert Carp, Kenneth Manning, and Ronald Stidham analyzed District Court decisions by appointees of presidents from Lyndon B. Johnson to Bill Clinton to determine the relative liberalism of judges appointed by recent Democratic presidents compared to those named by Republicans. Decisions were considered "liberal" if they expanded civil rights and civil liberties, interpreted labor or other economic legislation to favor workers and consumers, and if they supported rights for the criminally accused. The study shows that Johnson's appointees voted for a liberal decision in approximately 52 percent of the cases, which was matched by a swing to the right by Nixon's appointees—39 percent liberal—and Ford's somewhat higher 43 percent. Carter tilted the District Courts back to the left with a liberal 52 percent. The Reagan-Bush judges were the most conservative by far. Just a little more than a third of the decisions by Reagan's trial judges—37 percent—were liberal, and Bush's appointees voted for a liberal decision only 38 percent of the time.[1]

The Courts of Appeal

It has not been too different on the appellate level. The most elaborate study of the Courts of Appeals was done by Professor Cass R. Sunstein of the University of Chicago Law School and social scientists David Schkade and Lisa Michelle Elman, published in September 2003 by the AEI-Brookings Joint Center for Regulatory Studies.[2] It covers 4,488 appellate decisions and 13,464 individual votes by appointees of all presidents over varying time periods from 1970 to December 31, 2002. It does not break out the decisions by appointees of the different presidents, but aggregates all Democratic and all Republican appointees. It does, however, separate out the different subject matter of the cases.

The study found that judges appointed by Democratic presidents vote more liberally than Republicans in seven out of ten key areas: affirmative action, sexual discrimination including sexual harassment cases, campaign finance, environmental protection, contracts, Title VII employment discrimination, the Americans With Disabilities Act, corporate litigation, abortion, and capital punishment. Little difference was found between Republican and Democratic appointees in criminal, federalism, and "takings" law cases, the last of which deals with determining government's obligation to pay a property owner for the incidental harm to him from governmental regulatory or other action. The study did not deal with religious issues, free speech, or with issues of personal autonomy like gay rights or the right to die.

The study also found a strong polarizing effect when an appellate panel is composed entirely of nominees of one party, rather than split between two of one party and one of the other. Aggregating all 4,488 cases, the study found that a panel composed of three Democratic appointees issued a liberal ruling 61 percent of the time, whereas an all-Republican panel voted for liberal side in only 34 percent of the cases. A panel composed of two Democratic appointees and one Republican issued a liberal ruling 50 percent of the time, whereas a panel composed of two Republican appointees and one Democrat did so just 39 percent of the time.

On specific issues, the study made these findings:[4]

- *Affirmative Action.* Three-fourths of the Democratic

votes were liberal but less than half of the Republican votes were. On all-Republican panels, individual Republican appointees voted for affirmative action programs 37 percent of the time compared with 49 percent when Republican appointees held a two-to-one majority. By contrast, all-Democratic panels came out in favor of the plan 82 percent of the time and a two-judge Democratic majority supported affirmative action almost as often: 80 percent. An affirmative action program thus had about a one-in-three chance of surviving before an all-Republican panel but more than a four-in-five chance before an all-Democratic panel.

- *Sex Discrimination.* From 1995 to December 31, 2002, Republican appointees voted in favor of plaintiffs 35 percent of the time, whereas Democratic appointees voted for plaintiffs 51 percent of the time. When Democratic appointees sat together, 75 percent of the Democratic votes went for the plaintiffs, whereas plaintiffs won only 50 percent or fewer cases when the Democratic appointees sat with one or more Republicans. With all-Republican panels, plaintiffs lost almost 70 percent of the time.
- In sexual harassment cases in particular, Republican appointees sided with the plaintiffs 37 percent of the time, whereas the percentage for Democratic judges was 52. Interestingly, the study found that "in these cases, gender didn't matter. Female judges [were] not more likely than male judges to vote in favor of the plaintiff . . ."[5]
- *Americans With Disabilities Act.* All-Republican panels voted for the plaintiff only 18 percent of the time, whereas all-Democratic panels hit 50 percent. Having two Democrats on a panel also helped the plaintiff.
- *Environmental Protection.* From 1970 through 2002,

Democratic votes went 64 percent for EPA enforcement, whereas Republican appointees voted for the agency only 46 percent of the time. If the panel was all-Democratic the vote for the agency was 72 percent, but if all-Republican, only 27 percent.[6]

- *Title VII.* Here, the differences are smaller: 41 percent of the Democratic votes and 35 percent of Republican votes were for the minority plaintiff. These relatively low figures may be attributable to the decisions since 1988 by the Supreme Court majority which have made it increasingly difficult for plaintiffs to win these cases.

- *Commerce Clause.* One surprising finding is that Commerce Clause challenges to federal statutes through December 31, 2002, fared no better with Republican than with Democratic appointees, both of whom overwhelmingly voted against the challenger. Since 1995, Democratic appointees rejected the challenge and upheld the federal statute 99 percent of the time, and Republicans did so 95 percent, despite the Supreme Court's federalism rulings. This was, of course, before most of the twenty-nine circuit judges appointed by George W. Bush in 2001–03 took their seats, so things may change.

In abortion and capital punishment cases, panel composition made no difference—party identification remained strong, with Democrats strongly in favor of the former and opposed to the latter, and the Republicans the opposite.

These AEI-Brookings study findings are useful, but they necessarily have limitations. For example, the study aggregates all the votes on an issue over lengthy time periods. The environmental cases go back to 1970, abortion cases to 1982, the affirmative action cases to 1978, the Title VII cases to 1985, the "takings" cases to 1978. There is no way of knowing whether the liberal votes in any of these categories came primarily in the early years of the period in question, or were spread over it evenly. Thus one cannot know the impact of the Reagan-Bush appointments, especially since issues change over time. Nor can such a study indicate how far from the mainstream on either side a decision may be. Would conservative justices like Potter Stewart and John M. Harlan, who disagreed with many Warren Court decisions, vote with judges like Silberman, Wilkinson, and Douglas Ginsburg who are so far to the right on today's issues?

One further reservation about these findings is that the absence of a dissent does not mean that all the panel members agree on the outcome. A judge unhappy with the decision may go along with the panel majority to avoid being labeled an automatic vote for the losing position and not listened to, particularly if the judge is a minority party member. Also a Democratic minority judge who is writing for a Republican panel majority in a case favoring a civil rights plaintiff or a criminal defendant may have to write quite narrowly in order to avoid losing the panel majority or having the case heard *en banc* by the full court, on which his side may be in the minority. More than a few cases in the District of Columbia and Fourth Circuits have been reheard *en banc* because the conservative majority on the circuit was unhappy with a decision by a three-judge panel. A judge may also decide not to dissent in order to maintain good relations with the other judges or simply because writing a dissent takes time.

On the other hand, a monolithic panel will be inclined not only to arrive at a more ideological result than a split panel, but to write the opinion with far-reaching implications that the facts of the case may not fully justify. The presence of a potential dissenter who is willing to go along with a narrow ruling and can point out weaknesses in the majority's position can constrain such expansiveness.

A cautionary note on the overall significance of any study of the impact of ideology on decision-making is necessary. Because all federal trial court cases are subject to an automatic appeal if the loser so chooses, the overwhelming proportion of appellate cases, estimated by some at 90–95 percent or more, are not controversial. They are decided by the application of established law or by a decisional process that implicates no contentious issues. These can be technical questions of procedure such as the appropriate venue for a case, difficult problems in interpreting accepted law, or in applying the law to complex facts, none of which may raise ideological issues. This is particularly true with respect to criminal appeals where many issues are easily resolved, and to many private disputes governed by state law that are in the federal courts only because the parties are from different states.

Even where the issue is controversial, for most federal judges ideology does not always determine their vote. Apart from the obligation to follow higher authority, there are professional standards and constraints that often impel a judge to vote for a decision he does not like. For example, in spring 1988, when Anthony Kennedy joined the Supreme Court, he immediately set about trying to reverse a civil rights decision issued eleven years earlier that broadly interpreted the 1966 Civil Rights Act. Within a month or so after his arrival, he joined the other conservatives in ordering the parties to brief the question whether the earlier interpretation should be overruled. After the issue was argued, he wrote a reluctant opinion reaffirming the precedent because none of the established prerequisites for overturning a prior decision had been met.[7]

Another example is the decision by Rehnquist, Kennedy, and O'Connor not to overturn the *Miranda v. Arizona* interrogation case, even though all three had criticized and drastically limited it in earlier decisions. The consequences of overturning a decision that had become a part of American popular culture and known all over the world, and the green light it might have given to police abuses must have been at least a factor if not the most decisive one in overcoming their disapproval of *Miranda*.

Nevertheless, a significant number of controversial decisions are decided each year. Even if the proportion is only 5 percent, that comes to 1,400–1,500, or about 100 per year per circuit on average. Since some circuits like the District of Columbia Circuit, the Second, and the Ninth are larger and have many more cases than others, the larger circuits may have many more difficult cases than 100 per circuit per year.

To try to get at the ideological character and impact of the recent Republican appointees it is necessary to analyze specific areas and decisions, both thematically and as products of the different circuits. Little of this has been done on a rigorous analytic basis, but some case-specific data is available.

One such study is in environmental law. In summer 2001 the Natural Resources Defense Council, the Alliance for Justice and the Community Rights Council jointly issued an analysis of the Republican appointees' impact on environmental law. Most of these cases are from the District of Columbia Circuit, for it has been estimated that half of all environmental challenges are brought there, and some challenges can only be brought in that circuit.[9]

Although largely qualitative, the NRDC study also provides the following statistical data:

> From 1970 to 1994, Republican judges voted to deny standing to environmental plaintiffs in 79.2% of cases challenging EPA decisions. During the same period, Democratic judges voted to deny standing to environmental plaintiffs in only 18.2% of EPA cases. . . . From 1987 to 1994, three-judge panels consisting of two Republicans and one Democrat reversed the EPA on procedural

grounds raised by industry in 54–89% of cases. During the same period, panels consisting of two Democrats and one Republican reversed the EPA in between 2% and 13% of these cases....During the 1990s pro-industry claimants experienced a five-fold increase in their success in challenging EPA's scientific decision-making. Over the same period, environmental claimants saw their success rate decrease by 20%.[10]

The standing requirement—that a plaintiff must have a specific injury in order to get into federal court—has been used with particular effectiveness by conservative judges to dismiss suits by citizen groups. It is an easily manipulable doctrine, so much so that according to one observer who studied every standing case decided in the past several years by the Supreme Court and the federal Courts of Appeals, "judges provide access to the courts to individuals who seek to further the political and ideological agendas of judges."[11]

Judge David Sentelle has used the standing doctrine to be particularly rough on litigants. He wrote for the court denying the right of environmental organizations to force the Treasury to assess the potential environmental impacts of a large tax credit proposed for the dangerous gasoline additive MTBE, even though the plaintiffs offered detailed affidavits, expert testimony, and numerous reports showing that the tax credit could interfere with their use of wildlife habitats and harm their drinking water. When the dissenting judge complained that Sentelle's ruling would make it impossible to challenge any EPA ruling with widespread effect, Sentelle's answer was, in effect, "so be it."[12]

Of equal importance in environmental matters is the Court of Appeals for the Federal Circuit, which hears appeals from Federal Court of Claims rulings on claims against the United States for taking property without fair compensation. A "taking" can include regulations that so seriously impair the value of property as to be the functional equivalent of physically taking the property. Takings law is being used more and more to challenge environmental regulations, and the Court of Claims and the Federal Circuit have been receptive. In one example, Florida Rock, a large commercial mining operation, wanted to extract limestone from a large wetlands area in the Everglades region of southern Florida. The Army Corps of Engineers refused to issue a permit because of the pollution that goes with limestone mining and concern about destruction of the wetlands. Even with that restriction on mining, Florida Rock received offers for the property that would have allowed it to recover more than twice the original purchase price. The Federal Circuit still found a "partial taking," with a potential liability to the United States of tens of millions of dollars. One law professor called the Federal Circuit's opinion in *Florida Rock* "an extremely destabilizing decision, exposing all wetlands regulation, indeed all environmental and land use regulation, to compensation claims."[13]

Perhaps the worst District of Columbia Circuit Court environmental decision was the nondelegation decision by Judge Stephen Williams in 1999 and noted earlier in chapter 2. The 2-1 decision written by Williams struck down Clean Air Act regulations on smog and soot. The EPA administrator called the regulation "the most significant step we've taken in a generation to protect the American people . . . from the health hazards of air pollution." According to Williams, however, Congress cannot delegate broad authority to administrative agencies, a proposition accepted by the Court only twice, in 1935, and neither before nor since. The ruling was too much for even this Supreme Court, and it unanimously reversed with an opinion by Scalia. Had Williams's decision been affirmed, much of the government's health and safety regulation would be jeopardized.[14]

The District of Columbia Circuit has moved far to the right in many other areas as well. In testimony before the Senate Judiciary Committee in September 2002, Professor Michael Gottesman of Georgetown, a leading labor and constitutional expert who appears frequently before the Supreme Court, reported that in labor cases the District of Columbia Court of Appeals majority has continually voted for the employer, consistently striking down NLRB rulings for employees. "The ideological shift on the District of Columbia Circuit has resulted in a court that is all too happy to substitute its judgment for that of the NLRB, and in a manner that undermines the rights of workers and unions to form and join unions—the essential rights that the NLRA was enacted to protect," Gottesman told the Senate committee.

Gottesman's testimony is worth quoting at length:

> In fiscal year 1998, the last year for which statistics are available, the District of Columbia Circuit's affirmative rate was 20 percent lower than the national average—52 percent affirmative in the District of Columbia Circuit vs. an overall affirmance rate of 65.3 percent. Whereas in 1980, the District of Columbia Circuit heard only 3.2 percent of challenges to NLRB decisions heard by circuit courts—placing the District of Columbia Circuit next to last of all the circuits—by the year 2000, the District of Columbia Circuit ranked first among all circuits courts in the percentage of NLRB cases heard by the court. That year almost one in five cases—18 percent—were filed in the District of Columbia Circuit, virtually all of them by employers.

Some illustrative cases cited by Gottesman, "a small sample of an ocean of such cases," in his words, are:

> In *Pacific Micronesia Corporation v. NLRB*, the court overturned

the NLRB's determination that pervasive publicity about legislative initiatives to restrict the rights of nonresident workers prevented a free election among a group of (largely nonresident) workers in Saipan. In *International Paper Co. v. NLRB*, a panel of Reagan-Bush appointees overturned the NLRB's decision and ruled that the company's permanent subcontracting of employees' jobs during a lockout was not an unfair labor practice. In *Detroit Typographical Union v. NLRB*, a panel of Reagan-Bush appointees overturned the NLRB's determination that the *Detroit News* and *Free Press* had committed an unfair labor practice when they unilaterally implemented a merit pay proposal immediately prior to the beginning of a 19-month strike by newspaper employees. In *Mathews Readymix, Inc. v. NLRB*, the court overturned an NLRB determination that an employer illegally withdrew recognition from an incumbent union based on information from decertification petitions that were tainted by the employer's earlier unfair labor practices. These are a small sample of an ocean of such cases.

The D.C. Circuit has refused to defer to the Board's expertise in other areas as well. For example, the National Labor Relations Act gives the NLRB authority to determine the scope of an appropriate bargaining unit. Yet the D.C. Circuit frequently refuses to defer to the NLRB's bargaining unit determination and reverses its decisions.[15]

In civil rights cases, the Reagan-Bush judges have also turned the clock back. In a Title VII employment discrimination case they interpreted the prerequisites for punitive damages so narrowly that the Supreme Court, which has not been sympathetic to either Title VII cases or heavy punitive damages, reversed it. They have even struck down outreach efforts that obligated the FCC merely to *consider* the ratio of minorities to the majority in order to determine whether the agency was fulfilling its equal opportunity obligation. This case was severely criticized by the *Harvard Law Review*, and may be used to support recent efforts to block outreach efforts by universities and others.[16]

The District of Columbia Bush-Reagan judges have been equally hostile to the rights of prisoners. In one case, they found no violation when the District of Columiba prison authorities failed to provide Spanish interpreters during medical treatment. There was no "deliberate indifference" to the prisoners' needs, the Reagan-Bush panel found, ignoring District of Columbia policies that clearly showed such indifference. In another 2-1 case, the D.C. Circuit upheld prison regulations that disallowed electric guitars in part because they would involve expenditures for storage, electricity, or supervision, but primarily because "prison perks undermine the concept of jails as deterrents," a phrase that appeared in the legislative history of a law pro- hibiting the use of any prison appropriations for the "use or pos- session" of electric or electronic instruments. That decision produced a sharply worded editorial from the *Washington Post* which commented, "while the court majority is right that inmates have no inviolable constitutional right to play electric guitars, it came to that conclusion in a way that could let Con- gress ban books, mail or just about anything else from prisons by calling them just 'perks.'"[17]

Decisions striking down FCC regulations and allowing broad exceptions to the Freedom of Information Act are also common. Dissents by Clinton appointee Judge David Tatel appear frequently, but often only for himself, because Judge Patricia Wald has retired and the other Democratic appointees are not particularly liberal.

Because the District of Columbia Circuit is where many challenges to federal government action are filed, national security issues have also arisen from time to time. The Sen- telle-Silberman obstructionism of the Iran/*contra* investigation has already been noted. The September 11, 2001 attack has generated more. In one case, Sentelle and Karen LeCraft Henderson, a Bush Sr. appointee, overturned a lower court decision by Judge Gladys Kessler, a highly regarded Clinton appointee, and ruled, over a Tatel dissent, that the Freedom of Information Act does not require release of any information about the post-9/11 detainees—not their names, their lawyers, dates of arrest and release, or reasons for the detention. Some 1,200 people were detained, including those connected with immigration law violations, criminal matters, and material witnesses. "The need for deference in this case is just as strong as in earlier cases," Sentelle wrote. He added that when government officials tell the court that disclosing the names of the detainees would harm national security, "it is abundantly clear that the government's top counterterrorism officials are well suited to make this predictive judgment. Conversely, the judiciary is in an extremely poor position to second-guess" the government in this matter.

To Tatel, "by accepting the government's vague, poorly explained allegations, and by filling in the gaps in the government's case with its own assumptions about facts absent from the record this court has converted deference into acquiescence." Perhaps some of the requested material should have been held back, he observed, but "this all-or-nothing approach runs directly counter to well-established principles governing FOIA requests . . . [T]he government bears the burden of identifying functional categories of information that are exempt from disclosure, and disclosing any reasonably segregable, nonexempt portion of the requested materials." [18]

The most controversial and constitutionally dubious measure that the Bush administration has adopted in its antiterrorism tactics has been the denial of all rights and the virtually secret detention of Americans and others whom it has labeled "enemy combatants." Acting in patent violation of both international and domestic law, for which it has been condemned throughout the world, the administration has arrogated to itself the right to unilaterally label some detainees "enemy combatants" and deny them the right to counsel, access to their families, limits to the detention period, and any contact whatsoever with the outside world. It can try them before military commissions with no limits on what evidence may be introduced and with no right of appeal to an independent tribunal. Civilian lawyers who have offered to assist defendants in those tribunals have had numerous obstacles put in their way, including having to cover their own expenses to fly to the American naval base at Guantanamo Bay where the "enemy combatants" captured in Afghanistan are held, having their client interviews overheard, and facing other obstacles to effective representation. Efforts to challenge any of these conditions with respect to the Guantanamo prisoners have been met by government arguments that because the base is not formally part of the United States, no federal court has jurisdiction over what happens there, even though the United States has exercised total control over the area under a lease signed in 1903. In effect, they say, what the United States does at Guantanamo is outside the law and not subject to any judicial scrutiny. They have made a similar argument with respect to American citizens held in the United States.

The claim with respect to Guantanamo has been sustained so far by several courts, including the District of Columbia Circuit. In a decision handed down by Randolph, Williams, and Garland, the court accepted the government's argument. On November 10, 2003, the Supreme Court agreed to decide whether detainees at Guantanamo Bay may file a *habeas corpus* writ with any American court.[19]

What was said in 1987 about the District of Columbia Circuit by the Washington, D.C. *Legal Times*, is even more true today:

• • •

> [L]itigators [have] had to revamp their strategies to suit [the] 'Reaganized' bench....While the Court has by no means given conservatives and the administration everything they want, the D.C. Circuit has moved far closer to the Reaganite ideal: hesitant to overrule [Republican controlled] administrative agencies, grant nontraditional plaintiffs standing, create new rights, and exercise its judicial powers.[20]

As the District of Columbia vacancies fill up with Bush nominees like John Roberts, and if the theory about the impact of panel-majority is correct, the District of Columbia Circuit will move even farther to the right. For example, shortly after he joined the court this spring, Roberts dissented from a refusal by the full court to reconsider a decision upholding the constitutionality of the Endangered Species Act under the Commerce clause. Only Sentelle agreed with him.[21]

National security cases may not be a good way to test the impact of any president's appointees. Although most conservative judges are predisposed to favor the government in cases that pit the individual's rights against the government's claims of public safety, even liberal judges will go along with whatever the government asks in times of war or other threats to national security. The Supreme Court's abdication of any independent judgment in the *Korematsu* case, when the government claimed that it was necessary to intern hundreds of thousands of Japanese residents in order to protect the West Coast against a Japanese invasion, in the face of much evidence to the contrary, is the best-known example. The Court's opinion was written by one of the Court's foremost civil-liberties advocates, Hugo Black, and the 6-3 majority included such staunch liberals as William O. Douglas and Harlan F. Stone, as well as Felix Frankfurter.[22]

There are many other such instances. History has proved many times that during war or national emergency, the courts bow to the president and the military. It is thus hardly surprising that since September 11, 2001, the courts have rarely denied the government what it demanded.

Among the best-known rulings are those involving noncitizen immigrants, of whom about 1,200 were detained immediately after September 11, and two American citizens classified as "enemy combatants." Two important immigration cases arose out of an order by Chief Immigration Judge Michael Creppy that all deportation hearings be closed to the press and the public. The press challenged the order in Detroit and in New Jersey.

The Detroit case came before a Sixth Circuit bench consisting of three liberal judges: Damon Keith, Martha Daughtrey, and Ohio District Judge James Carr; the New Jersey case was heard in the Third Circuit by a panel of three Reagan appointees: Edward Becker, Morton Greenberg, and John Scirica. In each case, the trial court decided in favor of the newspapers. The Sixth Circuit affirmed, but a 2-1 panel of the Third Circuit reversed, setting up a circuit conflict that should be resolved by the Supreme Court. The Sixth Circuit decision stressed the importance of an informed public to a democracy, Judge Keith saying:

> Democracies die behind closed doors. . . . When government begins closing doors, it selectively controls information rightfully belonging to the people. Selective information is misinformation.

Judge Becker, however, concluded that "in recognition of [the attorney general's] experience (and our lack of experience) in these [national security] cases, we will defer to his judgment."[23]

The two cases involving American citizens arose in two very

diverse circuits with very diverse results: the ultra-conservative Fourth Circuit and the still liberal Second Circuit. The Fourth Circuit decisions involved an American citizen, Yassar Esam Hamdi, who was captured in Afghanistan and held as an "enemy combatant." The case pitted a Reagan district judge, Robert Doumar, against Wilkinson, Traxler, and Chief Judge William Wilkins, a Reagan appointee. Doumar ordered the government to allow Hamdi to meet privately with the public defender. The government refused and appealed, arguing not only that Hamdi be denied the opportunity to speak with a lawyer, but that the courts had no authority "to second-guess the military's determination that an individual is an enemy combatant and should be detained as such." Even Wilkinson refused to accept the latter proposition, saying that if they did, "we ourselves would be summarily embracing a sweeping proposition—namely that, with no meaningful judicial review, any American citizen alleged to be an enemy combatant could be detained indefinitely without charges or counsel on the government's say-so." The District Court was ordered to look into the question but to give the government's argument great deference and not to order counsel for Hamdi.

Doumar then ordered the government to turn over some documents to Hamdi. The government again appealed, submitted a brief "declaration" setting out its reasons, and won again from Wilkinson, Wilkins, and William Traxler in an opinion emphasizing the "limitations on judicial activities." This time, the court went further and held that the courts may not inquire into the basis for the military's decision that Hamdi was an enemy combatant since he was captured in a war zone and the government had set forth "factual legal assertions which would establish a legally valid basis for the petitioner's detention." Just as in *Korematsu*, the court would not ask for the evidence underlying the government's assertions. decision.[25]

• • •

During the week of December 15, however, two courts went against the trend. On December 18, a 2-1 panel of the Court of Appeals in New York ruled that the courts could not be kept out of the picture because Congress had not suspended the writ of *habeas corpus*, that American citizen José Padilla was entitled to counsel, that the president had no inherent power to indefinitely detain Americans not seized on the battlefied and that a 1991 law prevented the government from detaining Padilla. The panel consisted of two George W. Bush appointees and a Clinton appointee, with one of the Bush appointees dissenting on the inherent power and statutory issues; the other Bush appointee was Barrington Parker, Jr., who is an African-American Democrat, appointed a district judge by Clinton and one of the bones thrown to Democrats in Bush's May 9, 2001 nominees.[26]

That same week, a Ninth Circuit panel ruled that detainees at Guantanamo Bay could not be denied the right to file a *habeas corpus* writ in a federal court, an issue that is before the Supreme Court in the D.C. Circuit case. All three members of that panel were Democratic appointees.[27]

That the Fourth Circuit would give the government what it wants is hardly surprising. That court has long been considered the most conservative of all the circuits, and though it is beginning to get a good deal of competition for that distinction from the others, its pre-eminence seems safe, especially with Dennis Shedd and other recent Bush nominees filling up the court and making it less and less likely that a panel will have a liberal majority. Although it has four Clinton appointees on the court, Traxler was initially a Bush district judge and votes with the conservative majority, leaving only Blane Michael and Robert B. King of West Virginia, and Diana Motz of Maryland, as the regular dissenters.

Many of its decisions have already been discussed in connection with individual members like Luttig, Wilkinson, Karen Williams, and others. Some of the decisions have been too extreme for even the Supreme Court's conservative majority. The *Dickerson* case, where the Supreme Court refused to overturn *Miranda v. Arizona*, is one such case. There, the government had not requested that *Miranda* be overturned, but on its own the Fourth Circuit invited the government to do so, and then ruled that the *Miranda* warnings were not constitutionally required, had been undone by a 1968 law, and undermined by recent decisions. The Supreme Court disagreed.

Also in criminal cases, the only two instances where the Supreme Court found that a death row prisoner had been denied adequate representation were in decisions that reversed Fourth Circuit decisions; in both cases, the trial court had ruled for the defendant on the issue but the Fourth Circuit reversed. The judges of that circuit have also made it virtually impossible for a state prisoner to use *habeas corpus* to challenge his conviction in federal court, even when a death sentence is at issue. In his study of capital cases, Columbia Law School Professor James Liebman found that the Fourth Circuit overturned only 4 percent of the death sentences it reviewed—the average appellate court reversal rate was 40 percent. A Cornell Law School professor who represents death row prisoners described the circuit as "the black hole of death penalty cases . . . In the last 26 cases in which the death sentence petitioner prevailed at the trial level, the circuit reversed. How can the district judges be wrong every single time?"[28]

In other cases the Fourth Circuit judges have tried to limit the ability of citizen groups to sue polluters and get damages. In one such case, it was again too much for the Supreme Court, and a 7-2 majority slapped them down. The circuit also struck down the Driver Privacy Protection Act, which prohibits states from selling their rosters of registered drivers for profit. The judges said that the law had "offended our system of dual sovereignty" by telling the states what they could and could not do with their drivers' records. The Supreme Court reversed that too.[29]

A *New York Times* article in March 2003 summarized some of the Fourth Circuit's recent decisions as follows:

> Among its many decisions, the Fourth Circuit has upheld the minute of silence in Virginia schools; ended court-ordered busing in Charlotte; upheld state laws that stringently regulate abortion clinics or require parental notification or ban so-called partial-birth abortions; ruled that the Virginia Military Institute could remain all male as long as there was a separate but comparable education for women; upheld a Charleston, S.C., program that tested maternity patients for illegal drug use without their consent and turned the results over to the police; overturned a Virginia prohibition against license plates bearing the Confederate flag; ruled that the F.D.A. didn't have the authority to regulate nicotine as a drug; and, most recently, overruled a West Virginia federal judge's efforts to strictly limit mountaintop mining that buries Appalachian streams beneath piles of fill and waste.[30]

Although the VMI and the Charleston, South Carolina, drug program cases were also overturned by the Supreme Court, the circuit has been more in tune with the Supreme Court's conservative majority than most of the other circuits. One particularly notable instance was the circuit's decision striking down the Violence Against Women Act, which was affirmed 5-4 by the Supreme Court; the only Attorney General supporting the circuit was Pryor, and the lawyer who challenged the act was Jeffrey Sutton, now on the Sixth Circuit.[31]

The Fourth Circuit's extreme conservatism may well be an

example of the AEI-Brookings finding that panels composed of ideologically similar judges are more extreme than split panels: There are very few liberals on the Fourth Circuit to make a panel majority. As law school Professor Arthur Hellman observed,

> There is a conservative majority on the full court, and if they see a panel decision they don't like, they just take it *en banc* and reverse it. No other circuit enforces majority rule the way the Fourth Circuit does. It's gotten to the point that if there is a 2-to-1 liberal panel decision, you can predict with almost perfect certainty that it will go before the full court and be reversed. Liberal panel decisions are not allowed to survive.

A recent abortion case described by Neil Lewis of the *New York Times* is a good example of this. A federal trial judge blocked the Virginia law requiring underage women to obtain the consent of one parent before having an abortion. The state majority went to Luttig to get the ruling reversed, and he quickly agreed. The abortion-rights lawyers then asked for a three-judge panel to reconsider the case, and the panel overturned Luttig's order. Luttig promptly asked the full court to consider the case. In the meantime, the chief judge ordered that the ruling by the panel be withheld from the public. Eventually the full court upheld Luttig.[32]

The Sixth Circuit may be a further illustration of the polarization thesis, but its other side. When George W. Bush became president and during his first two years, the court was divided evenly, 5-5, between Democratic and Republican appointees. The result was that the decisions varied with the panel, and lawyers described it as "moderate" overall, though they expected it to become more conservative. The Sixth Circuit was where the affirmative action plan of the University of Michigan Law School was upheld, a decision the Supreme

Court affirmed. A panel of that circuit also produced the *Detroit Free Press* decision discussed earlier.[33]

On the other hand, when there was a conservative majority, it has issued extremely conservative decisions, some written by Danny Boggs, a 1986 Reagan appointee who is, in the words of one lawyer, "superconservative," and according to another lawyer, remains "very active in Republican politics." In one case, Boggs wrote for a panel that denied the protection of Title VII's ban on sex discrimination in employment to a homosexual who was subjected to consistent and harsh verbal harassment. In another case, Judge Alice M. Batchelder, a G. H. W. Bush appointee, wrote for a panel that included Boggs and Norris, another Reagan appointee, striking down the federal Child Support Recovery Act, which criminalizes the failure to comply with an interstate child support order. The panel ruled that the act exceeded Congress's commerce Clause powers. The full court, including another Bush appointee, overturned that panel.[34]

An example of how judges will sometimes find distinctions to reach a desired result where there really are no differences is a Sixth Circuit case similar to the Supreme Court's *Romer v. Evans* decision. In *Romer*, the Supreme Court struck down a Colorado constitutional amendment that barred state or local action to protect homosexuals against discrimination. Cincinnati had earlier adopted a charter amendment similar to the Colorado provision, but for municipal law and administration. The trial court found the amendment unconstitutional, but a panel containing two Reagan appointees and a very conservative Carter appointee, Cornelia Kennedy, reversed the trial court and upheld the amendment. After *Romer* was decided, the Supreme Court ordered the Sixth Circuit to reconsider its decision. Following a Scalia suggestion in the reconsideration action order—he had issued one of his harshest dissents in *Romer*—the panel reaffirmed its original ruling on the ground that the Cincinnati amendment involved only one city, not a whole state. With the arrival of Jeffrey Sutton and Deborah Cook, the circuit is likely to become even more conservative.[35]

One substantive area where almost all Republican judges have been consistently hostile is affirmative action for racial and ethnic minorities. The elementary and secondary school education cases, and the *Hopwood* decision have already been discussed in Chapter 1. In the District of Columbia Circuit, in addition to the *Lutheran Church-Mo. Synod* case discussed earlier in this chapter, the court struck down an effort by the District of Columbia Fire Department to increase minority representation in a city that is 75 percent African-American; this case was the occasion for the Silberman-Mikva exchange in which Silberman threatened to punch Mikva. Elsewhere, efforts to increase the usually small share of government contracts going to minority businesses have met the same fate, even before the Supreme Court's Reagan-dominated majority decided the *Croson* case which made it all be impossible to sustain such set-asides.[36]

Finally, two examples from the Fifth Circuit, which covers Texas, Louisiana, and Mississippi, and is the Fourth Circuit's closest rival for the rush to the right. The Fifth is where *Hopwood* was decided and it is the only appellate court to rule that Justice Powell's opinion in the 1978 *Bakke* case allowing racial preferences to achieve educational diversity was not a binding precedent.

In a 1999 death row case, Calvin Burdine, a Texas inmate filed a *habeas corpus* petition asking for a new trial because his lawyer was not only incompetent but had slept through parts of the trial. The trial court accepted Burdine's claim and set aside the conviction. A 2-1 panel of the Court of Appeals, with a Reagan and a Bush senior judge in the majority, reinstated the conviction, because the record did not reveal exactly when the lawyer had been asleep during the trial. This was too much even for the other conservatives on the Fifth Circuit, and on rehearing, they set aside the panel decision.[37]

One can multiply these examples many times, but it is hardly necessary. Those courts that are already top-heavy with conservatives like the Fourth, Fifth, Sixth, and Seventh will become even more so, as Bush fills the nineteen remaining appellate vacancies; the Ninth will probably remain moderately liberal, for the margin by which the Democratic appointees exceed the Republicans on that circuit is greater than the number of vacancies on the circuit. The Second Circuit now has seven Democratic appointees and five Republicans with one vacancy; one Democratic departure could shift that balance. And since so many of the Republican appointees are very young, the impact of these many conservative judges will probably last for decades to come.

• • •

1. Robert A. Carp, Kenneth L. Manning and Ronald Stidham, "President Clinton's District Judges - 'Extreme Liberals' or Just Plain Moderates," 84 *Judicature* 282 (2001).
2. Cass Sunstein, David Schkade, and Lisa Michelle Ellman, Ideological Voting on Federal Courts of Appeals: A Preliminary Investigation, AFI-Brookings Joint Center for Regulatory Studies, Working Paper No. 03-9, September 2003 (http://papers.ssrn.com/abstract=442480).
3. Id. at A1, Table 1, 35-43.
4. The findings on specific issues are at pp. 14-25.
5. Id. at 6.
6. This data was gathered almost entirely from D.C. cases where the bulk of environmental law is made. A more focused study on environment law developments appears below.
7. Patterson v. McLean Credit Union, 491 U.S. 164 (1988), re-affirming *Runyon v. McCrary*, 427 U.S. 160 (1976).
8. *Dickerson v. United States*, 530 U.S. 428 (2000).
9. Richard Revesz, "Environmental Regulation, Ideology, and the D.C. Circuit," 83 Va. L. Rev. 1717, 1717 n. 2, (1997);
10. National Resources Defense Counsel "Hostile Environment: How Activist Judges Threaten our Air, Water, and Land," Alliance for Justice, Community Rights Counsel, Natural Resources Defense Council (July 2001) p. 25;
11. Richard Pierce, "Is Standing Law or Politics," 77 N.C.L. REV. 1741, 1742-43 (1999)].
12. *Florida Audubon Society v. Bentsen*, 94 F.3d 658 (D.C. Circ. 1996) (en banc).
13. Id.
14. *Whitman v. American Trucking Assn's*, 531 U.S. 457 (2001).
15. Michael Gottesman, "The D.C. Circuit: The Importance of Balance on the Nation's Second Highest Court," testimony to the U.S. Senate Committee on the Judiciary, (September 24, 2002)(in author's files).

302   HERMAN SCHWARTZ

16. Kolstad v. American Dental Association, 139 F.3d 958 (D.C. Cir. 1998).; Lutheran Church - Mö. Synod v. F.C.C., 141 F.3d 344 (D.C. Cir. 1998).; 112 Harv. L. Rev. 988 (1999).; Michael, Dobbs, "At Colleges, an Affirmative Reaction; After Rulings, Recruiters Take a More Inclusive Approach to Diversity," *The Washington Post*, (November 15, 2003), p. A01.
17. *Kimberlin v. United States*, 318 F.3d 228 (D.C. Cir. 2003); Editorial, "Prison Blues," *The Washington Post*, (February 19, 2003), p. A28.
18. *Center for National Security Studies v. Department of Justice* 331 F.3d 918 (D.C. Cir. 2003). The Supreme Court has declined to review this case, prompting an unhappy editorial, "Keeping Detentions Secret," *The New York Times*, (January 14, 2003).
19. Al Odah v. United States, 321 F.3d 1134 (D.C. Cir. 2003), cert. granted sub nom, *Rasul v. Bush*, 2003 U.S. LEXIS 8203.
20. Karpay, Kenneth, "The D.C. Circuit's New Face," *The Legal Times*, (May 4, 1987), p.1.
21. *Rancho Viejo v. Norton*, ____ F. 3d ____ (D.C. Cir. 2003).
22. *Korematsu v. United States*, 323 U.S. 214 (1944).
23. *Detroit Free Press v. Ashcroft*, 303 F.3d 681 (6th Cir. 2002); *North Jersey Media Group, Inc. v. Ashcroft*, 308 F.3d 198, 220, (3d Cir. 2002)
24. The two "enemy combatant" cases involving American citizens are *Hamdi v. Rumsfeld*, 296 F.3d 278 (4th Cir. 2002); *Padilla v. Rumsfeld*, 243 F. Supp. 2d 42 (S.D.N.Y. 2003), aff'd in part, rev'd in part, 03-2235, ____ F.3d __ (2d Cir. December 18, 2003).
25. The two *Hamdi v. Rumsfeld* cases in the Court of Appeals are 296 F.3d 278 (2002) and 316 F.3d 450 (2003). Much to the Government's dismay, the Supreme Court has agreed to review this case, _____ U.S. __, (January. 9, 2004.).
26. *Padilla v. Rumsfeld*, 03-2235, ____ F.3d ____ (2d Cir. Dec. 18, 2003)
27. *Gherebi v. Bush*, 03-55785, ____ F.3d ____ (9th Cir. Dec. 18, 2003)
28. *Williams v. Taylor*, 529 U.S. 362 (2000); *Wiggins v. Smith*, 123 S. Ct. 2527 (2003) (inadequate counsel); Neil A. Lewis, "A Court Becomes a Model of Conservative Pursuits," *The New York Times*, May 24, 1999, p. A1, A2; James Liebman, "Overproduction of Death," 100 COLUM. L. REV. 2030 (2000).
29. *Friends of the Earth, Inc. v. Laidlaw Environmental. Services, Inc.*, 528 U.S. 167 (2000); Reno v. Condon, 528 U.S. 141 (2000); Deborah Sontag, "The Power of the Fourth," *The New York Times Magazine*, (March 6, 2003), p. 6
30. Neil A. Lewis, n. 28, p. A1, see also generally Deborah Sontag, n. 28.
31. *United States v. Morrison*, 529 U.S. 598 (2000).
32. The Hellman statement and the abortion case appear in Neil A. Lewis, n. 28.
33. 2002 Almanac of Federal Judges, 6th Circuit, p. 1; *Grutter v. Bollinger*, 123 S. Ct. 2325 (2003).
34. *Dillon v. Frank*, 952 F.2d 403 (6th Cir. 1987).; *U.S. v. Faase*, 227 F.3d 660 (6th Cir. 2000), (rev'd en banc, 265 F.3d 475 (2001));
35. *Equality Foundation of Quaker Cincinnati v. Cincinnati 54* F.3d 261 (6th Cir. 1995), 128 F.3d 289 (6th Cir. 1997).
36. *Hopwood v. Texas*, 236 F.3d 256 (5th Cir. 2000). *Hammon v. Barry*, 826 F.2d 73 (D.C. Cir 1987). See also Associated General Contractors v. San Francisco, 813 F.2d 922 (1986), *Croson v. City of Richmond*, p. 22, F.2d 1355 (4th Cir. 1987) aff'd (opinion by Wilkinson), U.S. (1989).
37. *Burdine v. Johnson*, 231 F.3d 950 (5th Cir. , 2000), vacated en banc, 262 F.3d 336 (2000)

Chapter 7
Concluding Observations

An obvious way to end these bitter battles is for the White House to consult the Democrats over the blocked nominees. These are only six at this time, for the Democrats have hardly been unreasonable. Moderate nominees have had no trouble being confirmed, particularly after consultation. Two nominees sent up at the beginning of December 2003—Diane Sykes from Wisconsin to the Seventh Circuit and Peter B. Hall to fill the remaining vacancy on the Second—received the approval of all four Democratic home-state senators. To the dismay of their allies in the liberal community, the Democrats have also confirmed numerous conservative Court of Appeals nominees like Edith Clement, Michael McConnell, Dennis Shedd, Timothy Tymkovich, Lavinski Smith, and D. Brooks Smith, to name but a few. A nominee's hostility to abortion has not been a bar, for many appointees have been openly and actively antiabortion. The Democrats have not blocked any district judges at all, no matter how conservative—it is the Republicans who blocked a vote for J. Leon Holmes. During George H.W. Bush's four years, and Ronald Reagan's last two, during all of which time the Democrats were in control, they also approved many conservative nominees to the appellate courts, such as David Sentelle, Michael Luttig, Emilio Garza, and the others discussed earlier. During the twelve Reagan-Bush years, they challenged only two Supreme Court nominees and a handful of lower court selections.

In fact until recently, the Democrats have been remarkably supine in their response to the Republican judgeship campaign and indeed, to much of the Republicans' counterrevolutionary agenda. Partly this is because the Democrats, unlike the Republicans, have little party discipline. Also, where judges in particular are concerned, this is because, as one Democratic staff member said in an interview with the author, the Democrats are concerned about the impact of an excessive number of judicial vacancies on the administration of justice. This may be self-serving on the staffer's part but by December 9, 2003, the vacancies had shrunk to about 4.7 percent, and after the sixteen months of Democratic Senate control, the vacancies had dropped to fifty-eight, or 6.3 percent. The fifty-eight included forty-seven vacancies that opened up after January 2001; the 110 vacancies inherited from Clinton had been reduced to ten.[1]

An additional factor is that Democrats are reluctant to fight over judges. There is no Democratic constituency for the issue comparable to the antiabortion, antigay, and Republican Party's business interests other socially conservative groups for whom the judgeship issue is vital. Democrats, on the other hand, want to legislate. They do not seem to realize—and some probably don't care—that, as Senator Hillary Rodham Clinton put it, the Republicans "are on an ideological march. They have no intention of playing fair. They want what they want when they want it."[2]

Now, however, Democrats have decided to fight back. Led by Leahy, Schumer, Kennedy, and Durbin, most of them have come to realize that a radical wide-ranging campaign is under way in which not only a woman's right to an abortion is being threatened, but also much of what was accomplished in the past century to make government more responsive to the needs of ordinary Americans. They have come to see that this campaign is also aimed at Congress's power to legislate for the common good. Angered by the Republicans' treatment of Clinton's nominees, outraged by the insistence that *all* Bush nominees be approved despite their extremist views and sometimes dubious ethics, resentful over Hatch's manipulation of the rules, and embittered by being called anti-Catholic, antiblack, anti-Hispanic and anti-whatever, the Democrats now seem ready to fight some of the more egregious nominations with whatever procedural weapons are available. They must. If they do not, it will amount to unilateral disarmament, for they know from their experience during the latter six years of the Clinton administration that a Democratic president will not be afforded the same deference, and the judiciary will be permanently tilted toward the extreme right.

The bitter exchanges over judgeships are thus likely to continue for many years to come. If George W. Bush holds the White House for another four-year term and the Republicans keep control of the Senate, the current situation will probably continue: many conservative judges will be confirmed and a few will be blocked with filibusters. If a Democrat takes the White House and the Senate remains Republican, there will be a reprise of Clinton's experience; Santorum has already pledged that he and the other Republicans will fight any liberal nominee, saying, "We'll have our opportunity someday, and we'll make sure there's not another liberal judge. Ever!" In the unlikely event—unlikely for the near future—that the Democrats retake both the White House and the Senate, Republicans will filibuster and obstruct in every way they can, though they will probably not be able to block more than a handful. If a president is determined and he or she has a friendly Senate, it is very hard to resist more than a few nominees.[3]

To many people, these bitter disputes may seem extraordinary, especially since we have not had such high-visibility fights over lower court nominees during most of our history. Yet the Framers would probably not have been surprised. The power to appoint judges was evenly divided between the president and the Senate, and whenever power is divided and the stakes are high, disputes are inevitable.

This is particularly true for federal judges. They were not intended to be like Cabinet or other executive branch officers who are in office to serve the president. As to such executive officers, a president should be given a good deal of deference, though even with respect to executive branch officials, the Senate has sometimes balked. But when senators are called upon to advise and consent to appointing the lifetime judiciary, whose independence from the other two branches and from the electorate is vital to the rule of law, independent senatorial judgment is not only permissible but constitutionally mandated. Federal judges are not given the unique privileges of life tenure and unaccountability so that they can promote a president's political and ideological agenda, and remain able to do so long after he is gone. As Charles Black wrote more than thirty years ago, "The judges are *not* the president's people. God forbid! They are not to work with him or for him. They are to be as independent of him as they are of the Senate, neither more nor less."[4]

Indeed, it was initially suggested that the Senate should name the judges, but that was rejected as unwieldy, and the president was given the authority to make the initial choice. The Senate was made an essential part of the process, however, for fear that the president might succumb to favoritism or other inappropriate motives. "The possibility of rejection" provided by the "advise and consent" power was intended to be an important part of the process, according to Alexander Hamilton, not a remote eventuality. As former Senator George Mitchell asked rhetorically, "If you take the position that 168 out of 172 is not good enough, that 98 percent approval is not good enough, then what's the point of having a Senate advise and consent process, if anything less than 100 percent approval of a president's request is deemed obstruction?"[5]

The Constitution allows a president to *try* to shape the federal judiciary so that it will affect his constitutional vision. It does not, however, entitle him to *succeed*, and senators with a different vision may and should use their "advise and consent" power to oppose him.

This is especially true today. The ultraconservative constitutional vision of the last three Republican presidents is not shared by a majority of the American people. Most Americans believe in vigorous enforcement of the laws barring discrimination against minorities and women, including gays; most Americans believe a woman should have the right to choose an abortion, though there are differences about parental consent requirements for minors and about how to perform certain late-term abortions; most Americans believe that Congress should be able to empower disabled and elderly people to sue state and local officials who discriminate against them; most Americans believe that all workers, including state employees, should be able to sue their employers for violating federal wage and hour standards; most Americans believe in strong and vigorously enforced environmental, health, and safety laws; most Americans believe that capital punishment should be administered fairly, with adequate legal representation and without discrimination against African-Americans; most Americans believe citizens should have ready access to justice. Few Americans believe the New Deal brought us a "socialist revolution," that older people "cannibalize" their grandchildren, or that the states should not be subject to the Bill of Rights, as Janice Rogers Brown does; that schools that discriminate against African-Americans should get tax exemptions, as Carolyn Kuhl argued; that Ku Klux Klan members should be treated like "minor pranksters," if they burn a cross on the lawn of an interracial couple, as Charles Pickering treated one such Klan member; that judges should let their hostility to abortion rights induce them to twist the law "unconscionab[ly]," as White House Counsel Alberto Gonzalez described Priscilla Owen's actions in an abortion case; should solicit and take campaign money either from businesses subject to their enforcement powers, as Pryor has done, or from litigants who appear before them, as Owen does.

Nor is a nominee entitled to a lifetime position on the federal bench just by virtue of being nominated. There must be a record of what the nominee has done and thought so that the Senate can know his beliefs and attitudes. The nominee must demonstrate the qualities of mind, temperament, experience, and integrity necessary to do the job properly. Passing judgment wisely on what others have done and not done calls for men and women who have lived for a significant number of years. Very young Court of Appeals appointees, those in their thirties, have not had enough experience of either law or life to pass judgment on their fellow citizens or on the rulings of trial judges. Ninth Circuit Judge Alex Kozinski, a brilliant man who was appointed to the Court of Appeals when he was thirty-five, has admitted that he "was then too young and inexperienced for the job."[6]

Part of the job description, which flows from the very nature of the federal courts in our country and of courts in every free society, is an understanding that courts have the responsibility to protect and promote the rights of individuals and minorities.

As Justice Lewis Powell once put it, "the irreplaceable value of [judicial review by the federal courts] lies in the protection it has afforded the constitutional rights and liberties of individual citizens and minority groups against oppressive or discriminatory government action." That is why the Bill of Rights was added to the Constitution—to protect individual rights "by the legal check which it puts into the hands of the judiciary," in Thomas Jefferson's words. In the *Federalist No. 78*, Jefferson's arch-enemy Alexander Hamilton also expected the courts to provide "the essentials to safeguard against the effects of occasional ill humors in the society."[7]

A nominee should therefore be required to demonstrate, with specific instances, that he or she has devoted a substantial proportion of professional time to serving the disadvantaged and those of limited means. Nominees should demonstrate also that they fully support our national policy condemning racial, ethnic, religious, and gender discrimination, and that they believe that remedial statutes, such as civil rights and other laws promoting human liberty and human rights and protecting the disadvantaged are to be to broadly construed as obligations prescribed by both congressional debates and Supreme Court decisions.[8]

Related to this as a disqualifier is a demonstrated and active hostility to generally recognized rights, such as the right to vote. If proven, the charges that Chief Justice William H. Rehnquist tried to intimidate Hispanic voters in Phoenix, Arizona, in the early 1960s and that Judge Sid Fitzwater tried to frighten black voters in Dallas in 1982 should have doomed their nomination. The records and statements of Pryor, Brown, Pickering, and so many other Bush nominees also justify their rejection for this reason.

For fifty years, the federal judiciary led the nation in seeking to improve life for those whom fortune has shortchanged. This was a major departure from the judiciary's record during most of our history when it supported the haves against the have-nots, the bigots against their victims. The rise of the radical right and the lock it has established on many of our most powerful institutions as well as on a good portion of the country, has already started to move the courts back toward the kind of judiciary that we had before 1937. The process is not complete, nor is the Right's success certain. Too much has been done to be undone easily or at all, and some of the Republican appointees are not interested in promoting a radically right-wing agenda. Much of what has been achieved by liberal and other forces is intact, and further progress through the courts is still possible, as the *Lawrence* gay-rights case shows.

Nevertheless, even if the radical right does not succeed in rolling back all the advances of the past fifty years, many Americans will be hurt by what they do achieve. Abortion and affirmative action, the two areas noted above, where the right-wingers seem to have lost, are good examples. The courts have not overturned *Roe v. Wade*, but the *Casey* case has made it far more difficult for women who are poor or young to find someone to perform a safe abortion. *Grutter* preserved affirmative action in higher education, and most affirmative action programs in employment are still in operation in the private sphere, but many lower courts have struck down state, local, and federal programs that provided modest advantages to minority youngsters below college level and to minority government contractors.

Even positive developments like *Grutter* and *Casey* may be temporary, however, for they are narrow, limited victories. The Republican war cry is "no more Souters" or liberals, and so long as George W. Bush or someone who shares his views is president, there won't be any. There will soon be at least some retirements at the Supreme Court, and there will also be many lower court vacancies, if only through normal attrition. If the new Supreme Court and lower court judges are like those that Bush has already nominated, *Lawrence*, *Grutter* and *Casey* would be isolated aberrations, and may be in danger.

Let me end on a personal note. I have spent my entire fifty-seven-year career engaged not only in the controversies over judicial nominations, but also in the civil rights, civil liberties, economic, and social struggles of the past half-century. I have also spent the past eighteen years working on human rights and constitutional and legal reform in the former Communist bloc and elsewhere in the world. That experience has confirmed me in my belief that a progressive judiciary committed to liberty, justice, and human dignity is vital to social progress. Though, the many professional and other constraints attendant to the unique position and privileges of judges discussed earlier limit what they may and should do, within those, constraints an active judicial role in promoting those great ideals is indispensable. At stake in today's judgeship struggles is whether American judges will play that role or resume helping those who already have power and wealth to get more.

• • •

1. Senator Patrick Leahy, 148 Cong. REC. 510344 (Oct 22, 2002)

2. Quoted in   E.J. Dionne, "The Democrats Take A Dive," *The Washington Post*, 11/25/03, p. A29.

3. Santorum is quoted in Editorial, *The Tri-City Herald* (Nov. 18, 2003).

4. Charles Black, *A Note on Senatorial Consideration of Supreme Court Nominees*, 79 Yale L.J. 657, at 660 (1970) (emphasis in original).

5. The Hamilton quotation is from *The Federalist* 76; the Mitchell statement is from an interview with Gwen Ifil, NPR, *News Hour with Jim Lehrer*, Nov. 12, 2003.

6. Matt Richtel, (Public Lives; To One Judge, Cybermonitors Bring Uneasy Memories), *The New York Times*, August 18, 2001, at A8.

7. The Powell quote is from *United States v Richardson*, 418 U.S. 166, 192 (1974).

8. The ABA Model Rules call for a substantial majority of 50 from every lawyer but a judgeship candidate should do much more. *Bob Jones University v. U.S.*, 461 U.S.

574, 581 (1983) (commitment to national policy against racial discrimination); S. Rep No. 101-315 at p. 36 (1990); Cong. Globe, 42d Cong., 1st Sess., App.68 (1871); *Griffin v. Breckinridge*, 403 U.S. 88, 97 (1971); *Dennis v. Higgins*, 498 U.S. 439, 443 (1991) ('1983); *Jones v. Alfred H. Mayer Co.*, 392 U.S. 409, 437 (1968) (' 1982); *United States v. Price*, 383 U.S. 787, 801 (1966) (broad construction of remedial statutes).

Acknowledgments

It is always a pleasure to acknowledge the help a writer receives from others and in this case, such acknowledgments are especially called for. I have received a great deal of help from more people than I can acknowledge here, but some deserve to be singled out.

First my thanks to those who ploughed through the manuscript to check for accuracy and completeness. Their help was invaluable and avoided numerous errors and misjudgments. I am certain they could not capture all my mistakes and for this I apologize in advance. Foremost among them was Lisa Graves, Staff Counsel to the Senate Judiciary Committee, who read virtually the whole manuscript. She is a superb editor and writer and knows an immense amount about the events described in this book. She devoted a great deal of time and effort to this project and I shall be eternally grateful.

My thanks also to Adah Shah and Marcia Kuntz of the Alliance for Justice, who also read chapters, corrected mistakes, and made suggestions. I have always depended on them for information about these issues even before writing this book and they came through again.

I always want to thank my dear friend Frederick Quinn, one of the few Renaissance people I have ever known. A distinguished author, clergyman, former Foreign Service officer, constitutionalist and a master stylist, he made numerous suggestions to make this a more readable book.

As always, I owe a high debt of gratitude to another dear friend, my agent, Milly Marmur. Her confidence in my work and her vigorous efforts on my behalf have been a source of encouragement and support for many years.

Without my student research assistants, I could never have gathered all the materials on which this book is based. Especially indispensable were the efforts of Kaleb Kasperson, now a lawyer in Florida, and third-year student Olga Kats-Chalfant. Jamie McDonald also helped as did Anne Leete.

Carolyn Wright typed this whole book. How she made sense of what I charitably call my handwriting is beyond me, with its inserted material squeezed into margins and all over the page. And all this was accomplished with continual cheerfulness and unflappability. I am deeply indebted to her, as well as to our staff Supervisor, Elma Gates, who stepped in frequently to help, as she has always done.

Dean Claudio Grossman was, as always, supportive with a summer grant and consistent encouragement.

I also want to express my appreciation for the work of Professor Sheldon Goldman, whom I have never met. His thoughtful, comprehensive and objective books, articles and biennial repots have taught us all and greatly deepened our understanding of this normally low-visibility process of appointing lower court federal judges.

And finally, as always, to my wife Mary. She endured months of my obsession with this project which often made me quite unavailable. Cheerful, even-tempered, encouraging, and loving, she made it possible for me to devote the all-consuming time and energy needed to do this book. Gratitude is too poor a word for what she has earned.

Index

on policy agendas, 35
on wealth of judges, 103
Gonzales, Alberto, 195, 199, 223–24, 308
Goode, Barry, 183
Gorelick, Jamie, 132
Gorton, Slade, 146, 152
Gottesman, Michael, 287–88
government regulations, 7, 34, 36, 43–44, 138, 194
Graglia, Lino A., 79
Gramm, Phil, 165–66, 181, 205
Grassley, Charles, 146–47, 234, 266
Gratz v. Bollinger, 55–56
Gray, C. Boyden, 100–101, 123, 126–27, 257
Greenberg, Morton, 293
Greenhouse, Linda, 106–7
Gregory, Roger, 180, 200, 205
Griswold, Erwin, 124
Griswold v. Connecticut, 86, 113
Grovey v. Townsend, 31
Grutter v. Bollinger, 13, 55–56, 251, 310–11
Guantanamo Bay detainees, 291–95
Guinier, Lani, 145
gun control, judges against, 248, 254–55

Haire, Susan B., 185–86
Hamdi, Yassar Esam, 293
Hamilton, Alexander, 21, 36, 307
Hammer v. Dagenhart, 8
Harlan, John M., 30, 40, 282
Harrison, Marion, 79
Hartz, Harris, 204
Harvey, William, 78
Hatch, Orrin
  blue-slip system and, 175, 198, 199, 240, 252, 260
  chicanery and new rules, 205, 240–42, 256–58, 260
  Clinton's nominations and, 140–46, 152, 160
  on control of Senate, 140
  on Durbin/Kennedy memos, 269–70
  on Estrada, 230, 231, 234

exploitation of religion, 256, 257–58
  on Hill, 127
  Jipping as speech writer for, 271
  on need for more judges, 208–9
  nuclear option threat, 250
  overview, 68, 134, 162, 172, 174, 176, 179, 184, 203, 212
  on Schumer's dumbass questions, 245
  on vacancy crisis, 157
"haves" vs. "have-nots," 24, 32, 149
Head Start, 41
health and safety programs, 2, 9, 28, 218, 263
Heflin, Howard, 75, 116–17, 127
Hellerstein, William E., 68
Hellman, Arthur, 298
Helms, Jesse, 60, 65, 71, 147, 179–80, 240
Henderson, Karen LeCraft, 290
Hewitt, Hugh, 210
Hibbler, William J., 167
Hill, Anita, 110, 125–28, 206
Hispanic Leadership Institute, 177
Hispanics. See minorities' rights; minority appointments
Hitchman Coal and Coke Co. v. Mitchell, 29
Hollings, Ernest, 237
Holmes, J. Leon, 268–69
Hoover, J. Edgar, 32
Hopwood v. State of Texas, 13, 300
Horowitz, Michael J., 78–79, 195
House Judiciary Committee, 251–52
Human Life Amendment, 214
human rights
  Brown v. Board of Education of Topeka, KS, 8, 35, 40–41
  judges against, 43–44, 56–57, 64–65, 80–81, 115, 247, 253–54
  judges for, 137
  Miranda v. Arizona, 35, 107, 113, 206, 283–84, 296
  Supreme Court support of, 34–35
  undermining, 5–6
Humphries, Martha Anne, 185–86

Reagan's agenda for, 68
regulations since passing, 7
Republican position on, 5, 244
Thomas's ignorance of, 124
Rogan, James E., 174, 183–84
Romer v. Evans, 98, 248, 299
Roosevelt, Franklin D., 32, 35–36
Rosenbaum, James, 251
Rove, Karl, 216, 257–58, 266–67
Rudman, Warren, 106
Rust v. Sullivan, 109, 244
Rutherford Institute, 234–35
Ryskamp, Kenneth, 113–17, 222

Saad, Henry, 252
Santorum, Rick, 152, 166, 210, 253, 259, 271
Sarbanes, Paul, 199
Sarokin, Lee, 155
Scalia, Antonin, 6, 62, 73, 84–85, 111, 128, 228
scandals, indiscretions causing, 168–69
Schattman, Michael, 165–66
Schkade, David, 278–82
school desegregation. *See* desegregation of schools
school prayer, 8, 67–68, 244
Schumer, Charles, 199, 200, 205, 234, 245
Scirica, John, 293
Searcy case, 224–25
secret holds, 175, 199
segregation, 80
seminars for judges, 220–23
Senate Judiciary Committee, 140, 159–60
Sensenbrenner, James, 251
Sentelle, David, 70–71, 72–73, 285, 289–90
Sentencing Guidelines, 250–51
separation of church and state, 38, 85, 92, 99, 254
September 11, 2001, attacks, 194, 208, 290, 293–94
Sessions, Jefferson B., III

on ACLU, 158–59, 163
on D.C. Circuit Court, 266
on Democrats' anti-Catholicism, 259
overview, 74–75, 146–47, 152, 174, 176, 201
sexual discrimination/harassment, 279, 280, 299
Shedd, Dennis, 202, 234, 237–38
Shelby, Richard, 128
Sherman Antitrust Act, 28, 31
Shestack, Jerome, 157
Silberman, Lawrence, 71–73, 147, 229, 289–90, 300
Simon, Paul, 108, 145
Simpson, Alan, 124, 128
Sloan, Sheldon H., 174
Slotnick, Elliot, 139
Smith, Bob, 152, 175, 176, 201
Smith, D. Brooks, 217–21
Smith, Gordon, 161
Smith, Levinski, 203, 234–35
Smith, William French, 52
Snowe, Olympia, 257
Snyder, Allen R., 183
Snyder, Christine A., 157–58
social counterrevolution, 1–2, 4–10, 239, 310–11
social revolution, 8–10, 41
Social Security, 2, 265
Solicitor General's office, 59
Songer, Donald R., 185–86
Sotomayer, Sonia, 163–64
Souter, David, 9, 105–9
the South, 4–5, 41–42
Special Court of Appeals, 70–71
Specter, Arlen
apology, support of Thomas, 128
opinions of, 166–67, 172, 220, 256, 259–60, 268
support for Thomas, 124, 127
Sprizzo, John, 153
St. Lewis Post Dispatch, 170
Stabenow, Deborah, 240
standing doctrine, 285
Starr, Kenneth, 53, 71, 168–69
state elections for judges, 155

Warren, Earl, 14, 40, 44
Washington Lawyers Committee for
    Civil Rights Under Law, 76
Washington Legal Foundation, 37
Washington Post
    on Bush administration, 194–95,
        239
    on Clinton nominees, 200
    on Durbin/Kennedy memos, 269–70
    on Hill, 128
    on judges, 72, 201, 209, 218–20,
        231, 262, 266
    on judicial nomination system, 211
Washington Times, 142, 214–15
Weekly Standard, 267
welfare recipients, legal services for, 57
welfare role, 100
Weyrich, Paul, 120
Whalen, Thomas, 135
White, Helene, 182, 200, 240
White, Penny J., 155
White, Ronnie L., 155–56, 167,
    170–73
Whitewater investigation, 71
Whittaker, Judith, 58–59
Wicker, Tom, 42–43
Wilkins, William, 293
Wilkinson, J. Harvie, 62–66,
    199–200, 293, 296
Will, George F., 106, 129n13, 143–44
Williams, Karen, 113, 296
Williams, Stephen, 70, 286
Winter, Ralph, 62
women. *See also appointment statis-
    tics of each president*
discrimination against, 57, 112, 182,
    279–80, 299
violence against, 9, 110, 253
women's rights
    Equal Rights Amendment, 58, 214
    gender equality, 31, 40
    judges against, 110, 260–61, 262
    judges for, 57, 161
Woocher, Frederic, 184
Wood, Gordon, 23–24, 25, 28
Wood, Kimba, 134

Wooten, Terry, 206
workers' rights.
    court decisions effecting, 9
    Fair Labor Standards Act, 9, 100
    fellow servant doctrine, 26
    judges against, 46, 212–13, 217,
        237, 246, 247, 254, 264
    judges for, 279, 281
    labor unions, 9, 28–29, 31, 61,
        230–31
    minimum wage, 9, 46, 144
    NLRB and, 287–88
    non-delegation doctrine and, 70
World Wars I and II, 32, 37–38
Wright, Angela, 206
Wynn, James, 180, 200

Yamashita, Tomoyuki, 37–38
Yazoo territory ruling, 21–22
yellow-dog contracts, 28–29